POSTED MISSING

POSTED MISSING

ALAN VILLIERS

POSTED MISSING

The Story of Ships
Lost without Trace in Recent Years

CHARLES SCRIBNER'S SONS

New York

Still They Go

IN the sixteen years since I wrote this book, ships large and small, oceangoing, short-voyage, freighters, tankers, coasters, fishermen, have continued to go missing at the rate of five to ten each year—one year, thirteen. Between January 1961 and June 1971, seventy merchantmen were officially posted missing at Lloyd's in London, and they ranged in size to more than 13,000 tons. In that decade alone, the records show that 1032 lives were lost in these ships—1017 of them crew members, 10 wives, 2 other women, 3 children. The ships were under many flags but they were all built, loaded, classed, surveyed, and controlled under proper supervision. Ships not in this category are not on Lloyd's records. There are no coffin-ships today, no wreckers and no 'pirates' in old or new guise—at least not at sea.

All seagoing ships, even the smallest, have their own means of communication, some of it automatic for emergency use. A considerable proportion of the world's commercial shipping keeps to defined sea lanes. There is a large and efficient organisation for sea rescue—salvage tugs, helicopters, Coast Guard cutters and rescue ships under many flags, and long-range aircraft. Within a wide range, ships may be tracked from electronic stations ashore. Radar permits them to avoid one another in a manner never before possible. Merchant vessels are surveyed, inspected, regulated as to sea-worthiness, manning scales, life-saving equipment, load-lines and everything else. Crews can be better trained technically —deck and engineer officers, seamen, engine-room personnel— than ever before too, in the more important seafaring nations.

This at least is the theory, though there is statistical and other evidence showing a worrying increase in the numbers of avoidable casualties among merchant ships, quite apart from those which just disappear. A great many of these casualties are directly due to human error: all are due to such error (perhaps series of errors) in one way or another. For the first quarter of 1972, for example, the Liverpool (England) Underwriters' Association reported that total losses of merchant ships on world routes in that three-month period exceeded a million tons for the first time on record—188 oceangoing ships of 1,056,904 gross tons. Over 40 per cent of these were graded as "constructive total losses"—that is, ships so badly damaged by strandings (hitting rocks, beaches, islands, through bad navigation), or collisions (hitting one another through bad ship-handling or misuse of the international Rule of the Road) or fire, that the estimated cost of restoring them to full sea-worthiness exceeded their worth when repaired. Obviously it was cheaper then to build new ships. The constructive total losses are written off. Twenty-six of these 188 ships were tankers of one sort or other, and their gross tonnage of 464,057 was almost half the total.

It is generally the smaller vessel which goes missing. Her voyaging remains fundamentally much as it has been since the era of the mechanised vessel became properly established, a century and more ago. In earlier days, powered vessels also carried sail, often a full suit, and they were handled by former sailing-ship masters and, to some extent, crews (apart from the engine-room gang). They were lost in large numbers but they rarely went missing: their low power would not keep them off lee shores in bad weather. Today and most of the 20th century, they have been full-powered. Sail has no part in their propulsion, but for many years steamers' deck officers were still required to be trained and at least theoretically qualified in sail. It was not until 1911 that a British seaman might qualify at all as a deepsea deck officer if he had no sailing-ship experience, regardless of the fact that the great majority would spend their whole careers in steam or, later, motor-ships. In Germany and other northern countries, the sailing-ship requirement lasted much longer, and these officer-aspirants were the chief source of recruitment of Cape Horner crews as long as those tough ships lasted under the German and the Finnish flags, well into the 1930's. Many large British companies like Cunard and Alfred Holt insisted that all their deck officers be certified masters in deepsea sail, before they accepted them as career officers—not at all a bad idea. It is now dead, in Britain anyway, though several important maritime countries—Norway, Denmark, U.S.S.R. among them, still maintain large square-rigged ships for the *ab initio* training of merchant seamen, and at least 20 others have such ships for naval personnel. Some of these ships have been built in the late 1960's.

Ordinary casualties there will always be, but one might think that by now the missing ship, if not an anachronism, should at least be very rare indeed. There are theories about dangerous cargoes, gases, chemicals and the like which might cause the sudden loss of a few ships, and there may be something in this. There have also been rumors and alleged reports that such-and-such missing or untraced ship "was seen in a Cuban port" or in North Viet-Nam or somewhere. All such rumors have proved to be groundless. There have been a few instances of supertankers blowing up mysteriously when empty and the small crews aboard were cleaning tanks for the next cargo. Few of this type—the 50,000-tonner and above— have sunk and none is missing, perhaps because there is too much ship to sink suddenly even if a third of the tanks are blown out of her. One may often—too often—see a bloated great ship of this sort sitting for weeks in the enormous dry-dock system built in recent years into the banks of the Tagus opposite Lisbon, because this is a handy port for the N. Europe–Good Hope–oil ports route to the Persian Gulf and Red Sea. One has seen there recently half-ships, two-thirds ships, ships with gashes in their sides of such extent it is remarkable that they stayed afloat at all.

The volume of international trade by sea has doubled in the 15 years since the late 1950's, and so (almost) has the total tonnage of oceangoing ships—from 124 million tons in 1959 to 210 million in 1972. The greatest increase has been in the outsize bulk-carrier, especially of oil, crude or refined.

In many of these ordinary casualties disregarding the large and mysterious list of "Missing") there is the implication of some inefficiency among at least watch-keeping deck officers. Of the 188 ships which were casualties in the first quarter of 1972, 49 of nearly 250,000 tons were lost by stranding, another 53 (300,000 tons) by fire, and a further 200,000 tons by collision. This last is readily understandable to me, for one has only to be trying to get some sort of sailing-ship through the shipping lanes anywhere to realise the life-and-death importance of keeping the powered vessel's lookout as well as one's own. In recent years, I have taken good care to keep clear of all of them, regardless of the Rule of the Road or what flag they fly. All powered vessels show bright masthead lights, easily seen: by law, the sailingship has none and so she is much harder to pick up by night. But she shows up strikingly well by day.

Many of these outsize vessels are Greek—far more than fly the Greek flag (a mere 20,000,000 tons) for another 17,000,000 tons fly the flag of Liberia, 2,500,000 the Cypriot, others the Panamanian. Greece has as long a sea history as any nation and longer than most. Greek seamen are trained well and have an excellent record. But ships under the aptly called flags of convenience can be another thing. I had to operate under one of them—the Panamanian —when sailing a frigate for Peter Ustinov to make his fine film of Melville's "Billy Budd." The ship was a Sicilian brigantine converted into quite a tolerable frigate. Her original Mediterranean flag proved impossible, so the change was made to Panamanian.

A Consul came from Rome with the necessary papers (chiefly a new certificate of registration for the ship), and handed this over without ceremony. He asked whether we had Panamanian certificates of competency in the grades in which we were employed. We had not, of course, never having needed them. This was soon put right for the Consul dived in his satchel, brought out a wad of folding 'tickets' in the form of small pocket-books, asked what we were, and handed out the appropriate book, which he filled in. He insisted on making mine out as Master of steamers up to 10,000 tons, and it was quite in vain that I pointed out to him that we were standing on the poop of a full-rigged ship of some 500 tons. This meant nothing, apparently, in Panama. We were all certified for 10,000-ton steamers: I noticed that my certificate, issued in January, 1953, was No. 36701. So there were another 36,000 'certified' Panamanian masters and officers about the seas somewhere, even then.

Ships large or small, under any flag, may still go missing anywhere. In 1968, thirteen did so, ranging from the wooden *Heidrun II* of Bolungavik in Iceland, 154 tons, presumably lost off Iceland within sight of her master's home, to the Liberian registered *Ithaca Island,* of Monrovia, 7500 tons, which sailed with her crew of 29 from Norfolk, Virginia, on the first of October, 1968, bound for Manchester, England, reported herself by wireless in mid-Atlantic on both the eighth and eleventh of October, and has neither been seen nor heard of since. An extensive air search was made, she was on a "beaten track," and all shipping was alerted.

The fishermen missing that year included the steam trawler *Kingston Peridot,* 658 tons, 20 men, which sailed from Hull for the Iceland grounds on January 10, 1968, bound on an ordinary winter fishing voyage, and never returned. She was heard of on the Arctic Circle off Grim's Island on January 26: then silence. She was fitted with both radio telephone (much used by fishing skippers) and W/T, and she was expected to keep in touch with her owners in Hull daily. The weather was atrocious, but this was the accepted thing on the Icelandic fishing grounds in winter. The old style steam vessel like the *Kingston Peridot* was perhaps vulnerable, compared with the modern fish factory-ship type which offers real shelter to her crew and hauls in her gear over or through the stern. She heads the sea without fighting it. The men work at the sheltered end of the ship, not the most exposed. Compared with these, the old-time "side dragger" is almost an anachronism. The older type trawler gets crews because many men prefer the shorter voyages she makes—three weeks or so, compared with the stern-trawler's two months. They are mostly family men with homes in their ship's base-port.

One advantage the old-style trawling skippers have: they are usually quickly missed by their friends fishing on the same grounds all round them. The silence of any is quickly noticed and may become alarming. Many set up their own groups which make a point of calling one another each day, as did Skipper Stephen MacNab of the Fraserburgh fisherman *Nautilus,* when he sailed from her home port on January 6, 1972. He reported by radio to his owners when fishing 80 miles southwest of Lerwick three days later, and has not been heard of since. Skipper MacNab had organised a group of skippers who undertook to contact each other at least once every 24 hours they were at sea, but he was the first who fell silent.

The Hull trawler *St. Romanus,* 600 tons, crew 20, sailed from the Humber on January 10, 1968 and went missing too, but it seems that she was somehow overwhelmed in the North Sea before she had got far on her way. She reported on the evening of the day she sailed as having made 120 miles on course: then silence. Search by air and sea found no trace of her. She was on a northbound trawler route: how could she drop unseen from the face of the busy North Sea? Easily indeed, as has been shown far too often. Definite evidence that she had been lost turned up at the Boat Show in London a month or two later, in the shape of a rubber life-raft in use there as part of a display. An expert visiting the show identified it as the raft he had delivered to the *St. Romanus* before she sailed. It was later picked up adrift, empty, on the trawler's track.

Fishermen must make a living: for this, they accept risks. Another deepsea trawler went missing in northern British waters that wild January. (At sea in those parts, there never is a docile January.) This was the *Ou Vas Tu*, 153 tons, of L'orient, which with her tough crew of ten Bretons sailed from France on January 8, 1968, for the grounds off the Hebrides, and six days later reported herself by radio as on Latitude 55.50 N., Longitude 8.20 W., to the north of Ireland. Soon afterwards (no further news coming from her and none of her compatriots or anyone else sighting her) descriptions of the little ship were being broadcast—"light green hull 30 metres long, 2 white-topped yellow masts, white bridge, grey upperworks: Official Number LO 5429." A French life-raft container marked OVT was picked up near her last known position. Air search was hampered by severe weather with very low ceilings day after day.

The only result of the air search was to turn up another mystery. Some wreckage sighted from the air in the area and picked up by helicopter was taken into Oban in Argyll. Some was marked PARIS FRANCE, and life-jackets bore the label "MOT VICTORY." What could this be? The French authorities were certain that these things had nothing to do with the *Ou Vas Tu*. "Paris France" may be considered an American geographical term. The "MOT VICTORY" might have some connection with a standard type of American war-time freighter: but how or why these things were floating about in the cold Atlantic no one, apparently, has yet explained.

[xi]

Search for the OVT was abandoned on January 24, 1968, sixteen days after she had sailed, and in due course she was posted missing.

The small wooden Icelander *Heidrun II,* 154 tons, of Bolungavik on the north-west coast of Iceland near Isafjordur, may have been a fisherman or a small freighter—possibly either as work offered. Her crew of six included a father and two of his sons. Early in February, 1968, she was on a coastal passage towards one of the ports in Isafjordur, which took her close by her home port. So the father thought it safe enough to take an hour or two off, as it was the birthday of one of the sons. Anchoring close in, they went ashore. They were away only an hour or two when it suddenly blew up from the worst possible direction, north-west, with hail and snow in violent squalls. The *Heidrun*'s temporary anchorage became at once a death-trap.

There was only one thing to do—get out of there! They rushed for the beach, the father and sons, but some of the crew were not there. Substitutes volunteered at once from the beach. All men of Bolungavik were seamen. The wind was screaming, whipping up stinging sprays, but there was shelter of a sort just round the corner. The *Heidrun II* never came round that corner. She disappeared into the violent flurries of a savage squall and was never seen again—not as much as an identifiable fragment of the ship, nor a bruised and broken body either. She was posted missing at Lloyd's on April 10, 1968. "With a crew hastily brought together . . ." said the brief official report. Seamen knew what that could mean, in an emergency.

The 360-ton Finnish motor-ship *Irma,* missing that same bad year of 1968, wiped out a family. Late in the fall month of October she was on a short coastal passage in the N. Baltic Sea, from Klaipeda (the former Memel) in Lithuania towards the Finnish port of Raumo, on the Gulf of Bothnia, with a full cargo of anthracite which for her was between 400 and 500 tons. It was October 23 when she sailed, late in the year for a small ship struggling northwards with a gutful of coal. She was a family ship: her crew of seven included the four brothers Grönquist, one of them master; another, mate. Three of the brothers had their wives on board. One had brought her child. So there were eight of the family in the complement of eleven. It was a wild time of the year for family cruising: probably the Grönquist wives—or some of them —were crew members.

The *Irma* reported herself by radio on October 25, two days after sailing. "All well," she said. "Anticipating arrival Raumo Saturday morning." Then silence: Saturday came: no *Irma* at Raumo or, apparently, anywhere else. She was required to signal ahead with her estimated time of arrival to be sure of a coal-handling berth and gang. Shipmaster Grönquist was a reliable and methodical man. It was quickly obvious that something was wrong. The weather was bad with fierce winds and plenty of heavy snow squalls.

The *Irma* never did send another signal. Air-sea search was begun quickly along her probable course—mostly air search, for local seamen knew the dangers of those waters. Wrecked men must be found fast.

On the 30th, a raft was found in a violent snow-squall tossing in the sea just north of the Åland Islands. On it was a frozen body, readily identifiable as Mate Thorvild Grönquist of the *Irma*. Further search over many days discovered no more bodies and no sign of the ship. A few pieces of flotsam were found on the rocks of the Åland Islands—that last home of the working Cape Horn ship—but this could not be positively identified. There was no trace of the three wives, the child, or the other brothers, or anyone else aboard. The registered owner of the *Irma* was a Grönquist, too.

There is something repellent in the thought of men (to say

nothing of women) being flung suddenly into a violent wintry sea: but they may drown as fast or die of a differing degree of exposure also in the tropics, like the crew of a small wooden motor-vessel oddly named *Speed Artist*. The *Artist* began her last passage from Trinidad towards Guadaloupe on December 9, 1967. She called at Barbados on the 10th of that month, sailed again and disappeared. Nothing was found despite the usual search by surface vessels and aircraft over many days. Nothing was found—not even another ship which had sighted her. So she was posted missing, too. She had a cargo of building blocks and the master's wife was signed in her crew. The *Speed Artist* was one of the very few missing ships of recent years which had no sending radio at all.

All these vessels were small, less than a thousand tons, five of them round the 500-ton mark or less. Much larger ships could go missing and did in that same recent year of 1968—like the *Tong Hong,* 3830 tons, of Hong Kong, and the *Ithaca Island,* 7500. The *Tong Hong* was a motor-ship 340 feet long with a crew of 38, British officers and Chinese seamen, and on her last passage she carried 5180 tons of ammonium sulphate, bound from Kawasaki towards Colombo by way of Singapore. She set out on October 25, 1967. She may be still going but no one has seen her since. She, too, sent no signals, left no trace. Search by aircraft and ships again discovered nothing. She was 23 years old, but she was kept up properly in class, well manned, and well looked after.

The *Ithaca Island* was considered a sizable tramp when she was built for Liberian ownership in 1947. She carried 10,000 tons or more with reasonable economy, and for 20 years tramped un-noticed round the world. Bound from Norfolk, Virginia, towards Manchester, she set off on her last voyage on October 1, 1968, with her crew of 29. She had radio, of course, and a week later, on October 8, reported her noon position as 45 deg. N. Latitude, Longitude 37.47 W.—not far north-west of the Azores, with the Gulf Stream helping her along. Three days later, she reported again, then just about in the middle of the North Atlantic. This was the last ever heard of or from her: she slid somehow below the North Atlantic without a signal, without a boat away—nothing. Why? How? Grain is not a dangerous cargo. The weather was stormy: a W.N.A. (winter North Atlantic) passage usually is. There is a special loadline for it, cut into the ship's plates both sides, marked W.N.A. and designed to give more freeboard—greater buoyancy—for such passages. Why did that passage, after the hundreds she had made, destroy her so utterly and suddenly that not even a W/T message could be sent? Or a boat, or anything got away? She was searched for quickly and diligently by aircraft and ships. She was in a shipping lane. Nothing: nothing: nothing, yet once more.

So in due course, on November 20, 1968, some seven weeks after she passed quietly seawards from Chesapeake Bay, the Lutine bell at Lloyd's rang for her and she was posted missing. Like all the others,* she has remained with all her people in the great silence of the sea.

A list of the thirteen ships gone missing that one year, with their tonnage, crew numbers, and lost voyages is of interest. They were all freighters, tankers, or fishermen.

The *Oostmeer,* a handy cargo tramp, was scarcely a year old when she sailed from Brussels in October 1968 with a heavy cargo of steel billets, bound for Monfalcone in North Italy. She was reported passing Gibraltar on October 29 and again off Cape Bougaroni two days later, near Djidjelli in Algeria. She was then on what was until a few years ago one of the busiest shipping lanes in the world—that between the Straits of Gibraltar and the Suez

---

* Not quite all. There was the body of Mate Grönquist of the *Irma.* The little German *Katharina* when she went somewhere in the vicinity of the island of Gotland in the Baltic in late December 1967, also left a body in the sea. This was identified as Engelbert Kampenga, a seaman aboard.

Canal. But the *Oostmeer* was never seen again, nor heard of or from, though her master was a meticulous man who had a firm habit of making some sort of radio contact every day. Because of this, his ship was quickly missed, but that made no difference. One of her lifeboats, marked with her name, was later found washed up derelict and empty on the coast of Sicily. She was carrying a heavy cargo, but what sort of calamity could strike her so suddenly in those waters that a well-found, almost new ship could slip below them for ever, without even time to send a signal?

	Ship	*Tonnage*	*Crew*	*Voyage*
Cargo	ITHACA ISLAND	7500	29	Trans-Atlantic
Cargo	TONG HONG	3831	38	Far East
Cargo	M.V. OOSTMEER	1134	9	N.W. Europe/
Trawler	KINGSTON			Med.
	PERIDOT	658	20	Iceland Fishery
"	SAINT ROMANUS	600	20	" "
Freighter	RAKUYO MARU	451	12	Onomichi for
				Tsukumi
"	KATHARINA	398	6	Baltic Sea
"	IRMA	361	11	Baltic Sea
"	ANNE URSULA	267	8	Coasting NW
				Europe
"	LIMFJORD	187	4	Baltic Sea
"	HEIDRUN II	154	6	Local, Iceland
Fisherman	OU VAS TU	153	10	N. of Ireland
Coaster	SPEED ARTIST	106	5	Local, W.
				Indies

During World War II, my squadron of Royal Navy LCI(L) was based for some months at Djidjelli for the Sicilian campaign. I came to know those waters well, especially in winter. Those LCI(L) were light steel welded boxes driven by American bus engines in a makeshift arrangement fit only for war. Yet we had no trouble, no losses to the sea whatever. My "captains" were bank-clerks, insurance men and the like, temporarily at sea only because of the war, and the engine-men were anybody who had ever worked in a garage. One wonders what could have happened to the 1000-ton Hollander? Nothing of her was found on the coast of Sicily, only the broken boat. Her disappearance—the 13th announced that year—brought the overall missing tonnage of good ships that one year to nearly 16,000, and the number of lives lost from missing ships in the one twelve-months to 178, at least three of them women.

Nor do Lloyd's statistics include all vessels—not ships of the U.S.S.R. or China, or seagoing "native" craft like junks, dhows, and the like, of which some thousands still sail in eastern waters: not yachts, for many of these are unregistered, not being merchant ships, though hundreds of them are engaged on ocean voyages at any time, some asking much of God. Lloyd's is essentially an insurance organisation. "Posting" a ship missing is a business finality. The insurances on ships and cargo (people too, if any) may be paid, and are forthwith, like everything else at Lloyd's.

There is drama in the "posting"—literally, in this sense, to put up a "poster," an announcement. First, vessels are listed as overdue: then, if there is no news they are up for inquiry. Does anyone on earth or sea in the far-reaching world of ships and shipping know anything of the such-and-such, 100 A1, which has been overlong on passage (or voyage) from such-and-such to so-and-so? Vessels can be stolen, disguised, renamed, spirited away (such cases are rare, but the steamer *Ferret* was stolen and pirated off to Australia earlier this century.) To prevent this and for identification in general, all registered ships have Official Numbers which, with their measured tonnage net and gross, are cut into their main beams where all may see. They go about their ways readily identifiable and thoroughly documented. Yet the *Ferret* slipped out of a port in England and disappeared. She was not "missing," merely stolen. It took a little time before the hawk eyes and long memory of Lloyd's agent in Melbourne saw through the disguise of the new small steamship coasting out of the port: but he did, once his suspicions were aroused.

It is unlikely that there have been any more *Ferrets,* though with the modern multiplicity of flags of so-called convenience and the profusion of new "national" fleets called into existence at times by small nations with no maritime experience whatever (in the international sphere) perhaps it could never happen again. Something of the sort may have been tried with a freighter during the Viet Nam war, which did not arrive where she was expected but was later reported as being seen in North Viet Nam waters. She was not posted Missing. No one was fooled.

To catalogue these fleets of missing ships could become monotonous were it not for the appalling tragedy each represents and the so frequently unanswered questions Why? How? Why do they all go unseen and in such *silence?* They cannot all slip suddenly beneath the sea like large stones, or just roll over and go straight on down. Yet several of the largest would appear to have done one or the other of these things.

Consider the cases of several ships, for example, gone from the face of the earth in the early 1970's, five of them aggregating over 36,000 tons, manned by 162 men, each with every necessary modern aid to navigation, safety, and communication, all gone to the bottom of the sea, whole or in pieces, without a sound, a signal or a trace—or a clue either. The motor-tanker *Milton Iatridis* of Piraeus in Greece, 10,000 tons, 30 crew, in 1970; the Philippino *Iligan Bay,* 5,300 tons of Cebu, with a crew of 39, last heard of on January 24, 1971, 120 miles north of Cabo Villano on the north-west corner of Spain on passage from Hamburg and Antwerp towards Manila; the *Kiki* of Famagusta in Cyprus, 3750 tons, crew 27, on passage that same winter of 1971 from Poland towards Yugoslavia with coke, known to have passed through the Straits of Gibraltar on January 31 but never seen again: the *Banalura* of Monrovia in Liberia, 8300 tons, crew 35, an iron ore carrier adrift on passage from an ore port near Spain's Atlantic border with France bound towards Kyushu, Japan—a long haul round the Cape of Good Hope, and a heavy cargo.

In the course of the voyage the *Banalura* had to pass through the typhoon belt round the Philippine Islands. It is known that there was a typhoon raging there at the time. On November 12, by which date she was in the typhoon area, the *Banalura* radioed that she was making only seven knots. She answered no further calls, and never has. The Hong Kong Marine Dept., the Japanese Maritime Safety Agency and the U.S. Coast Guard at Okinawa were alerted at once and searched industriously. Nothing was found. An ore-laden ship can sink horribly fast under the assault of a typhoon; no ship's boat and no man may live in the mad turbulence of such a sea.

The *Banalura* was posted missing at Lloyd's, after the usual melancholy signal on the Lutine bell, on January 12, 1972. That same day the bell sounded once more for yet another ship, the *Seng Lee* of Panama, 1694 tons register, which sailed from Kaosiung in Taiwan in September 1971 towards Brunei with a crew of 24 and two passengers. She had to pass through the S. China Sea and she was last heard of there, in the path of a typhoon. She had a cargo of cement, which is scarcely noted for buoyancy. She did not come through that typhoon nor was she ever seen again.

Two sizeable steamships posted missing on one day may not sound well in the matter of maritime safety in the 1970's. Cement may be heavy, but a well-found ship ought not to sink with it. Typhoons are endemic in the area, and a stout ship should live through as many as may assail her—so long as no hatch is stove in, and her engines and steering-gear continue to work properly. Yet right into this year of grace 1973 merchantmen large and small continue to sail to oblivion while making what should be ordinary passages—like the 850-ton *Puerto Limon* which sailed with her crew of 12 from Houston, Texas, on December 14, 1972, bound for Port Limon to deliver a cargo of fertiliser in bulk. Seen leaving Galveston later the same day, she has not been heard of since. So on February 7, 1973, she, too, was posted missing. There were local rumours of the usual sort, of course, and suggestions that she had been carried off to Cuba and seized there. There are people who know what goes on in Cuban ports: she did not arrive there, nor anywhere else.

So they go, the small ships and the large, taking their secrets with them almost as if they wanted to do just that—yet another of them the 13,000-ton *Anita* of Oslo, built in 1966, taken by the sea when Bremen-bound from Newport News with a full coal cargo in March, 1973. She sailed on March 23, reported all well by radio the following day, and that is the last heard of her. She was posted missing with her crew of 32 on May 16 the same year.

It was fortunate that she, too, had no company on that fatal list, for another bulk carrier—the *Norse Variant* which sailed within hours the same day on a similar passage—was also overwhelmed in the sea and, most remarkably, at the same spot. While they were hurriedly abandoning their own sinking ship, the *Variant*'s survivors picked up a life-ring and two life-rafts marked *Anita*, Oslo, drifting almost beside them. They were grateful, for they could use them. Because they survived—they had also the luck to be picked up quickly—the area where the *Anita* must have sunk was established. But the knowledge did not help her people or anyone else, and she was posted missing on May 16, 1973.

These two ships and others of the lost and missing were roughly in the area known sometimes as the "Bermuda triangle," thought by some (though not usually by mariners) to be particularly dangerous to ships. The "triangle" is that section of the North Atlantic enclosed by imaginary boundaries joining Bermuda to the U.S. coast westwards to Chesapeake Bay and south-west to the Florida Keys. Some speak of considerable ship losses in this general area. They speak truth, for it includes Cape Hatteras and hurricane paths and the Gulf Stream, which can be a menace for the south-bound in fall and winter.

But it is horribly obvious that ships large or small may be lost almost anywhere at any time. Any sea-girt land may wreck ships, any ocean swallow them. The rate of loss seems governed only by the rate of traffic. Frequency of high winds and storms can help and so can carelessness in securing for sea—any carelessness, in cargo matters as well as in seaworthiness.

As, apparently, in the case of the 10,000-ton special tank ship named *Milton Iatridis,* mentioned briefly earlier. This vessel (like many other tankers today) was carrying what could be dangerous cargo—caustic soda in liquid form, a huge tank full of it loaded at Canvey Island not far from London. She sailed from Canvey on October 26, 1969, with her crew of 30, and crossed the North Atlantic to New Orleans to fill her other tanks, not with any form of caustic soda nor petroleum products. This done (it did not take long), the Greek sailed again on November 14 bound first for a place called Kwinana, which is on the West Australian coast not far south of the Swan River. Two weeks after leaving New Orleans, she reported her position as approximately 2 deg. S. Latitude, 37 degrees W. Longitude—on the western side of the S. Atlantic off the bulge of Brazil: and that was the last ever heard from or of the *Milton Iatridis* and her 30 men. Again there was a rumour that her crew had seized the ship and taken her in to Cuba. (To sell that caustic soda?)

This was a loss which the responsible committee at Lloyd's (which takes nothing lightly at any time) looked into with exceptional thoroughness, but not because of the Cuba rumour. That was an unusual cargo. The ship was lost in a fine weather part of the Atlantic, very suddenly. She could otherwise surely have used her W/T, for it takes a little time to founder or to burn (but perhaps not to explode). If there had been a collision, another ship would be involved. But what about the cargo? Could it have blown up? How safe was caustic soda liquid? Safe enough, it seemed, if properly loaded and kept from contact with various substances, among them aluminum.

Many chemical cargoes can generate dangerous gases, caustic soda liquid among them. In contact with aluminum, it may produce hydrogen gas, and *that* is an explosion hazard. Investigation showed that the *M. Iatridis* was fitted with a heating system based on steam coils, and these coils were made of aluminum alloy. The hold with the caustic was so fitted. On the last day the ship was heard of, the caustic soda liquid had been in its tank for five weeks—plenty of time for the makings of calamity to build up, silently and secretly, down in the hold. No signal, no survivors, no wreckage: it is not an unusual story. The owners could not believe that a ship as well built and stout as their *Milton Iatridis* could just go missing in fine weather, in the 1970's, while quietly steaming on a commonplace voyage in a good-weather area of the sea. But no *Milton Iatridis* or any ship like her ever turned up in Cuba, or anywhere else.

It is to be hoped that the accident happened by night, for sudden disintegration and almost simultaneous foundering is a merciful way to go. But it was perhaps hard on a good and experienced ship-master to be blown to eternity by chemical formula, for his prior experience of such things was probably nil. He had been informed that there was some risk—yes. But there could be risk in all seafaring: so he had gone to sea. It was his life.

In the past ten years (1960–70) seafaring, like much else, has changed more than during the previous 10,000. The ocean lanes are filled with alarming processions of bloated great floating things of up to half-a-million tons—one ship, not a fleet—many of them twin-chimneyed, bulbous monstrosities pushing the sea aside, some of them unable to use more than three or four ports on earth, forced to suck oil from the innards of that earth into their cavernous holds while lying in the sea miles offshore, loading in a few hours. Then rush to sea, to pound along towards some similar inhuman anchorage to discharge, her people jammed in a multi-decked after-castle stuck as far aft as possible, above a very sophisticated (and perhaps temperamental) engine-room at times over-full of noise and vibration, and problems, too. Here a few able men tend a power plant that could provide light for a city. The ship steers herself. To get along the fore-deck the seamen need bicycles, riding them warily in anything other than calm. (A man can adjust his own motion to the ship's roll but a bicycle may not.) In the after-castles, built up in graceless steel deck upon deck like an Armada galleon's high poop, live the smallest possible crews: among them usually several women—a few of these crew-members, others wives.

The emphasis of all voyages is to cut port time to the minimum. The size of the ships is so great (even the 100,000-tonner) that if there were an open Suez Canal they could not use it, and many now cannot get their great bulks through Panama. Down to the Straits of Magellan they pound or past Cape Horn, adding thousands of miles to a voyage: putting in nowhere to break the long stress. Stress! That is the factor which can get men down, and ships—even 50,000 or 250,000-tonners. Gadgetry gone wrong (call it automation if you want) can cause hell anywhere. Tank-cleaning in these monsters can cause problems, too: but the tanks must be cleaned.

Not only tankers have swollen greatly in size and perhaps also in problems in recent years. There are new types of ship, some of them known among seamen by new names which seem not ship-shape at all—the RORO (Roll on—Roll off, the road juggernaut carrier): LASH (Lighter aboard ship: the big barge transporter which stows laden barges already full of cargo, rapidly laden and as swiftly discharged): the VLCC and ULCC (the very large and

the ultra-large crude oil carriers, serving refineries: some pro-
nounce ULCC as ULCER). These are now (1973) built up to
300,000 tons: there are VLCC's up to half a million. Soon there
will be great fleets of these and other maritime monstrosities, for
large shipyards in Europe and Japan are booked to capacity building them as far ahead as 1977. There are other maritime nasti-
nesses coming along in the shape of LNG's—*liquid* natural gas-
carriers, designed to load and carry their pleasant cargoes at
temperatures of minus 16 degrees centigrade. Here is plenty of
stress on hulls, too: the problems of building economically mer-
chantships of the strength to carry such stuff safely are great, and
expensive to overcome. Asking price for a small LNG (carrying
a mere 125,000 cubic metres) in mid-1973 was $80,000,000 in
U.S.A. and more in Japan. The money is found readily: but the
men?

LNG's, ULCER's, VLCC's and RORO's—these monsters
make the big-box-carrying container-ship seem almost prehistoric.
But nobody is 'building' VLHB's—Very Large Human Beings—
though plenty are fostering ulcers, not only at sea. Stress! Stress
upon seamen to hurry up, rush faster, turn round with greater
speed in ever more enormous, more expensive ship-monsters:
stress in the smaller ships too, the fishermen and all the hard-
working little fellows that do half the seafaring on earth—this also
increases. I suggest that the stress on many seamen today is
greater than ever before in man's seafaring history, and in this
may lie in part at least the explanation for this odd and continuing phenomenon of the Posted Missing merchant ships.

Oxford, Oct. 15 1973

Alan Villiers

Contents

CONTENTS

THE NINE LITTLE SHIPS

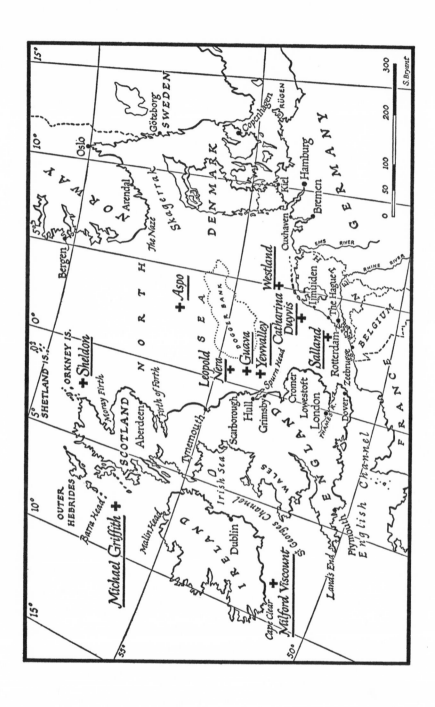

S.Bryant

CHAPTER ONE

"Will Require One Fireman"

> ## LLOYD'S NOTICE
>
> ## VESSELS FOR INQUIRY
>
> The Committee of Lloyd's will be glad of any information regarding the following vessel:—
>
> "YEWVALLEY," steamer of Glasgow, Official Number 160224, 823 tons gross, Master Potts, which is reported to have sailed from London for Bo'ness on the 30th January, 1953, with cargo of cement clinker, and reported by wireless off Cromer on the 31st January.
>
> Lloyd's, London, E.C. 3.
> 4th March, 1953

TEN minutes after the last grab had dropped its heavy load in the gaping hold, the little ship had left the wharf and sailed. No one watched her go. For nearly a quarter of a century she had been slipping out quietly from the multitude of almost inaccessible and awkward wharves at which she was required to load or discharge her unromantic cargoes. This was just one voyage more in a long career that had included six years of war. The January day was dull and blustery, with snow flurries, and the radio was speaking of gale warnings, though not then for the North Sea. Even the North Sea gulls were flying in to seek the shelter of inshore fields as the stubby little *Yewvalley* picked up her lines, belched a bit of smoke from the high funnel aft, thrashed the grey water for a moment as she manoeuvred off the wharf and was gone.

The coaster had only two hatches, one in the low well-deck forward and the other aft, on the long raised quarter-deck. A handful of hardbitten mariners was working to get the hatches on No. 2 hold. No. 1 had already been secured, for the grab had finished there first. Getting the hatches secured was no great job, for the steel beams had not been unshipped. All the men had to do was to get the wooden hatch-coverings in position, cover them with three stout tarpaulins, wedge the tarpaulins down and fasten the lot in place with locking bars. They were used to the job. They were at it every few days—hatches on, hatches off. The fact that when the hatches were off there was very little main-deck left did not worry them, nor did their knowledge that the bulk cargo had not been trimmed cause them any bother at all. The *Yewvalley* had been carrying bulk cargoes in perfect safety round the coasts of Britain, winter and summer alike, for many years. The grab-driver had stowed the cargo well enough, trimming it with his grab. Cement-clinker was heavy stuff. It wouldn't run, like bulk grain or slack coal. There was plenty of time to get the hatches thoroughly secure before the ship reached open sea. She loaded at a wharf near Tilbury, and the winding passage down the broad Thames from there to sea would take some time, even on the swift ebb helped by the west-south-west wind.

The *Yewvalley*'s crew knew their work. The sooner it was done the sooner would they go on the watch-and-watch system, which would give at least a few of them the chance to rest. The passage north to Bo'ness, on the Firth of Forth, would mean at least two nights at sea—maybe three—in the eight-knot ship at that time of year. No one in that crew of twelve was going to get much rest, in the best of circumstances.

[4]

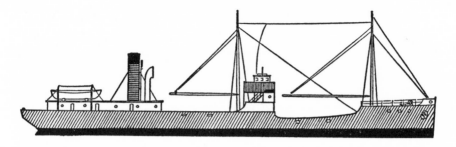

FIG. 1. Coaster with raised quarter-deck, like the *Yewvalley*

The *Yewvalley* was a typical British coaster of the older school
—no frills about her. She was utilitarian to a degree, nothing but
a steel box slightly pointed at both ends, with her one boiler and
the engines aft, the thin high funnel of the natural-draught coal-
fired ship rising from a grubby engine-casing which also housed
the two engineers, in minute cabins, and the small galley where the
cook-steward did his best to prepare meals. Above the casing were
the boats, which were adequate and in good order. From the fore
part of the engine and boiler casing for'ard to the short forecastle-
head the steel deck was broken by the bridge superstructure, a little block of cabins, a small charthouse and, above that, the wheel-
house which was all but filled by a huge wheel—huge because it
was often operated by hand, though the ship carried a steam steering engine.

The *Yewvalley* grossed little over 800 tons—823, to be precise,
with a nett tonnage of 404. Of her 195 feet length, 110 feet was
a raised quarter-deck, at the break of which stood the bridge. Forward of this was a short well-deck. Here was No. 1 hatch, nearly
forty feet long and more than twenty feet in beam, though the ship's
maximum beam was only thirty-one feet. This part of the ship was
awash nearly all the time at sea, when the ship was loaded. No. 2
hatch was even larger but it was on the raised quarter-deck. Two

[5]

stumpy masts swung a derrick each, served by a single steam winch. There was one long hold extending from the collision bulk-head forward to the foreside of the coal bunkers, but the hold was divided just below the bridge by a wooden partition. The *Yewvalley,* like most coasting tramps, was designed to handle her own cargoes in and out, if necessary, but really to be worked by cranes and grabs. Hence the large hatches for the grabs to work in, without impediment. Grabs are ungainly, bullying things of heavy steel, and they need room. They dump cargoes in and they bite them out again, five or ten tons a dump and five or ten tons a bite. They give quick turn-round. That is, they ensure the rapid handling of bulk cargoes, like coal and cement and chalk and stuff like that, so that a ship will be delayed a minimum of time to be charged wharfages and port dues, and so forth. Ships earn freights at sea, not in port. They must get in and out of port quickly. Loading costs money. The *Yewvalley* was generally in port about twenty-four hours. She was a sea-borne steel box built to carry cargoes, to have bulk commodities dumped into her with the utmost possible speed and hauled, dug, grabbed, or sucked out of her at the same rate. She was a North Sea coaster, a sturdy, well-found little wanderer fit to fight the sea—without malice, without 'romance'—to fight the sea and go on fighting the sea summer and winter, whether she was deep-loaded or running light, in ballast trim, bows high and squat counter low, where the four-bladed cast-iron propeller floundered. She had two touches of modernity. She had a Decca navigator to fix her position in bad weather, and she had a radio telephone. The master's orders were to use the telephone once daily, to send a report to the ship's owners in Glasgow.

Outside in the grey North Sea it was already dark, and the wind was freshening. But the wind was off the land and the bulge of Essex kept the sea fairly quiet. The *Yewvalley* dug her bluff bows into the short seas and clouded spray high over the bridge. The foredeck ran with cold water, but she was all right. Snow flurries obscured the coastal lights from time to time, but the ship had steamed up and down the English coast so many times that men said she knew the way by herself and could be left to take herself, if needs be. Master and mates—she had two mates—knew the coast, though the master, Captain James W. Potts, was one of those former deepwater-men who turn to the coast in late middle-age, for reasons of their own, perhaps to be home regularly and often, though for brief visits.

Captain Potts was an unusual coasting master. He was fifty-seven years old. He had been at sea more than forty years, a quarter of a century in command of Bristol Channel world-wandering tramps of Reardon-Smith's. Not ships like the *Yewvalley*—big fellows which went anywhere, and were apt to take a long time about it. His father had been a deepsea master mariner before him, out of the port of Leith, and so it was natural that the son, after schooling at George Watson's College in Edinburgh, would also go to sea. He rose to command many fine deepwater ships, like the *General Smuts,* the *Fresno City,* the *New Westminster City,* the *Bradburn,* the *Fort Fork.* He had a tough time in the war, like many master mariners, but he survived. He was in command of the *Tacoma City* which anchored in the river Mersey during the worst night of Liverpool's worst blitz. The *Tacoma City* had just arrived with general cargo and war stores from New York. After the bombing, naval control required him to move the ship which, they said, was in a dangerous berth. Captain Potts moved her to the berth the officials indicated, where, soon after her anchor was down, she blew sky-high, taking most of her crew with her. A boat from the training-ship *Conway* picked the captain up. After that he was given the *Prince Rupert City.* Off the north of Scotland she suffered three direct hits from a Focke-Wulf bomber attack and was fatally damaged. Again the captain was rescued, but he thought there was a chance to save the ship, which was not far off shore.

So he went back, with volunteers, but he was wrong. The weather worsened and she could not be saved. This time he barely escaped with his life.

After that kind of war (and it went on a long, long time) Captain Potts wanted to quit seafaring and realize an old ambition —an ambition strangely common among master mariners long at sea. He wanted to run a chicken farm. So he left Reardon-Smith's and went ashore, now the war was over and done with. But the Government he had so well served would not allow him an allocation of hens' food for his chicken farm, or a bit of wood to build his chicken-coops. No allocation, no farm: the captain tried hard, but it was no use. Then the chance came to go coasting and, thinking he would stay at that only until conditions improved and he could at last start that farm, he went. Captain Potts had been in the *Yew-valley* only since the previous September—four months. Expert ship-handler, expert pilot, like all the coasting masters; but unlike many of them, he was also an experienced shipmaster all over the world. The difficulties of east-coast navigation in a January gale were simple to him. The little ship plugged on.

It took all night to get round the bulge of Essex, though the wind remained off the land. The morning found the little ship making headway more slowly and the sprays were driving more stubbornly, more frequently and more heavily over the low forecastle-head. The weather had deteriorated, but it was still not really bad. There was no occasion to turn for shelter—yet. True, the fore well-deck was full of water now, though the wind was still in the west. If she were to run for shelter at every threatened North Sea blow she would never deliver a cargo. There were plenty of other vessels about, both northbound and southbound: the usual coastal stream of the flat-iron colliers—those awkward, ungainly vessels which have almost no superstructure and can hinge their funnels down to creep beneath the London bridges on the way to power stations and gas works far upstream—the trim little Dutch motor-ships which always look as if they carry a housekeeper instead of a boatswain, and a woman looks after them (generally a woman does, for the owner-master has his wife with him, almost invariably, and his stalwart sons help to run the ship); coasting and deepsea tankers, little fellows and big, the loaded ones awash in the sea and the ballasted ones high-sided, walloping their huge, high bows upon and into the steep and increasing sea. One after another they dipped and rolled, paying no attention to each other, like a line of automatons on a watery conveyor belt, with rarely a sign of a human being about them. In such weather, no one kept the decks. Wheel-houses were protected and so were glassed-in bridges. There was no occasion to go outside so long as everything stood.

Some of the ships came near enough for Captain Potts to read their names—the *Brockley* and the *President* among them. One coming up astern was more or less keeping him company. *"West-burn,"* he could read on her bows. She was making worse weather of it than he was, for the *Westburn* was in ballast, riding high. The wind now had a bit of northing in it, and the ships had drawn away from the shelter of the nearer land. With the wind at south-west or west-south-west, all England stood between them and the fury of the Atlantic gales. But if the wind went into the nor'ard, the sea went with it, and it would have a long fetch against them, too. It would get up, perhaps violently for a while. But it ought not to last. Westerly gales usually blew themselves out when they went to the nor'ard—usually, but not always. The water swirled round the high coaming of No. 1 hatch, but the steel battens and the steel locking bars above the hatches were doing their work—no sign of movement anywhere.

The *Yewvalley* plugged along like a half-tide rock, but she had done all this many times. There was one occasion when, finding herself in one of those peculiar and unpredictable patches of the shallow North Sea where the sea was much rougher than elsewhere for no accountable reason, she shipped a succession of heavy seas, even over the hatch on the raised quarter-deck. But she shook herself free of them again, like the old warrior she was. The wind was shrieking now and the snow squalls were more frequent. The wind screamed with a different note through the sparse steel rigging, the few funnel stays, and round the ventilators. The stokehold and engine-room ventilators were swung away from the wind, for their big mouths sucked in the cold snow and turned it to a miserable slush, which descended upon the lone fireman shovelling coal in the gloomy firehold. The fireman on watch, flung about in his noisy, dirty, heated dungeon, had had enough of it and meant to pay off as soon as the ship reached Bo'ness. Coasters were hard ships. He meant to find himself a better berth ashore, firing the boiler in some factory. There was plenty of work ashore these days.

About noon, in the lessening periods of fair to moderate visibility, Captain Potts saw that his ship was off the Cromer light-vessel. At one o'clock, she was still there. It was time then for his daily radio report to the owners. What was there to say? They knew what she had loaded—1,040 tons of cement-clinker—and where she was bound for. They would know the weather, too, what with the B.B.C. forecasts and all the weather information so freely available. But they wouldn't know about that fireman. Firemen were not so easily come by nowadays—not firemen used to the coast, and to coal-firing little ships that lived hard. Better tell the owners about that and have them begin to round up a useful citizen from somewhere round the waterfront in Glasgow, to meet the ship when she came in and so make sure there was no delay in her turn-round. He would need an ordinary seaman, too, Captain Potts decided. One of the deckhands also meant to leave. Owners don't like delay in turn-round: he had better ask for the men.

So he sent off his message, speaking carefully into the microphone. He wasted no words.

"Position 1300 off Cromer lightship weather heavy north-west will require one fireman and OS"—that was all, followed by his signature, "Potts." The message went through all right. He was not far from the station.

The weather continued to worsen and the sea to rise. By mid-afternoon, the *Yewvalley* appeared to be alone. The last they saw of the overtaking *Westburn,* she was turning back, to run for shelter into the nearest roadstead. Well, they could understand that. A vessel in ballast had too much hull out of the water to fight all that wind, and she was difficult to control when her bows kept jumping in the air and falling back into the sea again, never in the same place twice or at quite the same angle. The *Westburn* had been throwing her whole forefoot out of the water.

When the *Westburn* turned back Captain Potts might have given a thought to taking the same action, or he might not. The situation was different aboard his ship. Deeply laden, she had a good grip of the sea. He had no fear of the cargo shifting, or the hatches not being able to withstand whatever smashing blows the bad-tempered North Sea might hammer upon them. The ship had carried similar cargoes many, many times. Head-to-sea, as she would be if the wind went more to the north, she would be virtually hove-to. If the weather came on really bad, she was as safe that way as running— much safer, probably. If she tried to run, the sea could pick her up and throw her broadside, broach her to and—very likely—cause her to roll so far and so violently that the heavy, dead cargo *would* shift, and that would be the end of them. Plugging into it, eased down, not fighting but just keeping good steerage way, she ought to be all right. She steered best and handled best like that. True, she was smashing into the seas head-on—but she was no longer trying to push into them. Her big slow-moving propeller was giving her headway enough only to steer. At least she would not broach-to. Her cargo was all right.

The short January afternoon drew to a stormy close with the scream of the gale ever rising and the wind now howling out of the north-north-west. The *Yewvalley*'s steaming lights reflected themselves often upon the scudding snow—the two white masthead lights and the sheen of the coloured sidelights, green and red. There were no other lights, not even in the clearings—only the light of the Cromer lightship, which kept the same bearing hour after hour. The hard gale was picking up the tops of the seas now— the seas were twenty feet high, sometimes higher—and whipping the spray through the maddened air. No wonder those gulls had made for the fields! But a ship's place was at sea, doing her best to deliver such cargoes as were entrusted to her, going about her business as efficiently as she could.

After nightfall Captain Potts himself took the wheel, and stayed there. The sturdy little coaster needed careful nursing, now. This was not an ordinary gale. It was not blowing itself out but increasing in savage and almost continuous gusts until it was blowing almost at hurricane strength, as if it was trying to pick the ship up out of the sea and hurl her through the air. It was a malevolent and violent gale of wind and it showed no sign of easing. Captain Potts had been through hurricanes, cyclones, a typhoon. He knew what really dangerous weather was like. A hard gale of wind was common enough in the North Sea, but this was different. He nursed the ship along, now easing right down, now giving her a bit of power to keep her straight, shouldering into some huge comber of a breaking sea which would have rolled her over if it had caught her off course, slipping down the horrible, foam-streaked troughs, riding up on the crests of the tortured sea. . . . He hoped the old-fashioned rod-and-chain steering-gear would hold. That was a weakness. But it had held for twenty-five years, under the stress of many gales and of shot and shell, bomb-blast and mine. He hoped the hatches would stand all right, too. Well, they should. They had been designed to do just that. . . .

It was that rod-and-chain steering-gear that really worried him. The *Yewvalley,* like so many old-type ships, steered by means of a somewhat cumbrous system of rods and chains which, activated either by hand or by the steam steering-engine, clanked across the decks to the tiller, over a hundred feet away. In some places, the rods and chains ran in well-greased steel troughs. Elsewhere lengths of rod were exposed to the elements. Such steering-gear had been the downfall of more than one ship, as Captain Potts well knew. He knew equally well that it was a well-tried old system. It *ought* to stand. It was strong, and well maintained. There was no earthly reason why a rod, or a length of chain, should suddenly take it into its head that night to carry away. Mere weight of water would not break it, but sudden jerks and tremendous strains might. There was an alternative system of tackles to be rigged to the tiller-head in an emergency, and this system would be all very well if the rods-and-chains broke down in calm. In a gale of wind such as the ship was struggling in that night—well, those tackles were not even a gesture of hope. If the steering went she went, and those blocks and tackles would be as much use to the ship as her boats would be to the crew. Well, that was the way of it. That was the way old coasters were—and not only coasters. . . .

The mate was on the bridge, in the tiny wheel-house, with the captain. It was the mate's watch. From all that they could hear on the radio, the terrible weather the *Yewvalley* was experiencing was even worse elsewhere, nor was there any hope of early improvement. It was a bad night. The air was full of distress signals. But as yet there seemed no reason why it should be a fatal night.

Suddenly the sky cleared overhead, with the wind still shrieking and the seas breaking in a wild tumult of leaping, frenzied water. The horizon became clear shortly afterwards. Captain Potts was glad to see the clearing. Perhaps it indicated a let-up in the storm, and the morning would bring better weather. Now he could see the lights of other vessels, distantly. They were on safe bearings—no risk of collision. If they were all right, so was the *Yewvalley*. He thanked God that this stormy stretch of sea was no longer E-boat Alley, as it had been known during the war, when a swift torpedo from some lurking German E-boat was an ever-present menace, to say nothing of attack from the air. At least now it was a clean fight—the ship against the sea.

But what was that? One hand still on the spokes of the big wheel, Captain Potts opened the wheel-house door and looked out from the open of the bridge, though the spray and the sea flew over him there and the wind tore at his bare head, and the snow fingers bit like flying needles. What he thought he saw, at first, was *breakers*—the breakers of a reef, where no reef could be. The light of the Cromer lightship soon reassured him of that. No reef! The *Yewvalley* was on course, as she had always been all that long day and the wild night. Breakers? *They were breakers!* The sea was breaking, wildly, cascading over what looked—what looked now like rocks. Rocks? There were no rocks! It was a great ship, a lightless hulk, adrift, right in the very path of the coaster, dead ahead!

"We'll have to get her out of this! Hang on now! Warn the engine-room! She'll roll now like she was standing still before!" the captain roared to the mate, at the same instant throwing his weight on the wheel to pull it over, to get the ship round. The great drifting hulk, blown by the gale and driven by the furious sea, was almost upon the *Yewvalley*'s bows. Would she pay off in time? Could she avoid that deadly onslaught? She would go down like a stone if she did not: she might broach-to if she did! Captain Potts made the only possible decision—better any chance than no chance at all! She *might* get round. . . .

The little dripping bows began to swing—slowly, at first, all too slowly, as if reluctant to get out of the way of that menacing hulk. But then they came quickly—too quickly! The *Yewvalley* began to roll as if she would fling her boiler through the casing and the wheel-house off the bridge. The mastheads threw frightful circles in the wind-maddened air, their white lights stabbing now at the stars, now rolled towards the depths of the sea. The *Yewvalley*'s people could do nothing but hang on, holding their breaths. Would she come round? *Could* she come round? A moment now, and she would be in the trough of the sea.

Suddenly the poor little ship lurched violently. There was a terrible roar down below, audible frighteningly even above the wild scream of the gale—the cargo shifting! That rocklike stuff they had regarded as immovable was on the move, flung down to leeward with the ship's roll. Over it went and over went the *Yewvalley* with it, pinned down on her side, a plaything for the maelstrom of waters. The sea roared over her, smashed into the wheel-house, smashed the engine-room skylights and into the engine-casing, tore down below. Within a moment, lying on her side in the wild flurry of the roaring waters, smashed and open to the sea, the little ship slid below the waters, before her engines had stopped and while her great cast-iron propeller was still flailing round. Down she went, down. Within a matter of seconds, nothing of her remained. For a brief moment a white face broke the wild water. There was a cry upon the sea—and then, nothing but the roar of the gale. The lightless hulk, unmanned and unmanageable, dipped and rolled and drove upon her heedless way across the paths of ships—ships more fortunate than the *Yewvalley,* for they were further away.

The *Yewvalley* was lost beneath the sea, she and all her people, and nothing of her or of them has been seen since. She was officially posted missing at Lloyd's, on March 11, 1953, after the usual advertisements and inquiries.

The description of the last moments of the *Yewvalley* is a reconstruction of what may have happened, what probably did happen. In fact, no one knows what exactly did cause the ship to founder. She is missing. A well-found ship bound upon her lawful occasions does not just disappear from the face of the seas these days without some very exhaustive inquiries being made into all the circumstances. *Why* was she lost? *How* was she lost? Was anyone culpable? If there is some lesson to be learned from her loss, then it must be learned, and publicised in every possible way. The first step is taken by that wonderful organization for the protection of ships and those concerned with their insurance, Lloyd's of London. *Every* registered ship which plies for hire upon the seas today from Britain—and most other countries—is built to rules carefully compiled for her safety and the safety of the crew and cargo she carries. Not only is the ship built to rules and given a 'class,' but she has to retain that class if she is going to keep the seas. Periodical surveys both of hull and machinery are called for and they must be passed, though to pass them may cost large sums of money. Her proper maintenance is not a matter for her owner's whim. A well-built cargo ship, properly maintained and not knocked about by strandings, damage of the sea and so on, may last a good thirty years or even more. Every so many years, she has to take time off from carrying cargoes and come into dock for survey.

Not only Lloyd's is interested. The Government is interested, too —very much so. Competent and implacable men tear the ship apart (more or less) and stipulate what shall be done to keep her class. These things must be done and a certificate obtained to show that *all* official requirements have been complied with, or the ship will not be given a clearance from any British customs house. Much the same thing applies in America, in France, Germany, Holland, Norway, Portugal and other maritime countries. With no clearance, a ship cannot sail. If she does sail, she is a pirate (unless she is going to a break-up yard). Ships are usually sold for scrap when the sum necessary to be spent on maintaining their class exceeds a reasonable estimate of their probable earnings over the years of life left to them. It is a business proposition. Ships which are not scrapped must be seaworthy. They must also be properly manned; carry adequate life-saving apparatus, which must be in usable order, properly stowed, and exercised regularly; be safely loaded not only as to draught but in the matter of preventing shifts of cargo, whenever cargo likely to shift is carried. Every precaution is taken which centuries of experience indicate may help to maintain adequate standards of seaworthiness, in all respects.

Yet the *Yewvalley,* a ship classed $+100$ A 1 at Lloyd's, a ship properly loaded, adequately manned, seaworthy in every possible respect, *did* disappear from the face of the sea, with all her crew, within sight of the English coast. No trace of the ship was ever found, except a couple of lifebuoys off the Belgian coast, where they were picked up by a Belgian pilot vessel about a fortnight after she was lost. There was no trace of anyone who had been on board.

What *did* happen to that little ship? That night, dreadful as it was, seventy-eight other ships were at sea in the vicinity of the place where the *Yewvalley* was last reported. None of these went missing. Why only the *Yewvalley?* The North Sea is a great highroad for ships, big and small, especially along the British east coast and the coast of north-west Europe. On the face of it, it would seem impossible that an entity so solid as a ship could entirely disappear anywhere in such crowded waters and nothing ever be found to indicate her fate. (A lot of drifting lifebuoys are to be found in the North Sea. They are easy to lose overboard.) And why were there no signals? Captain Potts had only to switch on a microphone. He and his officers were thoroughly familiar with the procedures for maritime radio telephony. They were well aware of the distress routine, arranged to give urgent priority to just such a call as they might have been expected to send out some time on that wild night. But they sent nothing—not even a rocket, or a flare.

The *Yewvalley* was not the only ship which failed to survive that terrible night of January 31, 1953. That was the night the dykes broke in the south of Holland, and the cold sea swept in to wreak terrible destruction. Much of the low coastline of East Anglia was flooded, too. So was Canvey Island, in the Thames: London itself escaped but barely. The great storm pinned a mighty tide in the leeward corner of the North Sea, built up hurricane seas, lashed the coastal defences, smashed over and then right through strong dykes

[17]

and sea walls, ripped away sea defences, flung ships ashore, tore them from their anchorages, turned them over in dry-dock and smashed them against dock walls ordinarily thought to provide safe havens, wrenched even such securely moored vessels as lightships from their great anchors to send them careering about, a menace in the seas they should have safely marked. And the wind and the sea overwhelmed ships out in the open sea—the *Yewvalley* among them.

Yet it is surely the business of a ship to be fit to survive *any* onslaught of the sea. As far as it is humanly possible to ensure that all ships shall be so fit, in Britain the Ministry of Transport and Civil Aviation sees that in fact they are. It follows that when a seagoing ship, properly classed and surveyed and known in all respects to have complied with all the official requirements, does disappear after a storm, some searching inquiries are made. The first step is a preliminary inquiry. Competent and energetic men, themselves seamen and surveyors of great experience, go to the port where the ship loaded and the port she hailed from. Was she really properly loaded? Might a little carelessness have crept in? Or might the custom of the port be just a little slipshod in the matter of dumping bulk cargoes into the capacious holds of elderly ships a little too anxious for quick turn-round, regardless of all other con-siderations? Just precisely what was the reputation of the ship? Of her master? Her owners? Without any sort of inquisition—there is no such thing—a competent and patient seaman turned investi-gator can find out a great deal by going to the source of things.

But his search for the cause of the ship's loss is handicapped when the whole crew have gone with her. After all, they alone know the final answers, and they have gone where there are no official in-quiries. Nonetheless a great deal can be found out. If in the course of these preliminary investigations anything comes to light which may indicate any possible degree of blame on anyone connected with the ship or her running, or if there is the slightest possibility that a further, more exhaustive and public inquiry may conceivably serve any useful purpose, by discovering faults where no fault was suspected, or by uncovering culpability in anyone, or by indicating how the ever-present problem of assuring safety at sea may be carried even a little further towards complete efficiency, then such an inquiry is ordered to be held. In London the Minister of Transport makes the decision whether to hold such an inquiry or not. He has able advisers. The fact that the Minister may order an inquiry does not indicate that there is necessarily any suspicion of blame against anyone. In the case of the *Yewvalley,* for instance, the fact that eight other vessels, all thought to be seaworthy in all respects, also went missing about the same time, and a tenth vessel foundered in dreadful circumstances in the Northern Irish Sea with the loss of many lives, might well have indicated to the Minister's advisers that it was a good idea to inquire as exhaustively as possible into all these cases.

Four of the ships were British, three Hollanders, and one each Swedish and Belgian. The British ministry could be concerned only directly with the British ships. Nine ships missing after one storm! It was the greatest number ever to be posted missing upon the one day at Lloyd's this century. In the old days of weak, unsupervised ships, dependent upon sails to carry them safely through whatever hazards the grim North Sea could throw at them, such a loss would have called for no comment. Any onshore blow that accounted for only nine ships, indeed, would not have rated as much of an effort. In those days, a really wild gale left the shores both of Britain and the nearer Continent littered with the ribs of battered ships, and the bodies of drowned seamen. But in these days, the public does not expect to hear of nine power-driven, radio-equipped, properly classed, surveyed and supervised ships lost in a night—not only lost, but swept from the sea without a cry or a trace from any of them, and this in the narrow seas about the British Isles. The public does not expect its fish to be caught for it or its cargoes to be carried at the cost of so many ships and lives.

So there was an official inquiry, in due course, into the case of the missing *Yewvalley*. It was held in Glasgow, the little ship's home port, before the Sheriff-Substitute of Lanarkshire, sitting with two nautical assessors whose purpose is to see that the nautical evidence is properly given and its significance appreciated. This is the normal rule at such inquiries. The judge may be relied upon to sift through to the truth and to appreciate to the full the legal side of things, and the assessors are to help with the maritime technicalities. Any interested party is entitled to appear before the court, or to be represented. If there is any dirt to be exposed, the court is there to see it, and hear all about it. Courts of inquiry are extremely businesslike and competent affairs which suffer no fools gladly. They are out for the facts—*all* the facts and nothing but the facts, and guesswork does not interest them.

So it was in Glasgow on the 26th and 27th of March, 1954—over a year after the *Yewvalley* had been posted missing. The Sheriff and the assessors listened carefully to a description of the ship, who owned her, how she was maintained, manned, officered, loaded, fitted with navigation aids and life-saving gear. All relevant documents were produced for the court's inspection—plans of the ship, articles of agreement, crew lists, reports of surveys and so forth. Nothing was left to chance. The court was informed that the *Yewvalley* was one of four sister-ships in a fleet of seven vessels belonging to Messrs. John Stewart and Company Shipping Ltd., of Clyde Street, Glasgow. (One sister, the little *Yewdale,* had distinguished herself at the evacuation of Dunkirk, where she had shown herself a remarkably tough and able vessel.) She was built in 1928 by Scott and Sons at Bowling. She was a seaworthy and well-found vessel in all respects when she sailed from the Thames at the beginning of her last voyage. Her life-saving equipment was satisfactory and in good order. (The court by no means took that for granted but investigated each of the matters very thoroughly. Such things as copies of engineer's log books, the ship's official log, defect lists, survey reports, repair bills and so on throw a pretty clear light on both the state of ships and their maintenance. There was no fault to be found with the *Yewvalley*.) She had two lifeboats each 17 feet 6 inches long by 6 feet beam, either of which could easily have accommodated her entire crew, and she had a working-boat as well. She had life-jackets for everyone, eight lifebuoys, line-throwing apparatus, flares, rockets. All these things were subject to periodic inspection and had been so inspected, the certificates being produced. Her lights and sound signals had been inspected and passed (certificate furnished). There had been a special survey of the hull and machinery in May, 1952. The ship was classed +100 A 1 at Lloyd's, for four years from the time of the special survey.

None of the technical witnesses who gave evidence before the court could indicate any weakness or deficiency in the ship which could in any way have contributed to her loss, nor could any fault be found with the manner in which she was loaded, despite the fact that the cargo was trimmed only by the grab. There was no direct evidence of her draught, but she was not overloaded. The pier foreman who supervised the loading was unaware of the amount of water she was drawing, but her cargo was near-capacity and her draught would be normal. He had heard the mate report the draught for'ard and aft to the captain as he completed loading, and Captain Potts had said he was perfectly satisfied. There was another waggon or two of cargo he could have taken, and the foreman had offered him this. But he refused it. The pier foreman was a most experienced man, and the grab-loading was done in the normal manner, to get the heavy stuff evenly distributed in the holds, with the ship on an even keel and no undue stresses anywhere, flat enough on top to get the hatches secured. The captain could have ordered trimming, if

[21]

he had thought any trimming was advisable to even off the slopes or to fill in areas where the cement-clinker, perhaps, was not quite level. But he was quite satisfied, and he knew what he was doing.

Expert witnesses gave evidence about this cargo and its liability to shift. A ministry surveyor conducted experiments with the stuff, in a box, and he found that he had to roll the box fairly violently to an angle of 53 degrees before the cement began to run. A previous captain of the *Yewvalley* told how he had safely carried such cargoes many times, and he also paid a tribute to the ship. This was Captain George Peterkin Moir, who was in command of the *Yewforest* at the time of the inquiry. He described the *Yewvalley* as a well-found ship, in good seaworthy condition when he sailed in her, and a splendid sea-vessel. He had never had any difficulty with cement-clinker shifting. He had never known a suggestion of movement in such a cargo, even in a very rough sea. A former engineer from the *Yewvalley* said that the hatches and all their fastenings were good and well maintained and were always properly secured when the vessel went to sea. (There could be no direct evidence as to this on the voyage when the ship was lost. She left the wharf— as is normal practice in small coasters—with the hatches still unsecured. It was the usual thing to get the ship thoroughly prepared for sea on the way down the river.)

Extracts from the chief engineer's log books for the *Yewvalley* were produced to the court, covering a period of five years up to December, 1952, the month before she was lost. There had been some mechanical trouble. It would be very odd if there had not been, for the vessel was nearly twenty years old when the log was begun. She had been stopped at sea by engine breakdown once. This was during midsummer, 1949. There was no defect shown in the engineer's log which could possibly account for the loss of the ship. She had had a new propeller and a new propeller shaft. The steering-gear had been regularly overhauled. It had been thoroughly surveyed in May, 1952, along with the rest of the ship and her fittings.

There was no evidence that the *Yewvalley* had ever had a steering breakdown, but nonetheless the court noted that such a breakdown *could* be a possible cause, or a contributory cause, of the vessel's loss. There was not the remotest chance that an explosion of coal gas generated from her bunker-coal could have blown her up.

Nor was there any real chance that a stray Second World War mine might have sent her up, either. In the first place, it was highly likely that such an explosion would have been seen. In the second place, blown-up ships leave a lot of wreckage, and nothing whatever from the *Yewvalley* had come ashore anywhere, apart from those two lifebuoys. They showed no evidence of any explosion. In the third place, Admiralty pointed out that, since the area had been cleared at the end of the war, there had been only one mine casualty anywhere near the likely position of the *Yewvalley*.

". . . It is considered most unlikely that the *Yewvalley* either activated a ground mine or struck a moored mine," wrote My Lords of Admiralty in response to the court's inquiry. "Both British and German moored mines are fitted with a mechanism which renders the mine harmless should it break adrift from its moorings. The area in question has been very thoroughly swept, and since the War there has been only one casualty anywhere near the likely position of the loss of the *Yewvalley*. This was the loss of the ss. *Sarbegna*, which occurred as long ago as 7th May, 1949, in an approximate position of 52 21' N., 01 16' E."

This letter was read in court, but the learned sheriff refused to be satisfied even with that. Evidence was given that, despite what the Admiralty had said, the Hull trawler *Marach* had put into Grimsby Roads about a fortnight after the night of the presumed loss of the *Yewvalley*, with a live mine on deck which had been picked up in her trawl. During February, 1953, there were fourteen reports to Lloyd's of mines or objects resembling mines in the waters off the east coast of the United Kingdom. Four of these were said to be in the coastal traffic routes. Nonetheless, because of the absence of wreckage (to say nothing of the far greater likelihood of loss by stress of weather in some form or other), it was the official view that loss by mine, while it could not be entirely dismissed, was extremely unlikely. After all, a ship's own bow wave pushes a floating mine away, and any old moored mine was supposed to be harmless.

Evidence of the kind of weather brewing in the North Sea that night was presented by a Principal Scientific Officer of the Meteorological Office of the Air Ministry, whose business it had been to study British weather over the past twenty years. The weather was atrocious, though this was not the scientist's word for it. In the area where the *Yewvalley* was last seen, the wind on the night of January 31 reached the force of a strong gale, from between north-west and north-north-west. Further to the north it was stronger, and this helped to build up a very broken sea. Records that night at Spurn Head, which was not far from the *Yewvalley*'s position, showed an average speed of the wind which was exceeded only half a dozen times since records were kept—that was in over thirty years. The storm further north was the most severe for a hundred years. The seas were running twenty feet high, on the average, with perhaps some breaking seas of thirty feet. In water less than fifty fathoms deep such seas would be steep, and breaking. The visibility was poor during the snow showers, moderate between the squalls. Gale warnings had been given by radio.

As for the effect of that sort of weather on ships, the master of the collier *Bestwood,* a vessel of 2,850 tons with a crew of twenty-three, said in evidence that he had been coming down from Blyth with a full cargo of coal that night. The wind and sea were with him, but the *Bestwood* was struck by a "phenomenal sea which seemed to come from a direction other than the normal direction of the sea at the time, and it seemed to overwhelm the ship"—these are Captain Wolfe's own words—". . . and it caused her to heel and the cargo to shift." The *Bestwood* went over with the top of her coal cargo rattling down to leeward. She went over twenty degrees. The ship was about twenty-five miles south-east of Flamborough Head at the time. Her hatches held, and Captain Wolfe was able to get her round head to sea without the cargo shifting any further. There were no more such tremendous seas, though the state of the sea in general was bad enough. He staggered away for the nearest port, which was the Humber, and he just made it. The *Bestwood* had steel hatches; the *Bestwood,* too, had time to send off messages describing her predicament, and another ship stood by her.

The captain of the *Hudson Strait,* a vessel of over 3,000 tons, which was also bound south towards London from Blyth with a full coal cargo that night, said the sea was so high and broken that, even though the ship was deep-loaded, the propeller was coming out of the water. A heavy sea swept over the *Hudson Strait* and flattened the woodwork on the lower bridge, and flooded the midships accommodation.

The Ministry inquiries into the state of the seventy-eight ships which had been somewhere in the vicinity of the Cromer lightship at the time the *Yewvalley* was last heard of showed, from the logs of seventy-four of them, that of this number forty-one ships had run for shelter, four had their cargoes shift in greater or less degree, and twenty-five suffered heavy weather damage. Twenty-eight of the seventy-eight were northbound ships and forty-nine were southbound. Of the twenty-eight northbound, twenty-two ran for shelter and five were damaged by heavy seas. Of the forty-nine southbound, nineteen made for shelter. Twenty sustained heavy weather damage, and four suffered shifts of cargo. During the thirty-six hours following noon on January 31, thirty-two ships of different nationalities had sent out distress messages. All four ships whose cargoes shifted were carrying coal. None of these was lost. Four British ships and five foreign ships had been posted missing after that night. Only two of these sent out messages indicating that they were in any kind of trouble.

The really significant evidence came towards the end of the inquiry. A senior nautical surveyor of the Ministry of Transport told the court that among the ships in the vicinity of the *Yewvalley* when she was lost were two which were not on voyages, north-bound nor southbound, at all. They were adrift. One of these was an old oil-tanker, the *Olcades,* which had broken from the tugs which were towing her from Singapore to Blyth, to be broken up. She had no crew aboard, and no lights. The other was a lightship, the East Dudgeon light-vessel, which was adrift in the area on the night of January 31, without lights. The *Olcades* had broken adrift that afternoon from a position about sixty miles north-west of the last place where the *Yewvalley* was seen, and her drift before the wind and sea would have brought her into the path of the little steamer. The hulk of the *Olcades* was sighted off Bacton, near which place she grounded, shortly after noon on the following day. The East Dudgeon lightship was also adrift and her track was known fairly accurately. She, too, must have passed very close to the *Yewvalley,* if the *Yewvalley* had continued on her course. From a careful reconstruction of the *Olcades'* line of drift, she was more likely to be the real hazard.

The old oil-tanker was examined closely as she lay ashore, when the weather had quietened. She was battered about, but there was no sign on the ancient hull of any recent collision. It was unlikely that the *Yewvalley* could have come into collision with her without leaving some telltale marks. There was no indication that the light-ship had been in contact with any other vessel, either.

If a shipmaster, however, found himself, already hard pressed by the severe gale, suddenly faced by a couple of unmanageable hulks, or even one such hulk, bearing down on his vessel, "it would be rather an alarming sight," said the witness and, he added as an afterthought, "it might be somewhat unnerving."

It was not necessary for the *Yewvalley* to be struck to become a casualty of the storm. The witness made that clear. If the master quite properly took sudden avoiding action, that might well have been the cause of the disaster.

The court, after due deliberation, could only find that it could give no precise cause for the loss of the *Yewvalley*. By far the most important single factor was undoubtedly the "sudden storm of exceptional violence" which occurred round the British coasts on January 31, 1953. The absence of distress signals, the court went on, indicated that the disaster was sudden, and the absence of wreckage indicated that the ship went down as a complete unit and did not disintegrate.

"There can be very little doubt," it summed up, "that the predominant cause of this casualty was the exceptional violence of the weather, though the precise way in which the storm claimed this particular victim cannot be known." It was not impossible that the *Olcades* or the lightship might have been the cause of the *Yewvalley*'s undoing. In trying to swing away, "a consequent violent lurch accompanied by cargo shifting could have been quickly fatal. We think this possibility is as likely as any. . . ." These are the court's words.

As likely as any—aye, and seamen held that it was likelier than most. That phenomenal sea which struck the collier *Bestwood* might have helped. The same sea may well have struck the *Yewvalley* as she was in the very act of turning from the appalling danger of one or other drifting hulk. Or it might have knocked her over on her side as she was turning at last to run for shelter into Yarmouth Roads, and have sent her spinning down, without allowing her captain time even to flick his microphone on, or give a thought to the little farm he had hoped one day to own.

CHAPTER TWO

"The Usual Time in the Morning"

LLOYD'S NOTICE

VESSELS FOR INQUIRY

The Committee of Lloyd's will be glad of any information regarding the following vessel:—

"GUAVA," motor trawler of Lowestoft, Official Number 166722, 285 tons gross, Master Fisher, which is reported to have sailed from Lowestoft for North Sea fishing grounds on the 30th January, 1953, and was reported in approx. lat. 53 30 N., long. 3 E. on the 31st January.

Lloyd's, London, E.C. 3.
4th March, 1953.

SHIPS which were lost without trace on the night of January 31 to February 1, 1953, round the waters of the British Isles and in the North Sea were, in addition to the *Yewvalley,* the British trawlers *Sheldon,* of 278 tons, hailing from Grimsby, the *Michael Griffith,* 282 tons, of Fleetwood on the other side of England, and the *Guava,* 285 tons, of Lowestoft, in Suffolk, the motor trawler *Leopold Nera,* 58 tons, of Zeebrugge, the steam trawler *Catharina Duyvis,* 329 tons, from the Dutch port of Ymuiden, the Dutch coasters *Salland,* 297 tons, of Delfzyl, and *Westland,* 426 tons, of Rotterdam, and the Swedish steamer *Aspo,* 1,331 tons, of Stockholm. These nine ships carried crews of 108 men, and no passengers. Every one of them had wireless (though one had a receiving set only) and all had the usual rockets, flares and other distress signals. They all had boats, life-jackets, buoyant apparatus. Most of them were within sight of land—well populated and prosperous land, which manned Coast Guard stations, lifeboats, and rescue teams for the special purpose of assisting ships and seamen in distress. The longest voyage any was making was across the North Sea. The fishermen were all working the nearer waters. There were plenty of other ships in the vicinity of all of them. Only two sent any sort of message even indicating that they were in trouble, and all nine of them disappeared from the face of the sea.

In each case, they were listed first at Lloyd's as 'overdue' vessels when the dates upon which they should have reached their destinations, or returned to land their fish, had passed long enough to cause comment. Overdue is an ominous word but by no means fatal. Many ships are posted overdue which subsequently arrive, some of them after many days. Like the old sailing-ship *Lalla Rookh,* a barque of about 800 tons, for example, which left Brisbane in Queensland during March, 1905, and had not been seen or heard of by the end of the following September. She came in, in due course, at the end of the first week in October. She had been on the 'overdue' list a while then and was getting perilously near the 'missing.'

In those days, ships had no wireless to report themselves, and sailing-ships went by lonely routes far from the sight of other vessels, except a few wanderers of their own kind. From Brisbane round Cape Horn to the English Channel is a very long way, but the *Lalla Rookh* could and should have been less than six months in the sailing of it. She was no sluggard. However, she did arrive, and that was that. A ship is reported overdue as a warning to underwriters that no news has been heard of her. It is a domestic procedure at Lloyd's. The extraordinary newspaper which Lloyd's issue daily gives news of overdue vessels and of maritime casualties all over the world. On the average day there are about a hundred casualties— strandings, collisions, fires, weather damage, striking dock walls in a gust of wind and that sort of thing, and sometimes founderings. Comparatively few of the hundred ships are actually lost. Every now and then, one slips into the overdue list.

"Overdue Vessels," it is headed. It gives the facts, and the facts only—usually about little ships, like the *Lark,* from Holland.

> LARK, Oslo Feb. 19.—Anxiety is felt for the safety of the Dutch motor vessel *Lark,* which left Porsgrunn on February 10 for Stavanger, with fertiliser, and was last seen when she passed Brevik. In the night of Feb. 10–11 there was strong wind with heavy squalls from the south-east along the Skaggerak coast.

So reads a typical report. The source is given—one of the great news agencies, a shipping paper on the Continent, a Lloyd's agent somewhere. Such reports come from all over the world and concern all ships, big and small, and not merely ships which are insured at Lloyd's.

> SADIKZADENAZIM.—London, Oct. 8.—In reply to inquiries the owners of the steamer *Sadikzadenazim* write from Istanbul under date of Oct. 6: *Sadikzadenazim,* with a crew of 20 and a cargo of coal, left Zonguldak on Sept. 24 and up to now we have received no news of her and our authorities have considered her as sunk. The name of the master was Mehmet Ulsever.

So reads another message. The Turkish vessel with the long name was indeed sunk, and nothing further was heard of her crew of 20.

> BARBARA AND RONNIE.—London, Feb. 26.—In reply to inquiry, Lloyd's agents at St. John's, N.F., write under date of Feb. 18: No news has been received of motor vessel *Barbara and Ronnie,* 21 tons, since she left Ingonish on Dec. 18 for Petites, N.F.

MONT BLANC (aux.)—Land's End Radio, Aug. 25.—Following received from Brest Le Conquet Radio at 4 35 pm GMT: The authorities at Douarnenez request news of lobster fishing vessel *Mont Blanc* which is overdue. The vessel should have left the fishing grounds off Mauretania on July 21. The vessel is an auxiliary dandy, registered number Douarnenez 3146, 118 tons, painted white.

The Portuguese trawler *Exportador Segundo,* last heard of somewhere off Cap Blanc; the big American ore-carrier *Southern Districts,* of 3,338 tons, on passage from a Gulf port towards Maine; the Argentinian steamer *General San Martin,* of 9,389 tons, last seen somewhere to the westward of the Straits of Magellan; the German motor-ship *Melanie Schulte,* 6,367 tons, bound with iron ore from Narvik towards Mobile; the Peterhead motor fishing vessel *Quiet Waters,* 55 tons, fishing out of her home port in far from quiet waters—all these featured on the lists of overdue vessels, and none came in again. While they are overdue, underwriters who have insured the ships or their cargoes may wish to reinsure, and the rate at which such reinsurance can be effected is an indication of the hopes—in Lloyd's experienced view—of the vessel's ultimate safe arrival. In the days of sail, no wireless, and indifferent communications generally, ships came more easily on the overdue list and more easily off again, too. Now fewer come off. After all, if a ship can communicate her whereabouts she will do so, and she has no business becoming overdue if all is well with her. If she does come in again, the famous *Lutine* bell is struck, once, and once only, and the news of the overdue ship's safe arrival is announced from the rostrum. The *Lutine* bell is struck twice for other announcements of importance, of any sort. In these days, it is very seldom struck once, or twice either.

(The *Lutine* was a famous treasure-ship sunk with nearly £2,000,000 in gold aboard off Vlieland in October, 1799. Many attempts to salve the gold have failed, but the bell was recovered and presented to Lloyd's, where it hangs suspended over the rostrum in the underwriting room. The *Lutine* was originally a French thirty-two-gun frigate which was captured and commissioned in the British Navy.)

The next step is that the vessel is advertised for inquiry. She is then just that—a 'vessel for inquiry.' This means that the Committee of Lloyd's, anxious for the ship's well-being, place notices prominently in each issue of Lloyd's List for a week, asking anyone who has any information about whatever vessels are named to come forward and offer it. Before that stage is reached, Lloyd's agents have been alerted and have looked into all possible sources of news of the ship. In the old days, news used to come in. A ship might have been sighted somewhere, off St. Helena say, if she had come round Good Hope, or 'spoken' another—have exchanged signals. Or some fellow wanderer might have come in from a long voyage with the crew aboard, and news that the vessel had had to be abandoned. In these days no news is ever received in response to these inquiries. A vessel for inquiry is a vessel lost, and, after all the facts about her have been carefully considered, the Committee of Lloyd's weigh the case and decide whether the ship should be posted missing. The decision is not taken lightly.

Records have been kept at Lloyd's of all such vessels since October 29, 1873. The records are kept in large red books, each of about two hundred pages, and the first book was filled two years and two months after it was started, by no means only with the names of sailing vessels. There are plenty of steamers—of a sort —too. In the whole of the time from October, 1873, until today, there has been only one case where a vessel officially posted missing has subsequently arrived. This was the 1,600-ton ship *Red Rock,* of Glasgow, which was posted missing when over one hundred days out on a passage from Townsville, Queensland, in ballast, towards Noumea in New Caledonia. The *Red Rock,* which carried a crew of twenty-four, sailed from Townsville on the 20th of February, 1899, to load a cargo of nickel ore at Noumea. A week later, she was seen off Magnetic Island, which was not very far from her point of departure. After that, nothing was heard of the *Red Rock* until the 7th of June when, having been first reported overdue and then advertised as a vessel for inquiry, she was officially posted missing. Five days later, she turned up safely at Noumea.

Nothing was wrong with her, except that the crew were probably a bit hungry, which was no new state to them. She had had to beat to windward in ballast, high out of the water and difficult to handle, the whole of the way. The distance is less than a thousand miles, but nonetheless the Committee of Lloyd's then were perhaps a shade pessimistic about the *Red Rock*'s chances of survival. Perhaps none of them had ever had to beat about the Coral Sea in a big square-rigged ship in ballast. The whole of the way, the wind and the current and the very scend of the sea were against her. First, she had to get away from the dreadful Great Barrier Reef, which skirts the Queensland coast. Then she had to stay away from it, and all the other reefs—then, and for the following forty years, most imperfectly known and poorly charted—and beat right across the Coral Sea in the face of the south-east trade wind. *Everything* was against her. It was also the cyclone season, and a cyclone is a hurricane by another name. The area in which the *Red Rock* sailed that passage was the worst place for Coral Sea cyclones. Moreover, she could not be tacked—that is, driven into the wind on the many, many occasions when it was necessary to change course during the months of beating against wind and sea. She could not go about head-to-wind, in ballast, and so she had to go the other way—to wear ship, to jibe like a yacht (more or less). A square-rigged ship loses a lot of ground when she changes course that way—miles of it. The remarkable thing is not so much that the *Red Rock* took ninety-nine days from Magnetic Island to Noumea but that she made the passage successfully at all. There is no record of the fact, but it is also quite probable that she had none too much ballast in the first place. Her passage was to be made within the tropics. It was short—or should have been—and she was a

Scots ship with a Scots crew. The habit of sometimes taking too little ballast got a lot of sailing-ships into trouble.

If the Committee of Lloyd's were unduly pessimistic about the chances of the *Red Rock,* they did not make the same mistake twice. Even at that, no insurance had been paid out on the ship, for the rule then was that settlement was not made until two weeks after the vessel had been officially posted missing. There were plenty of Scotsmen on the floor at Lloyd's, too.

The brief facts about the *Red Rock* are recorded in Missing Vessels Book 9, which dates from the 1st of January, 1897, to the 31st of December, 1900. There are plenty of mysteries in it, mysteries that have never been solved, and, indeed, scarcely ever looked into, once the insurance changed hands. What happened, for instance, in the case of the barque *Bankholme,* of Liverpool, of 1,230 tons, which disappeared while on passage from Lobos de Afuera (off Peru) with a cargo of guano bound towards Antwerp, back in '96? She had a crew of nineteen all told, four of them boy apprentices. She had safely rounded the Horn, where many a fine ship went missing in the days of sail. She had safely sailed most of the South Atlantic, too, for she was seen and spoken off Martin Vaz on the 2nd of November when she was sixty days out. The worst of her passage was long over then. She was a good vessel, well found. Yet she, too, sailed off the face of the sea and was never again heard of. And the *Saratoga,* ship, with case oil from New York for Shanghai (she was allowed to be out 313 days before she was posted missing)—where is she? The *Glenfinlas,* ship, and the *Castlebank,* of Glasgow, barque—and many more—which sailed deep-loaded with Australian coal from Newcastle, New South Wales, towards the west coast of South America and never were seen or heard from again—what happened to them? In at least some of their cases it is possible that the cargo shifted, and the ships were flung upon their beam ends, with the cruel South Pacific seas smashing in their hatches and sending them down. 'Pacific,' indeed! That is a stormy road, the old coal road from Newcastle, N.S.W., towards South America. . . . The *Laurelbank,* of Glasgow, bound from Shanghai towards Portland, Oregon, for orders, 146 days out before she was posted missing: the *Caradoc,* ship, from Kobe towards Port Angeles: the *Celtic Bard,* Hong Kong towards Royal Roads in ballast: the *Dominion,* ship, Honolulu towards Royal Roads for orders (which should have been a short and sunny run): the steamer *Port Melbourne,* of nearly 5,000 tons, bound from New York across the Atlantic with a crew of sixty: the little *Glenora* of Windsor, Nova Scotia, 118 days out on passage from Turk's Island towards New York in the winter of '97 before she was posted missing—where are all these? Ship after ship, two hundred of them and more, fill the finely scripted pages—every one of them both tragedy and mystery.

In those days there was a greater acceptance of the risk of going missing. A voyage was a venture then, and ships fought alone. It was possible, too, for unscrupulous owners sometimes to send ships to sea which were not seaworthy. Over-insurance of such ships for the sake of criminal gain was far from unknown. Until comparatively recent years, one of the first things official inquiries and official investigators dealt with was this matter of insurance. The point is checked still. Was the ship over-insured? Was there any inducement for someone to lose her? If so, they wanted to know the reason why. In these days such cases rarely arise. Ships are not over-insured, not on today's rising markets. Crews will not go to sea in 'coffin' ships, under any flag. Any suspicion of unseaworthiness would make a vessel impossible to man. The slightest such suspicion, in any civilised port, calls for immediate official action.

Yet more than enough ships still go missing—on the average, at least one big, well-found ship each year, and a number of little ones of anything up to a thousand tons. Lloyd's 'missing' books are no longer filled with anything up to 230 names within a couple

of years or so, but they are still filled. There are still 'mysteries'—
unsolvable puzzles of ships lost at sea.

Consider the Lowestoft trawler *Guava,* for example, presumably
lost in the southern part of the North Sea about the same time that
the *Yewvalley* must have foundered. The *Guava* was a war-built
former Royal Navy minesweeper which had been sold as surplus
and converted for fishing. She was built mostly of wood, which
ought to float. She had plenty of freeboard, plenty of buoyancy,
plenty of strength, too, to survive a gale at sea—even a savage gale
of near-hurricane strength. The *Guava,* as converted, was a motor
trawler of 285 tons gross, 128 feet long by 26 feet beam and 12.4
feet depth. She was built at Pembroke Dock in 1945 and had been
used as a minesweeper briefly in the Mediterranean. Afterwards she
was one of a multitude of war surplus vessels bought for industry,
and she was thoroughly and expensively converted to fish out of
Lowestoft, on the nearer grounds. She was no skimped job. Her
high wooden bulwarks were cut down a bit to make it easier to
work the trawl. She had plenty of powerful pumps, and a good
main engine. Her steering system was electric-hydraulic, with telemotor control which could be switched to hand control, if ever
necessary, within seconds. She had an adequate lifeboat which
was carried on deck whence it could soon be swung or shoved
outboard, either by tackle on the mizzen boom, or manually. The
boat was certified for twelve persons and the *Guava* carried a crew
of eleven. She had, in addition, a good life-raft for twelve, and
plenty of life-jackets.

The *Guava* sailed from Lowestoft on what was to be her last
voyage, on the morning of Thursday, 29th January, 1953. Not
long afterwards an engine defect caused her to return for repairs. It
was not a main-engine defect but in the supercharger, which had
given trouble before. Indeed, the *Guava* had had more trouble than
enough with her auxiliaries and with this supercharger, and she had
had to cut several fishing voyages short on that account—so many

that she had a bit of a bad name among skippers and mates in the port. The reason for this was that the trawl winch was driven by a system of shafting and belts from one or other of the auxiliaries and, when these broke down, the winch could not be used and the vessel could not fish. In such circumstances, the *Guava* had to return to port for repairs. Fishermen are paid in part on shares of the catch, and they do not care for an inefficient fishing vessel. More than one good fisherman, and at least one skipper and mate, had left the ship for the very understandable reason that they could earn better livings in vessels which could be relied upon to keep their fishing gear at work while it was needed.

All these defects, while annoying to owners and fishermen alike, could have no real bearing on the seaworthiness of the ship. They affected her working capacity, not her ability to stand up to the sea. None of them could have had anything to do with the *Guava*'s mysterious loss. A trawl winch does not drive anything but the barrels for working the trawl. The defective supercharger was soon repaired on the trawler's return to port and, after a satisfactory test, off she sailed again—this time not to return. It was on the morning of Friday, the 30th of January, that the *Guava* finally sailed.

Like almost all offshore fishing vessels, the *Guava* was fitted with an efficient ship-to-shore radio telephone. She did not have to carry such equipment, and there was no obligation on the skipper to report to his owners daily as the *Yewvalley* was required to do. The radio was a safety device and a means of keeping in touch with fishing and fish-marketing conditions. Skippers from the same fishing port like to keep in touch with one another. They share the same wave-band and they exchange news. Friend calls friend at a certain time each fishing day, usually. Sometimes they have means of passing information unknown to other skippers, listening hard for news of fish. All the skippers listen ardently for news of good fishing, news which none broadcasts knowingly, for fishing is an ancient and still something of a secretive trade.

[37]

The skipper of the *Guava* that fatal voyage, George Fisher, had plenty of friends to call by radio telephone. The day after he left port he called his wife, about seven o'clock in the evening, when the weather was already pretty bad. This must have been his calling hour, for shortly afterwards he was also talking by radio to the skipper of a friendly ship, the *Ala*. What he said to his wife is not recorded, but he told Skipper Soanes of the *Ala* that the weather was bad and he had taken up his gear—'hauled' is the fishermen's word—and was going to 'dodge,' that is, keep his ship slowly under way, head to wind and sea, virtually hove-to. A vessel as seaworthy as a trawler, 'dodging' even into a ferocious gale, ought to be all right. All offshore fishing skippers are experienced 'dodgers.'

Later the same night—about 10 P.M.—Skipper Fisher told Skipper Soanes that he was still dodging and the weather was very, very dirty, as indeed it was. At that time the *Ala* was safely anchored off Southwold, where the strong and increasing winds and rough sea could do her no harm.

"I think you are in the best place," said Skipper Fisher to his friend, "and I wouldn't mind if I was with you. I will call you at the usual time in the morning." But in the morning no call came. No call ever came again from the trawler *Guava*—no call, no news, no wreckage, no bodies, not even a battered lifebuoy.

The arranged times for the two trawler skippers to exchange news were 8:15 A.M. and 7:15 P.M. daily. From 8 A.M. until 10 A.M. Skipper Soanes stood by for the call which never came. That day and the following four days, he called his friend morning and evening. The fact that he did not hear did not mean, necessarily, that his friend was lost. It might—indeed probably did—mean only that his radio was out of action, perhaps through some damage of the storm. But then the *Guava* did not come back at the end of her scheduled fishing trip. Men remembered that the night she was last heard of was one of the dirtiest they had ever known, even on that wild coast. The *Guava* should have dodged through it all right.

Many others did, in vessels without her freeboard or buoyancy.

As the days passed and there was no news of the *Guava,* seamen began to wonder. They recalled that the *Guava* had touched the ground earlier that month of January. She had grounded on the Newcombe Sands. Might the grounding have caused her serious damage undetected at the time but sufficient to cause her to open up and founder in a violent storm? The *Guava* had touched only, in quiet conditions, on a rising tide. She had not pounded. She was refloated with the aid of a tug, and, for the following forty-eight hours, she was carefully observed as she lay afloat at Lowestoft. Neither then nor subsequently was there the slightest evidence that she had suffered any damage. She was examined most thoroughly by a competent surveyor. After all, these trawlers are valuable vessels, and insured, and the insurance companies employ their own highly qualified men to keep an eye on them. It is in no one's interests that a damaged ship should continue to go to sea.

But the grounding, the history of minor defects in the auxiliary machinery, the fact that a skipper and a mate had left the ship— these things rankled round the Lowestoft waterfront. A fishing community—or any other waterfront group—thinks long and deep when one of its ships disappears mysteriously, without as much as a message to indicate that anything was wrong. In due course, an official inquiry was held on the 2nd, 3rd and 4th of November, 1953, before a judge and four assessors, who were master mariners, fishermen, engineering technicians. The court got down to business with the usual thoroughness and heard everybody. They could find nothing wrong with the seaworthiness of the *Guava.* The difficulties with her supercharger would not affect her seaworthiness, they found, except perhaps in one set of circumstances only. If the supercharger failed and had to be disconnected from the main engine (which could continue to operate very well without it), then the vessel might be without power for the few moments necessary to change over. Under such conditions, *if* they ever arose, the learned judge found it was "possible to imagine circumstances in which such a state of affairs might seriously embarrass those responsible for handling the ship in a sea way."

Seriously embarrass? Here is British understatement! It could have killed them. Left without power, heading into the wild sea and furious wind of the night of January 31! The *Guava* could have fallen into the trough and been catastrophically overwhelmed, smashed and filled and foundered. . . .

It is fair to add, as the court added, that not one piece of evidence was brought forward to indicate that such an accident did in fact happen. But it *could* have happened. *Something* caused the *Guava* to be destroyed, so suddenly and finally that not even a signal could be sent. What that something was can now only be guessed at, and the learned judge could not be interested in guessing. That is for the small body of trawler seamen who knew what might have happened, who had survived such nights themselves and knew by what slender threads, perhaps, their vessels had come through. "The cause [of the *Guava*'s loss] is unascertainable. The probable cause was the sudden overwhelming of the vessel by the force of the wind and the high confused state of the sea . . . and the possibility of the surge of a phenomenal wave cannot be excluded." So read the court's official findings. The weather evidence spoke of gusts to hurricane strength on the nearer North Sea fishing grounds the night the *Guava* was presumed to be lost. The phenomenal sea which struck the *Bestwood* and smashed the dykes of Holland further to the south might well have struck the *Guava,* too. If it did so just at a time when a defective supercharger was being disconnected and the main engines stopped—why, it is not to be wondered at that Skipper Fisher did not keep his promise to call his friend Skipper Soanes at the usual time in the morning.

CHAPTER THREE

Father and Son

LLOYD'S NOTICE

VESSELS FOR INQUIRY

The Committee of Lloyd's will be glad of any information regarding the following vessel:—

"SHELDON," steam trawler of Grimsby, Official Number 132128, 278 tons gross, Master Beesley, which is reported to have sailed from Kirkwall for Faroes fishing grounds on the 30th January, 1953, and reported by wireless from position believed to be about 60 miles north-west of Dennis Head same day.

Lloyd's, London, E.C. 3.
4th March, 1953.

MISSING Vessels Book 14 at Lloyd's, which contains the names and details of 222 ships lost without trace between the 10th of July, 1929, and the 22nd of December, 1954 (disregarding the war years), begins with a fishing vessel, ends with another. There are many others in between. Offshore fishing can be a hazardous industry. Fishermen are not like merchant seamen, who also accept the perils of the sea. They are a class apart, truly men who 'go down to the sea in ships.' The merchant seaman serves in ships in a clearly defined manner, on clear-cut voyages the duration of which is known, under conditions which are all carefully laid down. The employment of merchant ships is to carry cargoes which are loaded and discharged in safe ports. The ship goes to sea, but she does not work at sea. Her cargo is of and for the land. But the fisherman has to wrest his cargo from the sea, at such hours and in such circumstances as the sea permits. The fishing skipper brings to his profession a specialized knowledge, acquired through the years, and the fisherman must bring also a great capacity for the acceptance of hardships, and an immense endurance. He is so much at sea and of the sea that, in time, he may come to pay, perhaps, too little attention to the hazards of that bitter and deceptive element. He *has* to accept hazards to his ship, sometimes. Fish congregate in wild areas of the oceans, generally on banks and shoals where the storms pile the broken water high—especially winter storms.

Yet the market demands fish in winter, too. Offshore fishing is not in these days a seasonal occupation. It is continued off Iceland, off the Greenland coast, on the banks of Newfoundland, off Nova Scotia and New England, off the coasts of Norway, the White Sea, Bear Island, and off Spitzbergen—and a hundred other wild, inhospitable, storm-ridden spots—the year round. The very condition of the sea floor which is most attractive to fish is the ideal breeding ground for breakers, too, for the wild sea sweeping in on a rising floor, finding the progress of its mighty rollers checked, grows angry and dangerous. Yet most trawled fish are bottom-feeding fish. The trawl must take them where they are to be found, upon or near the sea floor, and so the trawler must drag his great net in a workable depth of sea. Out in the deeper ocean the seas run with a more even roll, though still at times with an almost overpowering menace. From fishing banks, in wild weather, the trawler must run for shelter, or—if he is forced—then the only alternative is to 'dodge.'

No wonder many of those 222 missing ships in Book 14, and of the more than a thousand others in six such books which have been filled at Lloyd's this twentieth century (disregarding almost ten years of wars) are offshore fishing vessels! The names know no limitations of flag or fishing ground. The first, in Book 14, is the 200-ton *Leine,* of Emden, which sailed on a Christmas fishing voyage towards the Barents Sea with her crew of thirteen and was never again heard of. She was a steam trawler—a bit small, maybe, for a winter voyage to the Barents Sea. But she had been making such voyages safely for years. The Newfoundland schooner *Partanna,* with a crew of twenty-four, most of them dorymen, sailed out of St. John's for the Grand Banks and never came in again, nor was as much as a dory ever found from her (though dories are wood, and all but indestructible, and surely some must have floated away no matter what the fate of the poor schooner).

The 217-ton Milford Haven trawler *Gordon Richards* was seen off the Fastnet on the 14th of January, 1938, and never seen again, nor heard from. The *Goth* (21 men), of Fleetwood, the *Côte d'Opale* (22 men), of Boulogne, the *L. A. Madsden* (6 men), of Fleetwood, the *Laermans* (10 men), of Ostend, the *Margaret Paton* (13 men), of Glasgow, the *Granz* (19 men), of Bremerhaven, the *Gay Lussac* (16 men), of L'Orient, the *Irene Alvarez* (12 men), of Vigo in Spain, the *Gudrun* (17 men), of Gloucester, Massachusetts, the *Milford Viscount* (13 men), of Milford Haven in Wales—all are missing, mysteries, gone in the sea with all hands, with many of their kind. The body of the radio operator of the Frenchman *Gay Lussac* came up in the trawl of a sister fishing vessel from his home port, and at least was given decent burial. The *Milford Duchess* brought up the echo-sounder of the *Milford Viscount* in her trawl, from the bottom of a particularly nasty shelf in the nearer North Atlantic three years after the *Viscount* had gone.

For the rest, nothing has been found.

Nothing has been heard and nothing has been found of the Grimsby trawler *Sheldon,* either, since she was known to be at sea during the dreadful night which brought the *Yewvalley* and the *Guava* and six other ships their doom. The *Sheldon* was an elderly steam trawler, built in 1912, operating out of Grimsby mainly to the Faeroe Island grounds. Grimsby is a great fishing port—they will tell you there that it is the greatest, with the most ships and the largest turnover of fish, of all fishing ports in the world; but they will tell you the same thing a bit up the river, in Hull. In their own way, both statements will be accurate. Hull is the greatest distant-water fishing port, Grimsby the greatest for the nearer banks. Hull has the largest trawlers and the greatest tonnage; Grimsby has the most ships. When it comes to fishing methods and fishing skills, there is little to choose between them. Hull ships or Grimsby ships, they know what they are at when it comes to the fishing business. There is no reason why either should go missing, anywhere.

Both run some elderly ships, Grimsby more than Hull because Grimsby has the greater number, and nearer-waters fishing is not quite so exacting or competitive a business. There is no reason why elderly fishing vessels should not remain efficient. They are well built, and they have to be thoroughly well maintained. The career of the *Sheldon* had been interrupted by two world wars and she had been on extensive naval service in at least one of them. After such service, a ship is usually pretty well reconverted, regardless of cost, as the taxpayer is paying. The *Sheldon* was in good trim in all respects. She was the usual older steam-trawler type—a low, long seat in the water, with a good sheer to her to get bow and stern well clear of the sea and yet leave the main-deck low enough to work the trawl with maximum efficiency and ease, and a graceful, sea-kindly, staunch little hull. A high thin funnel carried the fumes from such coal as she had to burn to keep her one boiler going, at the same time providing natural draft to fan her three fires.

She was only 130 feet long, 22¼ feet maximum beam, a shade over 12 feet deep, and her little 89 h.p. reciprocating engine could send her along fast enough. Her registered tonnage was 278 gross and 122 net. She had the usual big steam trawl-winch, small hatches to accept the fish she caught, and all the ordinary fishing-gear. As for navigational and fishing aids, she had just about everything that could be jammed into her little bridge—radar, direction indicator, two echo-sounders, one of them designed especially to help in the location of shoals of fish. She had all the charts, life-saving apparatus, fire-fighting gear, properly adjusted compasses, lights and sound and radio signalling apparatus she could have needed. She was fitted with an efficient radio telephone, in the use of which her skipper and mate were both well skilled. It was the practice to overhaul all these aids after each voyage. Experts came down and looked at them, and gave them all the maintenance or repairs they needed.

Fishing trawlers are essentially working ships and whatever is put aboard them is put there for use—hard and continuous use, if necessary. The *Sheldon* had been working long enough out of Grimsby to establish a reputation; if she had any vices, they would be known. She had the name of being an excellent ship and good in any sort of sea, however violent. She had never had any difficulty in getting crews, and men liked to stay in her. Her skipper, Mr. W. R. Beesley, thought enough of her to have his son along as mate. Both the Beesleys were qualified skippers. The son had command of the ship on voyages when the father took his leave or stayed ashore for any reason.

On what was to be her last voyage, the little trawler sailed from Grimsby fish docks in the very early hours of the 26th of January, 1953, with a crew of fourteen, all told. It was really the middle of the night when she undocked, for the tide served then. Seven other trawlers undocked on the same tide, but the *Sheldon* could not go straight to sea as she had not her complete crew aboard. It is easy for a man, on a brief visit ashore, to sleep in a little about 3 A.M. on a bitter January morning. The third hand and the cook were adrift. The third hand came rushing down to the lock gates in a car just as the ship was going out, and Skipper Beesley—a magnificent ship-handler, like all trawler masters—nosed the black bow along-side just long enough for him to leap aboard. The lock gates were brilliantly flood-lit as the eight little ships jostled together on their way to sea. Onlookers noted nothing in any way unusual about the *Sheldon*. She was in her ordinary trim for a fishing voyage to the Faeroes. Her ship's husband—the marine superintendent for the owners, who had a lot of trawlers—was on the pierhead, too, watching her go. She was in his care and he was there to see her, though it was so bleak an hour and she sailed, on the average, once a fortnight. The *Sheldon* anchored in the river out of the way of traffic there, and waited for the cook. He turned up, in due course, and the trawler sailed.

She did not get far. A couple of days later, bad weather forced her to take shelter in a place called Lambs Bay, in the Orkney Islands. The weather then was not all that bad, but it was too bad for fishing, and there was no point in battering the little ship about the sea to no purpose. It was better to take it easy for a while, and go on to the fishing grounds when the weather made up its mind to improve. While the ship was sheltering, two of the hands reported to Skipper Beesley that they were sick and wanted medical attention. These men were one of the deckhands and the cook who had already de-layed the ship's departure from Grimsby. Now he said he had dermatitis. Skipper Beesley got his anchor up and went into Kirk-wall, the nearest port, to have this pair attended to. They had to be landed, on medical orders, and that left the *Sheldon* too short-handed for a winter fishing voyage. The skipper telephoned his owners in Grimsby and asked for two replacements. These were sent, arriving at Kirkwall from Grimsby on Friday, the 30th of January. By this time two more of the crew had reported sick but these had minor ailments and, as soon as the replacements were aboard, the *Sheldon* sailed to carry on full speed to the grounds.

Already fishing on the Faeroe grounds was the Grimsby trawler *Burfell,* the skipper of which was Mr. F. Goddard. Skippers Goddard and Beesley were old friends, the sort of friends who would even exchange good news about fishing over their radio telephones. (Any skipper would pass on bad fishing news, true or not.) They had an arrangement to call each other by radio twice daily, at 10 A.M. and 10 P.M. So Skipper Beesley duly spoke to Skipper Goddard at 10 that Friday evening. The *Burfell* then was on the grounds off the north-east of the Faeroes. The very bad storm which later was to sweep so disastrously down the North Sea was already working up off the Faeroes then, and the *Burfell* was having a bad time of it. Skipper Goddard, already forced to 'dodge' in a north-north-east gale, was mildly surprised to hear from his friend that he was coming along at full speed with a moderate south-south-westerly behind him. The *Sheldon* then must have been somewhere between the Orkneys and the Faeroes.

That was the last time Skipper Beesley ever called anyone. He did not call back in the morning at 10 A.M., or in the evening, and, try as he might, Skipper Goddard could not raise him—neither then, nor at any subsequent time. Somewhere, some time between 10 P.M. on the 30th and 10 A.M. on the 31st, the *Sheldon* disappeared.

There was no evidence of this at first, of course. There never was any evidence apart from her failure to arrive anywhere. But Skipper Beesley was a man who kept his word. When he did not call, knowing that the weather had been so appalling Skipper Goddard was a little worried. He was more worried when he heard that another Grimsby trawler, the *Cunningham,* Skipper Shepherd, was also between the Orkneys and the Faeroes that night, and had been struck suddenly by the most ferocious squalls which grew rapidly into a whole gale of wind, with gusts up to hurricane strength. The *Cunningham* had also experienced light south-south-westerly winds at first. He was on the same course as the *Sheldon,* about three hours astern of her. About five o'clock on the morning of Saturday, the 31st, the *Cunningham* was struck by the first violent squall, with the wind swinging round and coming up with alarming force and suddenness. The sea was high and confused, and the only thing the *Cunningham* could do was to 'dodge.'

A ship can heave-to in bad weather with a sea anchor out, if she has sea-room, and drift slowly before the storm while her hull shoulders the sea: but a trawler does not heave-to in this manner because, for one reason, she rarely has that much sea-room. If she drifted she would be in too much danger of going ashore, on a lee shore at that. Hence the 'dodging' procedure. The vessel has way enough just to keep steering, head-to-sea (some ships take certain states of the sea better when they shoulder them and do not head directly into the wind). If she has too much way, the heavy seas will break over her and damage her. If she has too little way, she will not answer her helm. So dodging is a skillful and painstaking manouevre of seamanship, requiring patience, endurance, experience, skill in the engine-room and a good hand at the helm. If a trawler tries to run before too great a weight of sea, her rather low stern may be swamped and the seas break over her from aft. Then they will swirl round the open working-deck, smashing about, pressing her down with the weight of water and doing damage. If they do not decide to run for shelter early, many fishing skippers prefer to dodge. Another factor which gives them some preference for keeping the sea is that in such gales the visibility is generally poor almost to the point of uselessness. How is a skipper to be sure he is running his vessel safely between the headlands of some sheltering bay, and not on them? He cannot see. He may have radar, but he also has much else to do besides watch a radar screen, and often he has not any spare officers to watch it for him.

The *Cunningham* safely dodged out the storm. The violent north-north-easterly became even more violent, and shrieked and howled throughout the whole forenoon of the 31st. Then it gradually eased, and at last went round to the north-west and moderated. The *Sheldon* was not officially missed for another week. Skipper Beesley had a lot of friends among his brother fishermen, and they noted that his ship was no longer on the air. He had been a man of regular habits, reliable: when he said something he meant it. And so, after a while, not only Skipper Goddard was worried. On the 6th of February, another skipper, who had wireless telegraphy in his vessel as well as the radio telephone, sent a message to the *Sheldon*'s owners in Grimsby. Had they heard anything of the vessel? They had not.

Because of some freak of radio, the ordinary telephone will not reach through from the Faeroe grounds, and the owners had not expected to hear anything directly from their vessel. They, in turn, became anxious when a trawler skipper who ought to have been hearing Skipper Beesley's broadcast at least once daily sent messages about the ship's safety. The only way they could get in touch with a ship of theirs which did not carry telegraphy was by first sending a message to a ship which was so fitted, and then this ship could pass on the message by voice radio. This was done. Nobody knew anything about the *Sheldon*. Since it is a reasonable assumption that by that time Skipper Beesley, his son the mate and all the crew had been dead for a week, it was scarcely likely that anyone would.

It was just possible, of course, that she might have been driven ashore and that the crew, or some of the crew, had survived. In that case, the Coast Guard service in the Faeroes would have news of her. They were asked, and they had not. Ships throughout the area were asked to keep an eye open for anything of the *Sheldon* or her people. It was a bit late, but that was no one's fault. It could not be helped. A trawler going about his business on the Faeroe grounds or anywhere else was supposed to be self-sufficient. Even the fact that radio silence was continued *might* mean only that the radio had been put out of action by the storm. With some skippers, it could mean that they were on fish and doing extremely well, and did not want other trawlers to hear about their luck and come hurrying to take too much of the harvest.

[49]

The business of searching for small ships in distress in great storms, in any circumstances, is rarely productive of results. It is a comradely gesture. If the unfortunate *Sheldon* had not, for any reason, lived through that night of storm, then it was certain that her boats had not survived either, even if they could have been launched. In such circumstances, carrying the ordinary lifeboat is a gesture, too. It has little hope of surviving what the ship will not, even if it can be launched. But no seaman worth his salt hears of a ship in distress or missing without at once determining to do what he can to aid her. There is a search, usually a long, wide and most thorough search, even if it is highly dangerous to make it and it is well known to be hopeless.

So it was in the *Sheldon*'s case. The search began late, but that made no real difference. Beyond a battered lifebuoy marked "*Sheldon,* Grimsby," which was picked up on a Shetlands beach by a man not searching at all, nothing was found. She and all her people were long gone, then, where searching made no difference.

The only thing that remained was to hold an official inquiry.

That too, like the search, was really a gesture. The *Sheldon* had a clean record. In her case there was not even a brief history of minor defects, or any defects. She was a good old battler which could only be overwhelmed by that chance combination of dreadful maritime circumstances which sailors and insurers know as an 'Act of God.' Her survey certificates, her registration, her classification, her insurance, her hull, machinery, life-saving gear, equipment of all kinds were all in order. From her history and her state, no one could suggest any possible cause for her loss. The court having been convened—again, only because that night had claimed so many ships with such appalling, sudden finality, and not with any real hope of finding out anything or because anyone suspected that there was anything to find out—the Commissioner of Wrecks and his assessors went thoroughly into every conceivable aspect of the case. The

court assured itself that there was no possible known fault attributable to anyone.

Elderly as she was—and the court made no comment on the
Sheldon's age—the little trawler was as fit for the sea as she could
be designed, regulated, surveyed and certified to be. Her crew was
a good crew, and adequate. Her skipper was a good skipper, and
more than adequate. His son was equally a good skipper. Two former skippers of the *Sheldon* came forward and spoke of the ship's
good qualities.

"Completely seaworthy in every respect," was how Skipper
Whittleton described her, and he commanded her for many voyages. She behaved very satisfactorily, he went on, even in the worst
of weather. He recalled a heavy north-north-east gale once when
she was the last ship to be forced to dodge, although there were
twenty other trawlers about at the time, several of them big fellows
from Hull. He had left the *Sheldon* only because he could do better
in a larger ship. The deckhand and the cook who owed their
presence in the court—and on earth—to the fact that they had been
landed sick at Kirkwall, both declared on oath that everything
had been normal aboard up to the time they left. There was no
trouble and there was no defect—nothing to cause an accident.
Marine surveyors, insurance experts, meteorologists, fishing skippers, all gave evidence.

The meteorologist described the storm in the area of the Orkneys
and Faeroes as unusually severe. Such instrumental evidence as
was available—mainly from Lerwick in the Shetland Islands—indicated an average hourly velocity of the gale of 65 knots, with
gusts to 85. From all that could be pieced together afterwards, it
looked as if the centre of the storm must have passed very close by
the *Sheldon*'s probable position. The sea would be particularly bad,
both because of the rising ground there and the force of the wind
and, even more so, because the wind had previously been blowing
fresh from the south-west and south-south-west for some time and

had brought up quite a sea from that direction. There would, therefore, be a high, cross, confused and breaking sea up to thirty feet high. The wind had in fact veered suddenly, from at least four to eight points, and increased very much in strength, within a matter of minutes. Though the change in direction had been forecast in the weather bulletins (the ordinary bulletins on the B.B.C. Home Service), there would be nothing to indicate *when* it might change direction, or that it would jump so suddenly and so violently. The nearest weather-reporting ship had recorded the wind changing and jumping from 28 to over 60 knots within half an hour.

Several trawler skippers gave evidence supporting the weather expert. "As bad a night as I have known," said Skipper Goddard. He tried to run before it back for shelter, but that was hopeless. "She was just running herself full," he said, "and of course then I had to pull her up to the wind. I could see if I didn't we were going to get some damage." He dodged through the worst of it, then made for shelter and was lucky enough to reach a place called Klaksvig, in the Straight Fjord, on Bord Island in the Faeroes. Here he anchored, and thanked God. Skipper Goddard was of the opinion that any skipper caught in that weather would have been forced to dodge. He had been lucky to get a chance to run for shelter, but that was when the worst had passed. And he was not then near where the *Sheldon* was. She was worse off, because of that rising ground which would so increase the fury of the dangerously high sea.

The skipper of the *Cunningham,* who had also dodged through the night, explained that he, too, was better off than the *Sheldon.* He had in the first place a larger ship, and he was not on the rising ground. Even so, he had had as much as he could cope with. At first he tried to dodge at half-speed, but the wind was so violent that the ship would not steer. So he had to increase to three-quarters speed. His ship suffered some damage.

Both skippers, asked by the court, expressed the opinion that a steering-gear breakdown aboard the *Sheldon,* or any other sort of breakdown at the height of the storm, would have been very bad indeed. "He would fall off," said Skipper Goddard, not liking to imagine such a state of affairs. "He would fall off, and he would just have had an unfortunate sea go right over the top of him." But Skipper Beesley would have sent out a distress message, surely, in such a case? he was asked. Yes, he replied, if he had the time, and his radio was still in order. The skipper of the *Cunningham,* when asked, said he thought some accident of the kind must have happened. "Either his steering-gear failed or he washed something adrift, so he fell off broadside to the sea," he said. "I think he would have just taken a big sea and, probably, washed everything away just in one. That was the state of the sea. . . ."

That was the state of the sea, in the opinion of veteran skippers with half a century of experience shared between them. Just one great sea smashed aboard, through some unpredictable and irreparable accident, and the engine-room skylights would be stove in and perhaps the whole superstructure, too, the boiler-room and engine-room flooded, the whole ship awash on deck and below, left to lurch a moment violently in the maelstrom of the broken water, buoyancy going, and then to lurch on horribly down, all buoyancy gone from the stricken hull for ever. . . . Father and son and ten good Grimsby fishermen would go to their deaths in the twinkling of an eye.

The court found that it could ascribe no reason for the loss of the steam trawler *Sheldon,* but it was "firmly of the opinion that the most likely cause was the exceptionally heavy weather experienced in the vicinity about the time when radio communication with the *Sheldon* ceased, the wind in not far distant localities being of greater force than that recorded during the previous 60 or 70 years, and its effect on the sea could well be heightened by an opposite running tide and in places where there was rising ground, a position in which the *Sheldon* would quite likely be at the material time."

So the case was closed, and the *Sheldon*'s hull lies rusting somewhere on the road to the fishing grounds off the Faeroes, as so many other trawler hulls lie rusting and rotting on every fishing bank round the whole Atlantic Ocean. Father and son, good skippers both, share the same unknown grave in the sea.

CHAPTER FOUR

A Lifebuoy on the Beach

```
┌─────────────────────────────────────┐
│                                       │
│          LLOYD'S NOTICE               │
│        ─────────────────              │
│       VESSELS FOR INQUIRY             │
│        ─────────────────              │
│    The Committee of Lloyd's will be   │
│  glad of any information regarding    │
│  the following vessel :—              │
│    "CATHARINA DUYVIS," steam trawler  │
│  of Ymuiden, 329 tons gross, Master   │
│  Glas, which is reported to have      │
│  sailed from Grimsby for North Sea    │
│  fishing grounds on the 20th January, │
│  1953, was 18 miles north-west of     │
│  Ymuiden on the 31st January and      │
│  reported by wireless on the 1st      │
│  February.                            │
│  Lloyd's, London, E.C. 3.             │
│            4th March, 1953.           │
│                                       │
└─────────────────────────────────────┘
```

NOT only Grimsby ships bring fish to that busy port. All kinds of ships—German, Faeroese, Danish, Swedish, Belgian, Dutch, Icelandic (unless there is some current quarrel about fishing boundaries between British and Icelandic trawlermen) land their catches at Grimsby. It is a great international market for fish as well as a port sending out its own trawlermen. The ships crowd into the fish docks on every tide, often packing themselves in so tightly that there is room for little more than their bows nosed up to the fishy quay and they look like sardines stowed in a can. The fish they bring are sold at once, by auction on the quay, and go off to great centres such as London and the big midland cities. Grimsby and Hull are big fishing ports because they are centrally situated to serve the larger British markets, and they are also convenient ports for the fishing grounds of the North Sea and Arctic waters. On the other side of England, Fleetwood in Lancashire is the principal fishing port. It is convenient as a base for ships operating on the banks off the Western Isles of Scotland and the Faeroes, and it is a well-placed market for the teeming towns of Lancashire which are crowded all round it. Ships from all three ports have been compelled, in recent years, as the nearer banks have become fished out, to go farther and farther afield for their cargoes. More and more foreign-flag ships have come to share the market. The trade is free.

Among these foreign ships, the steam trawler *Catharina Duyvis,* of Ymuiden in Holland, was a regular visitor to Grimsby Dock. She was a fair-sized ship, over 300 tons gross (the precise figure was 329 tons), twenty-five years old. She had a sort of a plump and well-fed look about her, as many of the smaller Dutch ships have, as if she found the sea life comfortable and to her liking. She was well kept, as Dutch ships are, both big and small. Where other vessels seemed so frequently to mess up their decks whenever they took in the necessities of coal and ice and never seemed to find time to clean themselves, the *Catharina Duyvis* was a model of well-organized cleanliness. Every nut of coal was swept into her bunker-tops almost as quickly as it was deposited on her decks, and she was never seen in other than an orderly and well-cleaned state. She had an experienced skipper and a good crew of sixteen Hollanders, as clean and well nourished as she was. She caught good fish and she landed them in prime condition. She had a good name everywhere.

The *Catharina Duyvis* landed fish in Grimsby in the latter part of January, 1953 and, on the 20th of that month, left the port for the last time. She was bound for the North Sea fishing grounds and should have been back again within, at most, a fortnight. On the 31st, caught in the same bad weather which worried so many ships, her skipper reported that he was obliged to heave-to. He was then about twenty miles to the north-west of his own home port of Ymuiden. In the clearings between the savage snow squalls, he could see some of the more powerful of the Dutch coastal lights. It was eight o'clock in the evening when the skipper reported his ship hove-to. She came through that night all right, although it was terrible weather, and at one o'clock the following afternoon the skipper was on the radio again, this time speaking to another trawler called the *Flamingo*. The weather was still very, very bad, but the skipper said nothing of any difficulties. His ship was dodging along all right, not doing too badly. He would be glad when the wind had blown itself out and he could get on with fishing again, but for the meantime he was content to wait. He was horrified to hear of the awful effects of the storm on his own country, where the dykes had been smashed in the south and great areas devastated, with appalling loss of life and property. He would, he said, call the *Flamingo* again at ten o'clock that evening, to hear how things were going.

But the *Catharina Duyvis* never called again. Nothing whatever was ever heard of her, or seen. Though she was not twenty miles from a friendly coast—her own coast—and though she had wireless to ask for help, or to indicate at least that she needed assistance, she made no signals, left no wreckage, not as much as a lifebuoy tossing on the sea, and the sea cast up no bodies from her, anywhere. Like the *Yewvalley,* she was in the shipping lanes. There was no real need to organise a special search for her (though a search was made), for ships were constantly crossing and recrossing the waters where she must have been, all of them keeping that sharp lookout which is enjoined upon ships at sea. They saw nothing. The fate of the *Catharina Duyvis* is a mystery. She was posted overdue, then a 'vessel for inquiry.' Then on March 11, 1953, along with seven of the other ships swallowed up in the sea that same weekend, she was posted missing at Lloyd's in London. The insurances were paid over, in due course, and the uncomplicated affairs of her sixteen-men crew were settled.

Apart from the widows she had made, her owners, the workers and fish merchants who knew her in the Grimsby and the Ymuiden docks and her fellow trawlermen on the grounds, she was forgotten. Her name was added to that long, long list of unsolved mysteries of the sea, the greater mystery because she disappeared so utterly and suddenly in a crowded shipping lane so near to a crowded land. Did a mine take her? It *might* have done, but the chance is extremely remote. At least there would remain wreckage. A mined ship does not go down in one secure piece. Did she strike some old war wreck, with which too much of the floor of the shallow North Sea is littered? Not likely. There was depth enough to keep her clear of such dangers, in the area where she was known to be: again, that would have meant at least some degree of disintegration. If identifiable wreckage comes ashore from a ship in north-west Europe or round the British Isles, it will be found and identified. The coasts are expertly watched and there are plenty of watchers. Was she, then, overwhelmed by a mighty sea, thrown over as the collier *Bestwood* had been off the East Anglian coast, by a phenomenal sea? But that sea had passed her way *before* her last radio call. Why should the *Catharina Duyvis* be overwhelmed, and not other ships? She was not alone in the southern North Sea that night—far from it. She was not the only vessel dodging out the storm. She had no structural defects, no weaknesses of design or build, of hatch or steering-gear or power, of trim or manning. Why should she go?

There is no answer. There never will be an answer, now.

As for the little *Leopold Nera*, at least she left some trace—a more eloquent and more readily identifiable trace even than a lifebuoy washed up on a beach. The *Leopold Nera* was a little fellow, a Belgian motor-trawler built in 1937 and sailing out of Zeebrugge, with a gross tonnage of less than 60. She carried a winter crew of five men, and fished the nearer North Sea grounds. There were plenty of offshore fishermen no bigger than she was, not only out of Zeebrugge but from Scotland, Denmark, the east-coast ports of England, the northern and western ports of France, and from

> "LEOPOLD NERA," motor trawler of Zeebrugge, 58 tons gross, Master Rappe, which is reported to have sailed from Zeebrugge for North Sea fishing grounds on the 23rd January, 1953, and was reported in lat. 54 20 N., long. 4 40 E., on the 31st January.
>
> Lloyd's, London, E.C. 3.
> 4th March, 1953.

Holland. With Skipper Rappe in command, the *Leopold Nera* sailed for the last time from Zeebrugge on the 23rd of January, 1953. She was reported from a spot not far from the *Guava*'s last-known position at five o'clock on the morning of January 31. That was the last ever heard of her.

But another trawler from Zeebrugge, a friendly ship to the *Leopold Nera*, was fishing that area some weeks later. The skipper was a friend of Skipper Rappe, and the crews of the two ships had known one another. They hauled their gear and the trawl brought up something that was not fish. It was a body, and it spilled out on their deck with the flapping plaice and skate. It fell out from the cod-end, face uppermost. They knew that face.

It was old Louis van Dierendonck, of Heyst, a village on the coast near Zeebrugge. Sixty-year-old Louis Dierendonck had been mate of the *Leopold Nera*.

The Hollanders lost other ships besides fishermen in that wild storm, apart from the numbers of vessels damaged or destroyed when the dykes broke. Two of their small cargo ships featured on the lists of overdue vessels, too, soon to become 'vessels of inquiry,' and then 'missing.' The Hollanders have developed a splendid type of small motor-vessel, with engines and accommodation aft and the main deck filled with two or three large hatches, as is the modern way. They are small ships, hailing from a host of little ports as well as from the great ports of Holland. They are run so efficiently that they have scooped up a considerable proportion of the North Sea short trades and the British coastal trades—so much so, indeed, that now and again there is something of an outcry against them, not only from British coastal shipowners.

Usually small grey vessels which somehow contrive always to look shipshape and Bristol fashion (clean and neat and seaman-like) the little Hollanders have solved what might have seemed an insoluble problem, of making the hard-worked little coaster, all hold and enormous hatches, look like a ship and home as well, and a well-kept home at that. They are not houseboats. There are often curtains in the windows of the charthouse, which is not as small as usually is found in other country's ships, because it may be—probably is—a living-room as well. The wheel-house often is a living-room, too, and is kept like one. Flowers grow in pots hung in the skylights and secured to the bulkheads. These are family ships, often financed by a family and its relations, with the help of a banker in some little port. They work hard, and there are hundreds of them. They are to be seen in the Mersey, Humber, Clyde, Tyne, Tees, the British Channel, far up the Thames in London, beyond the bridges: upon any day in the week, several of them are certain to be seen going and coming up-Channel, down-Channel, into and out of the Thames, anywhere round the coasts of Britain and much of western Europe.

Their enormous hatches do not worry their crews at sea. The power is down below, right aft, and they are steered from the comfortable wheel-house on the bridge. All hands live aft. The cooking is done aft, and excellent cooking it is. Once they are secured for sea, no one need venture on the fore-deck. The hatches are thoroughly strong and well secured. They are covered with, first, a sort of moveable deck of wooden covers (confusingly called 'hatches,' too) made of heavily bolted planks at least two and a half to three inches through, and these fit closely over steel beams shaped to take and hold them, and to form part of the main transverse strength of the vessel. Above these wooden covers (which are very strong and usually have ringbolts or hand-grips sunk into them), a minimum of three stout tarpaulins is fitted, each just so much larger than the hatchway it is covering to allow of a good drop all round to be tucked carefully into a row of steel cleats welded to the sides of the hatchway, which are called coamings. These coamings are strong and high, as high as the ship's bulwarks. Sometimes they are higher. When the tarpaulins have all been properly tucked into the rows of cleats all round the coaming, steel bars made to fit there are rammed home to keep the ends of the tarpaulins from working loose, and these steel bars are then firmly wedged in position by means of wooden wedges, blunt ends forward where the sea will hit them and so knock them in and not out, one wedge for each cleat. Those on the thwart-ships coamings are sledged home with their thin ends inboard. When wooden covers, tarpaulins, steel bars and wedges are all in place, another system of steel bars is fitted over the whole and locked in position, one such locking bar to each transverse set of hatches.

A hatch may be over forty feet long even in a small ship of only a few hundred tons. It follows that there is a good deal of hard work involved in shipping and unshipping its coverings. It is done most carefully, by experienced seamen, who are well aware that their lives may depend upon the effectiveness of their work. In the old days of sailing-ships, cargo hatches were much smaller—very much smaller, because then ships were never in such a frantic hurry either in ports or at sea—but they were secured as well, or better. Often wooden breakwaters were built up on top of them, lashed there with chains and wire, to break the force of the sea. A ship is vulnerable in her hatches, as seamen well know—none better than the family men in those little short-sea traders.

THE NINE LITTLE SHIPS

"SALLAND," motor vessel of Delfzyl,
297 tons gross, Master Teekman, which
is reported to have sailed from Par for
Stockholm on the 29th January, 1953,
with a cargo of china clay, and passed
Prawle Point same day.
Lloyd's, London, E.C. 3.
4th March, 1953.

The motor-vessel *Salland,* 297 gross tons, of Delfzyl on the river
Ems, by the German border, was just such a little vessel as the Dutch
merchant service might be proud of. Built in 1952, she was equipped
with everything she could possibly need. Her master, Captain Teekman, was part owner. He was proud of his ship and spared nothing
for her improvement. Her crew of seven included some of his and
his wife's relations. Seven was an adequate crew. She was an efficient and an easily run ship. The crew all worked together, sharing
the necessary duties and getting on with them, without anything of
the ineffectiveness of work-to-rules. There was a good spirit in the
little ship and life aboard was harmonious.

But she barely had time to settle down before she was lost, for
the *Salland* was not a year old when she sailed from Par, in Cornwall, on a late January day in 1953 and never came in again, anywhere. She had loaded a full cargo of china clay—clay used in the
making of porcelain—for Stockholm. China clay is heavy stuff, and
her well-deck was deep in the water. Her route lay up-Channel,
along the Belgian and Dutch coasts, and through the Kiel Canal
into the Baltic. It was a tough January voyage for a ship of less
than 300 tons, and it was a tough January. But it was a voyage such
as thousands of small ships had made before her, and since. She was
well fitted for it. She went to sea in perfect order except for just one
small thing—her sending radio was defective, leaving her fitted to
receive only. And so she made no reports.

The *Salland* sailed on January 29 and passed Prawle Point, not far beyond Plymouth, later the same day. She was seen there, plugging along inshore, with everything apparently in order. (If anything was not in order she could easily have put in somewhere. There were plenty of safe harbours in the vicinity.) The *Salland* plugged on into the night, her lights burning brightly. Her lights, on masthead and bridge, were the last ever seen of the *Salland*. How far she might have gone on her voyage no one can say. What dreadful sudden termination came to her upon that voyage no one can say either. But there was one piece of evidence—bad evidence. Some of her hatches came ashore—the wooden covers of those enormous gaping holes in her long hold. In the course of time, nine of the *Salland*'s hatches washed up on the sand at a little hamlet called Noordwyk-aan-Zee, which is on the Dutch coast not far past The Hague.

Hatches float away from a ship only when the hatch is smashed, and the most likely reason for those hatches to be adrift was that they were stove in by the sea. Not the steel locking bars nor all the wedges and the three tarpaulins had kept the sea out. Why? Carelessness? It was scarcely likely. Captain Teekman was a most careful man, and it was a winter voyage. Could there have been a failure of a locking bar, the washing-out of a few wedges, the ripping away of a corner of the tarpaulins and a succession of dreadful seas which washed out a hatch? *One* of those wooden hatch-covers gone would be enough for tragedy. The sea would smash down into the hold, where the heavy cargo left a lot of room for it, and the little ship would plough on under—underneath the surface, with the pretty curtains in the chart-room and the wheel-house windows, and the geraniums in the saloon skylight. The flowers and the men would die together in the sea, and the men would die first.

The sea washed out nine hatch-covers—one thwart-ships row— and, after them, threw the little lifeboat up uselessly on the beach at Katwijk nearby, an empty lifeboat, very new, with the fresh-

[63]

painted name of *Salland* of Delfzyl plain to be seen upon the counter.

And so the *Salland* was posted a missing vessel at Lloyd's on the 11th of March that year, along with all the others, after her due term as overdue and then as a vessel for inquiry.

> "WESTLAND," motor vessel of Rotterdam, 426 tons gross, Master Penning, which is reported to have sailed from Wismar for King's Lynn on the 29th January, 1953, with a cargo of kainit, and passed Cuxhaven on the 30th January.
>
> Lloyd's, London, E.C. 3.
> 18th March, 1953.

The *Westland* of Rotterdam was not a sister-ship to the *Salland*, though in many ways she was a similar vessel. She was larger and older, and her big hatches had withstood many a North Sea battering. She was built in 1931, grossed 426 tons and carried nearly 600 tons. Under the command of Captain Penning with a crew of seven, the *Westland* sailed from Wismar on the Baltic coast of Germany in the morning of the 29th of January, 1953, and, a little later, passed through the Kiel Canal. She was bound for the small port of King's Lynn, a port up the river Ouse in Norfolk in England—just such a little port as the Dutch motor-ships serve so well. She was taking a full cargo of fertiliser for the farmers of that area. The *Westland* was seen passing Cuxhaven the following day, and everything was in order. After that, she, too, disappeared. No hatches, no lifeboats, not as much as a lifebuoy ever drifted ashore from her —nothing at all. She sent no messages and she left no trace.

Though it is a reasonable assumption that the *Westland* went in the same storm as all the others, her name did not go up as a missing vessel at Lloyd's until two weeks after the names of the other eight. There was no particular reason for this, except that she was not overdue as early as most of the others were. She was not missed until after she should have arrived at King's Lynn and, as the weather was known to be so bad, time enough was allowed for her expected arrival. But she did not come.

> **"ASPO,"** steamer of Stockholm, 1331 tons gross, Master Mansson, which is reported to have sailed from Oskarshamn on the 22nd January, 1953, and Kalmar on the 26th January, for Hartlepool, with a cargo of pitprops, and reported by wireless in lat. 55 57 N., long. 4 E., on the 1st February.
>
> Lloyd's, London, E.C. 3.
> 4th March, 1953.

China clay, fertilisers and cement-clinker are heavy cargoes, weighing a ship down. There are plenty of other cargoes more fit for a winter voyage (though ships must take what offers at any season). The largest vessel of the nine which disappeared in that January storm, however, was laden with timber. She was the Swedish steamer *Aspo* of Stockholm, a vessel of 1,331 gross tons, built in 1920 for the Baltic and North Sea trades, which include a good deal of timber-carrying. The *Aspo* loaded a full cargo of 482 fathoms of pit-props—lengths of pine used to prop up the galleries in coal mines, to allow miners to work—at Oskarshamn on the coast of the province of Kalmar in Sweden. Because the pit-props are light cargo and she could not carry enough of them in the holds to make the voyage pay, the *Aspo* filled her decks as well. That is the custom of the trade. Baltic timber is always carried that way, and ships are designed for it, with their well-decks as clear as possible in order to make the stowage of vast stacks of props or other timber as easy as it can be. There is a sort of ship called the 'Baltic' type, with her masts at either end, one on the forecastle-head right forward and the other right aft on the poop, with their winches grouped about them and the decks broken only by the usual great hatch coamings. When they are loaded with timber they look like sawmills more than ships.

[65]

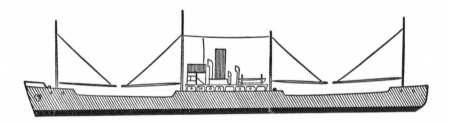

Fig. 2. "Baltic" type

The stowage of deck cargo is well understood at Oskarshamn, and they lashed something over a quarter of the *Aspo*'s pit-props on her roomy decks. The resultant stack, held in place by stout wires and chains, was high and it looked ungainly. But it was well secured by stevedores who knew their business. There was adequate visibility from the bridge, and the ship, designed for just such stowage of just such cargoes, was perfectly stable. She was bound across the North Sea for Hartlepool and, on the 22nd of January, 1953, under the command of Captain Mansson, with a crew of 22 all told, she sailed. She came out of the Baltic through the Sound and the Kattegat, wandering pleasantly along, a black old steamer beneath a great stack of yellow pine, belching a bit of smoke now and then as her firemen put on a pitch of coal. The sight of such timber-laden steamships is a common one in the Sound, and no one paid attention to the old *Aspo*.

The *Aspo* was no record-breaker. She was a good staunch old ship, and her cargo should have floated her anywhere. There is, however, one serious drawback with these high-stowed timber cargoes on a winter passage. They *can* make a ship quickly unstable, if anything happens to upset her trim, and they can roll her down on her side in the twinkling of an eye, without any shifting of the cargo itself at all. Out in the North Sea, the *Aspo* battled along in wild weather that voyage. After a while, she began to leak a little. Then she began to leak a lot. The pumps could not cope with the water she was making—why, no one will ever know—and, because this in-rush of water upset the ship's trim and the water could run freely in whatever hold it had entered, the ship began to take a list—a slight list at first, and then she lurched violently, listed over heavily, and stayed there. The water continued to rise in the hold, making her list the more. The *Aspo* was rolling her side in the sea, which was leaping and smashing and breaking all round her. The position became grim—very grim. She could roll over at any moment. If she lurched any further she would go.

The date was February 1. The *Aspo* had wireless telegraphy, not just a radio telephone like so many trawlers. She could send all the messages Captain Mansson wished to send, without difficulty. So at half past four on the afternoon of that day she sent out a message that she was making water badly and required immediate assistance. Two hours later, she repeated this message, and gave her position. This was Latitude 55.57 north, Longitude 4 east—about midway out in the North Sea between the coasts of Denmark and Scotland. The weather was bad with violent winds and a very heavy sea. There were plenty of other ships about and they did not hesitate, sore pressed as they were themselves, to go to the *Aspo*'s assistance. The nearest was the Swedish steamer *Kalix*.

The tragedy of the *Aspo* is that the *Kalix* actually saw her, despite the appalling conditions of wind, sea and visibility, and was ma-noeuvring to get to windward near enough to take off the crew when a particularly vicious squall of wind and snow came down, completely blotting out the already semi-obscured area. When the squall passed—and it did not take long—the *Kalix* could not find the *Aspo* again and, though she stood by all night and searched then and all the next day, her people did not again see anything whatever of the old steamer. Neither did anyone else.

Maybe the *Aspo* had rolled over in the squall: very likely she did. With safety so close at hand, and brave men standing by to rescue her crew, she rolled over and was gone. Could none of the crew swim? Her people had no chance to swim! No man can swim in the North Sea in a January gale and, for that very reason, the older mariners would never learn to swim at all. Swimming, they held, only prolonged the agony. A man dies fast in a cold raging sea, and his sodden clothes would in any event soon pull him under, to suffocate the last breath out of him which the spray-filled air had allowed him to suck in.

No one was saved from the *Aspo*. There were some pit-props about in the morning. Later, there were many pit-props, but these might have come from other ships as well. Carrying pit-props to the collieries of England employs many vessels. A couple of days later, searching ships which had relieved the *Kalix* sighted a lifebuoy among the floating props. They recovered the buoy with difficulty. It was marked "*Aspo*, Stockholm." The following day, one of the *Aspo*'s lifeboats was found drifting, empty, in the North Sea not very far from the Danish port of Esbjerg. It was odd that the boat survived intact, but none of the men did. There was not even a body lying in the bottom of the boat.

So in due course the *Aspo* became officially overdue, then a vessel for inquiry, along with that tragic list of others. "The Committee of Lloyd's will be glad of any information concerning the following vessels," it began, and there followed a list of eight names headed by the *Aspo,* because the names were in alphabetical order, and the *Yewvalley* was last. But all the information there was ever likely to be on any of those ships was already in: the fate of the *Aspo* was too tragically easy to guess. On the 11th of March, she, too, became a missing vessel.

There was in her case, however, rather a curious aftermath. While fishing in the North Sea later in the year, the little cutter *Bradsted* of Esbjerg felt her gear foul a wreck. There are a good many wrecks on the bottom of the North Sea, and fouling one with an expensive trawl was not as unusual an accident as trawler skippers would like it to be. But when he had managed to free his ship's gear the *Bradsted*'s skipper noticed that a bundle of papers had floated up and the papers were tossing about on the greasy grey sea. He went close and picked them up—maybe they would help identify whatever wreck it was he had touched. They were old bills of lading. The ink had faded from them and they were soaked by the sea, but the rubber stamp of a ship could still plainly be seen on all of them. The name it gave was *Aspo,* of Stockholm.

The *Aspo* really, then, though posted missing need remain a missing vessel in fact no longer, for seamen know where she is buried. The mystery remains as to why she was overwhelmed, why she took in all that water. She was classed $+100$ A 1 at Lloyd's and she had passed a rigorous survey only six months earlier. She was a thoroughly experienced timber-carrier.

> "MICHAEL GRIFFITH," steam trawler of Fleetwood, Official Number 145118, 282 tons gross, Master Singleton, which is reported to have sailed from Fleetwood for fishing grounds off St. Kilda on the 30th January, 1953, and was reported, in distress, 7 miles south of Barra Head, on the 31st January.
> Lloyd's, London, E.C. 3.
> 4th March, 1953.

One other ship went down that same week-end and she, too, managed to get out a distress message, asking urgently for help. She was the little old trawler *Michael Griffith,* 282 gross tons, of Fleetwood, and she was caught while trying to make a commonplace passage from her home port towards the fishing grounds off the island of St. Kilda, on the west coast of Scotland. She was caught in the same storm which caused the doom of the railways steamer *Princess Victoria,* on the ferry service between Stranraer and Larne, in much the same area.

The *Michael Griffith* was not, as was said at the subsequent court of inquiry, the best ship out of Fleetwood. She was far from being the worst, either. Built in 1919, she had had half a dozen owners. Like the Grimsby trawler *Sheldon,* she had been on extensive war service in the Second World War, with complete reconversion afterwards. She was classed 100 A 1 at Lloyd's, was properly fitted and maintained, and everything was in order. Skipper Singleton liked her well enough, and had no difficulty in getting crews—a good sign of a ship with a satisfactory reputation. The insurance and the classification societies surveyors had kept an eye on her, as they do on all classified and insured ships. There was no slightest evidence that she was in any way neglected, nor could anyone hazard a well-informed guess as to why she should be overwhelmed.

And yet she was overwhelmed, and disappeared with all her crew, and Skipper Singleton—apparently—had time only to send out a general call by his radio telephone that the ship was "full of water, with no steam." His exact words, as written down by another listening trawler some miles away, were: "All ships, from *Michael Griffith,* 7 to 8 miles south of Barra Head—full of water—no steam—am helpless—will some ship please come and help us." That was all. It was emphatic enough. The only way the *Michael Griffith* could normally—or abnormally—have become full of water was by being knocked down by such a powerful sea that either the engine-room doors or the ventilators were stove in, or the ventilators sheered off, or the casing itself broken adrift and the water poured down below. In that condition—full of water and with no steam to work her pumps or give her way, she was powerless, finished, at the mercy of a sea which had no mercy then, and never has.

Several trawlers searched for the *Michael Griffith,* reaching the area as quickly as they could. Three of them—the *Braconbank,* the *Wardour,* and the *Sata*—made a particularly thorough search, despite the fact that they were hard-pressed themselves, and the weather became steadily worse. Both the Barra and the Islay lifeboats went to aid in the search, though the Islay boat had already been out in answer to another distress call, and the Islay boat stayed out so long in that frightful blizzard that two members of her crew were overcome, and died. She found nothing. None of the searching ships found anything. Aircraft from the Royal Air Force joined in the search and so did a destroyer, H.M.S. *Tenacious*. One of the aircraft stuck at it twelve hours but saw only the other trawlers which were also searching. The *Tenacious* made a thorough search, which was equally fruitless.

It was all quite unavailing. Nothing of the *Michael Griffith* was found. A week later, a lifebuoy came ashore on a stony beach near the entrance to Loch Foyle. It bore the name *Michael Griffiths, Fleetwood*—Griffiths, not Griffith. The additional *s* was the work of some careless longshore painter. It was the *Michael Griffith*'s buoy, all right. The ship's husband recognised it when it was brought to Fleetwood for his inspection.

There remained the official inquiry. This was held at the town hall in Fleetwood on three days towards the end of April, 1954, more than a year after the ship was posted as a missing vessel. The inquiry was unusual only in that Skipper Singleton's widow chose to attend it, to represent her late husband. The judge, as always, went exhaustively into every possible detail about the ship and her last voyage, accepting nothing at its face value, verifying everything. But there was no fault to be found with the ship. There had been some murmurings round the waterfront at Fleetwood about her. There always are such murmurings when a ship is plucked away like that, by the sea, when the ship's prime purpose for existence is to be fit to defeat the hazards of the sea—*all* the hazards—at all times. The *Michael Griffith*, like the *Guava,* had come back after a false start on her last voyage to repair an engine defect and—again like the *Guava*—had been remarkably quick about effecting the repairs. But it was a straightforward defect which had been properly attended to, though Mrs. Singleton at first had questioned this. The

THE NINE LITTLE SHIPS

court found that the defect had been properly put right and all was well aboard the trawler when she finally sailed.

The court, indeed, could ascribe no reason for her loss, other than the exceptionally heavy weather and the violence of the seas in the area where she had last reported herself. A former skipper of the *Michael Griffith* who had commanded the ship for five years, mainly spent on fishing voyages off the north-west of Scotland, praised her highly. He had, he said on oath, once had her in a three-day stretch of terrible weather every bit as bad as that which sank her (he was at sea in the same area, about seventy miles away, at that time too), and she behaved perfectly.

"She was perfect," he said. She had hand steering and it took two men to hold her, when the wind chopped round from south-west to north-west, blowing a whole gale, and brought up a confused and dangerous sea. For the three days the sea ran so high and so confused that "they did not know which sea to meet," but she only "wet her decks and took no heavy water at all." That was a substantial tribute. The same skipper said that the area where the *Michael Griffith* was lost, however, was a much worse place than where he met the bad weather. It was, he said, "a good place not to be," explaining that when the tide ran against the wind (as it was running at the time of the *Griffith*'s last signal) even on a quiet day there was a severe swell. He added that the *Griffith* would dodge through anything, so long as she was kept head-to-sea. She had to head into it. In really bad weather, none but skipper, mate and boatswain touched the wheel.

It was agreed that, if for any reason the ship fell into the trough of the sea, she would very quickly be in grave danger. She had a bunker-hatch, engine-room doors, openings in the stokehold ventilators to swing the ash-cans out. There had to be these things. All ships are vulnerable to the sea to some extent. If the sea can make a clean break over them, there are openings which must be used by the crew that the water will find. The sea must have rushed in to put out the *Griffith*'s three fires at once, and rob her of steam. Once in, the sea would wash around down below and the whole engine-room would quickly become unusable. Without headway, no steering-gear was any use. The little trawler fighting for her life off Barra Head was in exactly the same condition as the other stricken ships that day, elsewhere round the coasts of Britain. She would not fight for long.

The court, as was to be expected, could only, in the end, find that it was unable to find anything. It could not "find the cause of the loss of the *Michael Griffith,* but the most probable cause was exceptionally heavy weather." The wind at the time was north-west Force 10—a bad gale—and the squalls reached hurricane force, with a very high and confused sea. Whether the ship lost power and in consequence fell off and was filled with water, or was struck by a great sea which broke a way to the engine-room and doused the fires, no one could say. In any case the matter was academic. The precise order of events could have no further interest for anyone. The *Michael Griffith,* Skipper Singleton and all her crew had gone where another Court would ask the questions, or accept the poor men with no questions at all.

The ship's official log book, wherein a master must record various matters to show compliance with the Shipping Act, indicated that Skipper Singleton had had a trawlerman's opinion of lifeboat drill. The *Michael Griffith*'s boat had been swung out twice in the six months before she went down, though the act required that a proper lifeboat drill be carried out at least fortnightly. The entries of drill were in the log all right, but it was obvious that the 'drill' had been somewhat perfunctory.

The court did not care for that. But the truth was probably that Skipper Singleton, no matter what any act might say, was well aware that his crew could get that boat out at any time it was required and the weather allowed it. If the wind and sea made such a manoeuvre impossible, then no amount of drill, however well performed or meticulously recorded, was going to make any difference. In the event, the boat had as much chance of surviving, even if it could have been launched, as a Thames punt. But the court recommended that owners be required to see that regulations regarding boat drill were carried out in the spirit as well as the letter.

The lifebuoy came ashore off Loch Foyle in Ireland a week after the ship was last heard from.

From four of the lost little ships, lifebuoys came ashore eventually, mute messengers from the dead. Ships' lifebuoys are painted with the vessel's name and home port in order that they may bring news, if they are found and the ship is not—bad news, and final. Poor little ships! Nine of them, gone bravely out to sea manned by brave men, humdrum little ships at which not even the most ardent ship-lover would take a second look, hard-working little ships going quietly about their business in the nearer sea lanes. Old ships—perhaps too many old ships—and new ships, motor-ships and steam-ships, little tramps and trawlers, now they were gone. Nine in the one great storm! There have been other great storms. There will always be storms. There will always be little ships to put out to sea and fight them too, and there will always be some lost, always some mysteries of the mysterious sea. But nine snatched out of crowded waters almost in the one night, nine well-built, not over-loaded, adequately manned, properly supervised ships taken by the murdering sea with all the men aboard them—that is a high price to pay for the conduct of our business in great waters. There were many bewildered widows—Scots, English, Swedish, Belgian, Dutch—after that January gale, besides poor Mrs. Singleton of Fleetwood, who came—she did not quite know why—to represent them at the official inquiry into the disappearance of her husband's trawler with all its crew.

Mrs. Singleton sat in court throughout the three days of the sitting, which was a trying time for her. Once, and once only, at the beginning, she said her piece. "I speak today for the wives," she began, "that they may not be hurt as I have been hurt." She might have said more, much more, but the learned judge stopped her at that stage—properly so, from the legal point of view. The widow could ask questions of the witnesses, he directed, but the time for an address would come at the end of the proceedings.

By that time, three days later, having heard so much of technicalities and details much of which though relevant meant little to her, the widow could only offer a brief tribute to the memory of her husband, which she did, and sat down. She had no witnesses to call before that court, though her case was eloquent.

PART

2

BATTLESHIP

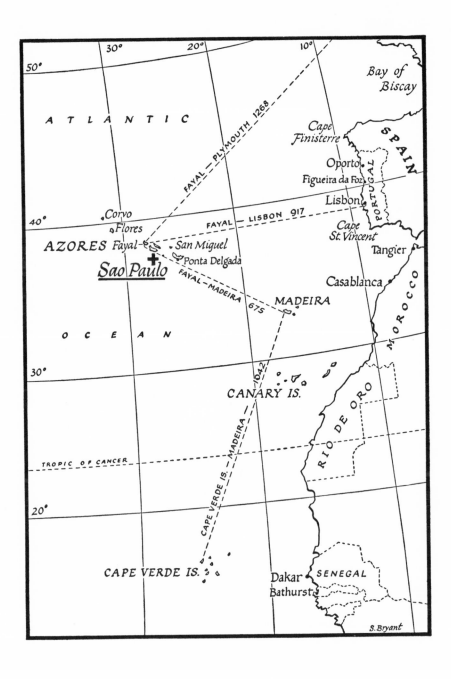

CHAPTER FIVE

The Battleship *Sao Paulo*

ON the face of it, it would seem difficult to mislay a battleship. It would be, one might think, rather improbable that a battleship could be lost in time of peace in the North Atlantic Ocean, or any other ocean, and the whole great compartmented construction disappear beneath the sea, gone utterly from the face of the waters and the knowledge of man. A battleship, after all, does not have to carry any cargoes anywhere. Little ships, struggling to make a living, even big ships, fighting in the sea with heavy loads of iron ore or coal or some such lading, ships whose business is the constant making of their working voyages no matter what the condition of wind and sea—yes, some of these may go missing. But a battleship's only excuse for existence is to provide a floating gun-platform—a *floating* gun-platform, fast and workable and rapidly manoeuvrable in the sea. Because it must be prepared for combat with other floating gun-platforms, it must be so compartmented and filled with watertight bulk-heads that, if not actually unsinkable, it must be able to stand tremendous punishment and yet survive. It is the most pampered of all ships, planned carefully, built carefully, maintained, rested, fostered, groomed like an expensive thorough-bred horse. It is the most expensive of all ships both to build and maintain, and it has the greatest care. It ought to be able to laugh at hurricanes and smile at a mere Force 10 gale. It ought, indeed, to be the most seaworthy type of vessel imaginable.

And yet a 20,000-ton battleship *is* missing in the North Atlantic, gone without a vestige remaining, sunk in the sea somewhere off the Azores with not even a floating lifebuoy left as a temporary mark above the watery grave. It is true that this battleship was not in commission at the time but under tow, a dead ship bound for the breakup yards. She was still a battleship. In some ways her loss under such conditions is the more inexplicable. All she had to do was float.

The missing battleship is the Brazilian *Sao Paulo,* and she was lost off the Azores in an early November blow in 1951. The *Sao Paulo* was built by Messrs. Vickers Armstrong at Barrow-in-Furness in England in 1910, for the Brazilian Navy. Messrs. Vickers Armstrong knew how to build a battleship, and the big-gunned vessel had a long and reasonably successful career under the Brazilian flag. Her life was not arduous and she was not scarred in battle. She was an efficiently maintained unit in a well-run navy. No fault was ever found with her seaworthiness, or her stability, or any other point of importance about her. In the course of time, as battleships do, she became outmoded. Her ram bow and old-type cruiser stern began to look old-fashioned. Her near 20,000 tons, although it had been quite a displacement back in 1910, began to be small as battleships go. She was 500 feet long between perpendiculars—that is, not counting the ram bow—and 83 feet maximum beam, with a moulded depth of 42 feet 3 inches. Her designed draught, in commission, was 25 feet of water. She had three continuous decks, the weather-deck, main-deck, and middle deck, with a lower deck under that which was not continuous. The vessel was divided into seventeen main watertight compartments by transverse watertight bulk-heads, very solidly built, like everything else about her. She had practically a double bottom, and her sides were armoured with a belt of Krupp armour plate nine inches thick which extended from the upper deck to several feet below the water line, and this armour belt was backed on to three inches of teak, which in turn backed on to ¾-inch steel plating. Her main armament con-

THE BATTLESHIP *SAO PAULO*

sisted of twelve 12-inch guns mounted in six barbettes, two of these on the fore-deck, two on the after-deck, and one each on the port and starboard sides amidships. Her secondary armament included eighteen 4.7-inch guns, fourteen of which fired through gun-ports in the side armour, seven guns each side. Each of these side guns used an aperture six feet by four feet, and these were designed to be made watertight in a seaway by means of heavy hinged steel shutters. A large deckhouse, built up on the flush deck, formed the midships superstructure, and this extended between the for'ard and the after pairs of 12-inch barbettes. One enormous tripod mast rose between the two huge funnels and, altogether, the *Sao Paulo* was a fine and powerful representative of the older type of battle-waggon.

She was extensively refitted in 1921 but she had been outmoded for years when at last, in 1946, she was laid up in the sunny harbour of Rio de Janeiro. Two years later, she was put into dry-dock for examination and cleaning. The hull was as sound as ever and she was still a good ship. But she was obviously useless as a battleship and, when she was taken back to her moorings, it was to lie there, largely neglected. She was not docked again, and the green grass and the barnacles flourished on her expansive under-water body. Nobody bothered to clean them off. What could be done with her? Of what use are old battleships? Gradually bits and pieces of her drifted ashore—some officially, maybe some not. Parts of her were 'cannibalised'—as the expression is—to help maintain newer vessels. Her furniture and many of her fittings disappeared. With the postwar shortages, there were good markets for such things as brass and copper, and she had plenty of both. The brass and copper fittings began to disappear ashore, too—some officially, maybe some not. She had brass scuttles, brass round the deck glands, brass fastenings and cleats everywhere. All these were necessary fittings, but they went. She was not to go to sea any more: why bother? Even some of the heavy steel shutters for the secondary armament went, too. A good many of the openings in her upper deck and in the deckhouse had been fitted with brass fastenings in some form or other. These went, too. There are plenty of metal merchants with boats in Rio harbour to gather what harvest they may from ancient ships, liberally provided with expensive brass built into them in spacious days.

So the *Sao Paulo* of 1951 was not the *Sao Paulo* of 1910, or of 1921, or 1941 either. But she was still a massive great hulk and she should surely still have been practically indestructible. The fastenings, if necessary, in all her deck openings could be resecured. These were comparatively minor matters.

After the Second World War the demand for metal in Europe was insatiable. It was worth while, then, to buy old ships almost anywhere, and tow them to Rotterdam or Genoa or Antwerp or the Clyde, or any of the great ports of northern Europe, to break them up. So in due course scrap-steel merchants flew out in passenger aircraft to look over what offered in the ports of Brazil. A sister-ship of the *Sao Paulo* was bought for breaking-up in Italy and was successfully towed to Genoa. Battleships are extensive pieces of scrap and, in due course, the *Sao Paulo* also found a buyer. This was a firm called the British Iron and Steel Corporation (Salvage), of London, and a representative made an on-the-spot appraisal of the ship's scrap value. True, he would have preferred to see her without any of the nonferrous metals removed, but there she was. There was still plenty of good scrap in her, thousands of tons of it. All his firm would have to do was to have her towed to Britain. It was expensive and unnecessary to recommission her. Battleships were never designed to be economic in crews, and it would take a hundred men to run her engine-room and fire the old coal-burning boilers, even just enough of them to give the old ship a sea speed of eight or nine knots.

So, in August, 1951, the scrap-metal experts bought the *Sao Paulo,* as she lay in Rio harbour, flew out a 'runner' crew from

Scotland and arranged for her to be towed back to the country where she was built, by two of the best tugs they could find. Before the battleship could be towed the hull had to be made reasonably seaworthy again and, as it was proposed to tow her well north in the fall of the year, she had to be properly fit for the voyage. The *Sao Paulo* was put in dockyard hands and made ready for her last voyage, and the powerful ocean-going tugs *Bustler* and *Dexterous* hurried out from England.

In the beautiful harbour of Rio de Janeiro anything can be done, but it may take time—a great deal of time. It was, it seems, difficult to get the necessary work finished in the *Sao Paulo* before the tugs arrived. Salvage and long-distance tugs are expensive vessels to hire and, if the battleship were not ready within reasonable time to be towed away, her scrap-metal would become more expensive than enough. The new owners employed agents to help them, and their experienced rigger—Mr. William Painter, the managing director of the Ensign Rigging Company—knew what he wanted done and how it ought to be done. He had to have all those openings made secure again and, above all, the apertures for the 4.7 guns (which had been removed ashore) must be thoroughly closed. He had to see that the 12-inch guns could not move (they were still in the ship for they were fit only for scrap). He had to see that there was nothing aboard which could slop about and upset the ship's stability—water in the watertight compartments, old coal in the stokeholds, and so forth. He had to see that the watertight doors were in fact watertight, that the many manhole covers on the compartments in the double bottom were properly in position, and watertight, that there was no way for a November North Atlantic gale to smash seas over the vessel and find vulnerable spots where the water could gush in and upset her stability.

It was not the water flooding her and so causing her to founder which was his worry. If he had a worry at all—and he probably had—it was stability. A little sea sloshing about in the wrong place *could* upset that. After all, the ship was high and she had a lot of windage. A hard beam wind could list her and if, rolling in a great seaway such as the North Atlantic could well bring up—and must be expected to bring up, in October or November—the sea found some of her openings vulnerable (such as those hinged steel shutters on the 4.7 apertures, or the too-many openings in the big steel deckhouse) then it might be too bad for the old *Sao Paulo*.

Mr. Painter knew his work. He had not handled many old battleships (few people had, for long ocean tows), but he had been looking after old ships on long tows and so forth all the days of his adult life, and so had his father before him. He had a mate, a Mr. Adams, and seven able seamen who were also riggers. With patience, with energy, with competence and with drive, he set about the laborious and trying business of inducing the Brazilian naval dockyard maties somehow to do the necessary work to assure the vessel's seaworthiness for the long tow. It was hot and difficult, sometimes to the point of exasperation. Why hurry over a useless old hulk? The local attitude, though the workmen were competent enough when they were on the job, was sometimes not very helpful. The custom of the port was not, perhaps, conducive to the rapid execution of efficient work upon an ancient vessel, or any other vessel. Just precisely how well the *Sao Paulo* was prepared for sea no one can now say and there never was much direct evidence on the subject, but at any rate she was properly furnished with a certificate of seaworthiness by the local Bureau Veritas surveyor. He was an expert marine surveyor, and he went over the ship thoroughly, taking some days to do the job. A battleship is not to be looked over in five minutes.

The *Sao Paulo* was not ready when the tugs arrived from Britain, though Mr. Painter, having contracted to get the ship home, had worked energetically on the job. The master of the tug *Bustler* and his chief engineer also helped, as soon as they arrived. The work was begun on the 5th of September and, on the 18th of that month, the Bureau Veritas surveyor duly furnished the seaworthiness certificate. The ship was ballasted with water ballast and was in good trim for the long tow. Two good lifeboats were put aboard as well as life-jackets for the runner crew. Her original radio equipment—such of it as remained—was unusable, and a portable set was therefore put aboard in order that Mr. Painter could talk to the tugs, and a communications drill was worked out between him and the radio officers in the tugs. The necessary steaming lights were rigged, to indicate to all vessels met by night that a large ship in tow was passing by. The bottom was not cleaned, but the rudder was fixed amidships and the boilers, propellers, and the machinery (all of which was merely scrap) fixed in such a way that none could cause any trouble during the tow. The boilers were empty, and the propeller shafts were disconnected inside.

The runners made themselves a bit of a rough place to live—'doss-house' would be the best word for it—in the accommodation and, although they were men well accustomed to old ships and the roughest of sea housing, some of them objected that the lack of comfort was extreme and would become a hardship when the tow reached windy northern latitudes. However, they accepted things as they were, though there was a little trouble. After all, they wanted to get home. A stranded Britisher, with his wife and young child, volunteered to work a passage home in the ship, the wife doing such cooking as might be possible, but the accommodation was altogether too rough for a young mother and child and—fortunately for them—this family was left behind.

Two seamen from the *Dexterous* were also left behind, since they deserted at Rio, and one of the runners named De Vos was seriously hurt in an accident aboard and, though he asked to be taken home in the ship, he was left behind in Rio, too. On the 20th of September, which was the equinox, the two tugs, whose gear was

[85]

of the best, began the long tow, and the once-proud battleship, now barnacled and dingy, was moved slowly out of the magnificent harbour with naval tugs assisting. She was as fit as she could be made for the voyage, and the few who watched her go expected to hear no more of her except that she had duly arrived. The *Bustler,* a rescue tug of more than a thousand tons gross and 205 feet long, could have managed the tow by herself. She was towing with 100 fathoms of 22-inch manila attached to 350 fathoms of 5-inch wire, the tow-line secured to a length of the battleship's anchor cable at the one end and the *Bustler*'s patent towing-winch at the other. The *Dexterous,* which was a strong 600-ton tug, had been sent out to make doubly certain that the tow would be completed in good time, probably because of the expectation of bad weather at the time of the year the ships were expected to be passing through the wilder reaches of the North Atlantic. The *Dexterous* was using 70 fathoms of 10-inch nylon secured to some 230 fathoms of 5-inch wire. The two tugs towed one on either bow, and the *Bustler* (Captain Jonathan Adam) was in charge.

For forty-five days the old battleship wandered along placidly at the end of the two long tow-lines, and her crew of runners had enough to do, watching her trim and in general looking after her. They did not have to steer nor run any engines except a portable generator put aboard for the steaming lights, but they were busy with such things as the manhole tops, better securing doors and fittings against the coming bad weather, coping once or twice with some water slopping about on the tank-tops. The route was up through the south-east trade winds, which were behind the ships and helped them along, then through the doldrums of the equatorial calms, and so northwards into the north-east trade winds. The north-east trades were fresh and cut down progress. Twice the *Sao Paulo* was noticed to have a slight list, once with one of the for'ard barbettes slewed slightly out of position and once (as Mr. Painter reported over his walkie-talkie) because of some water slopping out of one of the double-bottom compartments. Both these slight lists were corrected, and Mr. Painter at no time reported anything seriously wrong in the ship.

By mid-October the *Dexterous* was in need of bunkers and, slipping the tow temporarily, put into Dakar in West Africa. This diversion took only a day or two and she was soon back on the job. The *Bustler* was a diesel tug with more endurance, and she plugged along. The rate of advance was not great and, early in November, a gale got up from the north-west which slowed the ships down almost to a stop. The wind howled around the *Bustler*'s radar and through the *Sao Paulo*'s high tripod mast, round the rusted old funnels and in and out of the big steel deckhouse. The sea got up, and the two tugs jumped and bounced about, leaping and rolling. After a day of this, with the conditions steadily worsening, the flotilla was hove-to, with the two tugs—still one on either bow of the battleship —headed into the wind, to keep themselves and the tow head-to-sea. All three ships were rolling, pitching, lurching, but they were not trying any longer to make headway, waiting for the weather to blow over. The ships were then close to the Azores, which were on their route.

It was nine o'clock on the morning of the 4th of November that the flotilla hove-to. The battleship, watched closely from the bridges of the two tugs, was doing all right, and there was no foreseeable reason why she should not continue in that manner. She was rolling and pitching, as any ship would in the increasing sea. But there was nothing violent about her motion. Mr. Painter reported over his walkie-talkie at two o'clock in the afternoon that he had just been round the ship and found everything all right. There was, he said, a slight trickle here and there through those closed 4.7 gunports—the temporary closings, put on in Rio—but he described this as negligible. That was his word—negligible. Nothing to worry about.

The gale continued to shriek with an increasing strength. The squalls of rain and violent wind howled and screamed, but the great sea ran true. It was good deep water, out there, with no shoals to bring up a tortured mess of breaking water. The seas were breaking and, sometimes in the squalls, the force of the wind seemed to lift the very tops from the breaking seas and to send them flying bodily through the air, which was full of spray and sea and flying foam. Visibility was bad—very bad in the squalls, which were of increasing violence and duration. It became obvious that this was to be a really heavy blow. Still, the three vessels should come through all right. That was what they were built for. The two tugs had all the power they needed, and the big hulking battleship had only to stay afloat.

A howling squall came with an early dusk, shutting out everything except the contorting walls of water leaping and roaring round the ships. There had been many such squalls, but this time the tugmasters sensed that something was wrong. They could feel a difference in the behaviour of their ships. There came a slight lift, an easing in the driving spray and rain, a lull in the squall. And there, close behind them now, was the great hull of the battleship swung broadside in the sea. She was rolling her rails under, her great tripod mast whipping like the pendulum of an enormous grandfather clock in a violent earthquake, her twelve-inch guns now flung towards the heavens and now pointed to the depths of the sea.

Instead of being safely hove-to, the *Sao Paulo* was a dead and uncontrollable bulk in the trough of the sea! She took a wild sheer, refused to respond to any pressure of the tow-lines, lay and rolled and wallowed. The fierce wind now gave her sternway, while the breaking seas roared all round and the squalls shrieked. The battleship drove astern with all the windage of her enormous upperworks, pulling the two tugs together, helpless, like harnessed horses held hopelessly to some huge steam-roller headed inexorably downhill. Fumes belching from their funnels, rails rolling under, the stinging sea-spray everywhere, the *Bustler* and the *Dexterous* tried to bring the giant under control again, tried to steam away from

[88]

one another. Hopeless! The wind and sea roared with a demoniac laughter at them. Now the *Bustler* was within yards of the *Dexterous,* pulled on that all-powerful tow-line. Up the smaller tug climbed upon the crest of a breaking sea to crash down a moment again within feet of the *Bustler*'s rolling rail, while the battleship, like a cat with two fat mice, played with the tow-lines! Another sea, another few moments of this, and it would not be the battleship that was in trouble. The tugs would be ground together and—very likely—fatally damaged. They could not stand being flung together in collision in that storm.

In these circumstances there was one thing and one thing only to be done. The *Dexterous* must slip the tow-line. This had been agreed between the tugmasters beforehand. The *Bustler* could hold on through the night, or until the conditions of wind and sea permitted the tow to be resumed. With the *Dexterous* free of the tow and able to look after herself, the other tug would be all right. So should the battleship.

So the *Dexterous,* wasting no time, prepared to slip. Even that operation was extraordinarily difficult, in the dreadful sea. While the chief engineer was still preparing to slip, the towing hawser parted—he thought because a shackle gave—throwing the whole strain on the *Bustler* before she was ready for it. Almost at the same instant, the *Bustler*'s tow-line parted, too. The master and the carpenter tried at once to recover the line but it hung a dead weight in the sea, as if it had the battleship's cable still on the end, so up and down that it came into contact with the tug's thrashing propeller and so was cut and lost. By this time the weather was so bad that both tugs could do nothing but remain hove-to. It was dark then. The wild gale continued. The *Dexterous* was suffering damage in the sea.

Though their own position was not enviable, both tugmasters tried at once to get into touch with Mr. Painter in the *Sao Paulo* to let him know what had happened and that they were standing by.

Though his last signals, a few hours earlier, had been loud and clear, they could not raise Mr. Painter.

No one ever raised Mr. Painter again, nor was the *Sao Paulo* seen, nor her two boats, nor the body of a runner, nor as much as a piece of life-jacket that had been aboard. Though the *Bustler* had her powerful radar going as quickly as she could, there never was an echo from the battleship. Though the tugs stayed and searched for days and there was a week-long search by ships and aircraft, not a trace of the *Sao Paulo* was ever found. She had disappeared from the face of the waters as if some mighty force had plucked at those broken tow-lines and dragged her, in an instant, down beneath the sea.

The pale autumnal sunshine lit the high-ceilinged room, cream-walled, elegant, carpeted underfoot and hung with candelabra above. Between forty and fifty men were assembled there, headed by a mild little man with grey hair who sat upon a bench with two large men beside him—the nautical assessors. The rustle of bundles of white paper, the quiet voices of the grey-suited men, now and again a penetrating question from the smaller man with grey hair—these were all that broke the peace of the October morning. Outside there was not wind enough to bring the autumn leaves down in the well-kept park. A window in the Carlton House apartment was partly open to admit the warm southerly air. Few traffic noises penetrated the pleasant London backwater. It was almost three years since the *Sao Paulo* had so mysteriously disappeared, and now these two tables full of counsel and the mild little man (who was a judge) and the expert witnesses were assembled together to try to find out why. This was the court of inquiry, the formal investigation ordered by the British Ministry of Transport.

The *Sao Paulo* and her lost crew seemed remote from all this, their tragedy now reduced to bundles of white paper tied up in pale red tape, and the dry voices of men. Plans of the battleship (which were more than the riggers had been able to find in Rio), charts, weather information, details of the tugs and so forth, littered the long tables. In the back of the court sat a row of men with strong faces—seafaring men, watching with an air of great interest and slight bewilderment, as if they found the proceedings somewhat incomprehensible, or perhaps doubted the ability of this array of legal gentlemen to solve this or any other mystery of the sea. These were men thoroughly aware of the power of screaming gales and storm-lashed, violent seas. They might well wonder at the purpose of the quiet court.

And yet the court had a function to perform. A big ship had been lost, with eight men. Why had the ship been lost? Had everything been done, and properly done, to guard against the loss of the vessel? If not, who was at fault? If no one was at fault, could any mistake be discovered among the methods of preparation for the tow or in the tow itself, or the manner of handling the tugs, which would guard against another such calamity in the future? The ship was supposed to be seaworthy. The tugs were good tugs: and yet they had lost their tow. Why? Had the tugmasters done all that could properly be expected of them, and that little more that a good seaman should? Was there any question that they had improperly abandoned the tow? It was late in the year when the old battleship was taken away on her last passage. Was it not a little too late? Not for the South Atlantic, of course—not for the beginning of the run, but for the end. Would it not have been better to have waited for the following spring? Having decided to tow through the autumnal weather of the North Atlantic, was the ship properly prepared? Really properly prepared that is—not with a piece of paper declaring her to be seaworthy, but thoroughly seaworthy in all respects to survive whatever weather she might encounter, and such hazards of the sea as might be expected to affect a large vessel under tow.

The legal gentlemen were assembled to find out these things, if they could be found out, and, quiet voices or no quiet voices, they would thrash the problems out, thoroughly, competently, without fear or favour. Two assessors were on the bench for the same purpose with the judge, and he was not dealing with his first sea mystery. The learned judge, indeed, was an expert in such matters, had probed to the bottom of many sea tragedies. As always in these cases, he would be seriously impeded by the absence of the chief performers, the lost crew. But in this case there were witnesses up to the last hours of the tragedy—the tugmasters and their crews. There was a man who as one of the rigging party had helped to prepare the ship for sea, the injured man who had been left behind in Rio. He had had time enough to recover and he was in court.

Counsel from the Ministry of Transport outlined the case, described the *Sao Paulo* and the tugs, in great detail, put in plans, certificates, documents in such volume, indeed, that the judge once or twice had a little difficulty numbering them, to keep up with him. Counsel said that difficulty had been met in getting information from Rio de Janeiro, which did not astonish the row of seafaring men seated in the back. Indeed, he indicated that it was not until Her Britannic Majesty's Ambassador to Brazil had presented the authorities with a questionnaire that any useful information was obtained from the Brazilian Navy at all. (Why should they bother? The ship had been disposed of. She was Brazilian no longer. They were not naval tugs which towed her away.) It had taken years to find out anything and, even then, they had not found out very much. There was no direct evidence about the extent of the work done to prepare the ship for sea. What evidence there was, was in part conflicting. The Brazilian Navy had done the work of closing the gunports. There was no oral evidence from the people who had done this work.

Counsel gave the whole story in all the detail he could. When the tow-lines parted, he said, the *Bustler* flashed light signals in the direction where the *Sao Paulo* should have been, but there were no answering flashes, nor was the walkie-talkie set used. The *Bustler*'s radar showed the *Dexterous,* but not the battleship—only sea clutter. In the morning the *Bustler* returned to the place where the hawsers had parted and remained there, despite the weather. Royal Air Force, United States Air Force, Portuguese Air Force aircraft had searched an area of some 140,000 square miles, operating both from the Azores and from Gibraltar, and they had seen nothing of the lost ship or her crew. The aircraft searched by instrument and visually for three days, from the 7th of November until the 10th. The *Bustler* remained searching as long as she could, but the *Dexterous* was too badly damaged to remain and had to go into Ponta Delgada for repairs. On the way back to Britain, the *Bustler* lost one of her crew overboard. No one from the *Bustler*'s crew at the time of the tow was now in the ship. This sort of thing, and the difficulty of obtaining information from Rio, had delayed the inquiry, which had been ordered by the Minister as far back as early February, 1952.

Life-saving arrangements, counsel went on, had been properly attended to, but there was some conflict of evidence about the size of the boats. One was at davits on the port quarter and the other under a derrick amidships. Precise information on the boat's equipment was lacking. There was no line-throwing equipment. That was in the tugs. The *Sao Paulo* had twelve red and twelve blue flares ready for use. The *Bustler* carried two radio operators and was fitted with radar with ranges of three, ten, and thirty miles. Captain Adam, of the *Bustler,* inspected the *Sao Paulo,* and he and Captain McDonald of the *Dexterous* arranged for the filling of some tanks, to give the ship a deeper draught and trim her by the stern, but there was no precise stability information available for the court. When the battleship was last seen from the tugs on the late afternoon of the day she disappeared, there was nothing apparently wrong with her. There was no observable alteration in her trim. Mr. Painter had himself reported that she was all right only a couple of hours before the lines parted. The *Dexterous* was keeping walkie-talkie watch but heard nothing more. The *Bustler* had searched until the 20th of November and was joined by the rescue tug *Turmoil,* which was sent from England to assist the search. As soon as the tow-lines parted, the *Bustler* had warned all shipping to keep a lookout for a battleship adrift in the gale. But nothing was ever seen, beyond a piece of wood (which might have come from any ship) floating in the sea. A ship had reported later that she had seen mysterious flashing lights, but this was in a position some 230 miles south-east of the place where the tow parted. A vessel called the *Pansio* also reported having seen flashing lights which she investigated, but found nothing. The *Pansio* at the time was about 160 miles south-east of the place where the *Sao Paulo* broke from her tow.

The case having been opened, witness after witness came forward—the man who bought the ship for scrap (who admitted that in a letter to him Mr. Painter wrote he had "never had a job with so many hitches" and one of his runners refused to make the trip when he saw the accommodation provided); Mrs. Painter, the widow, present in court also because she was a director of her husband's company, then in liquidation; the captain of the *Bustler* (who said that even after the *Sao Paulo* had broken adrift he was in no anxiety about her, or those aboard); Captain McDonald, of the *Dexterous;* the chief engineer and a radio operator from the *Bustler;* the surveyor from Bureau Veritas who had given the seaworthiness certificate—all these took the stand and were heard.

Captain Adam of the *Bustler* said he had made an examination of the *Sao Paulo* before leaving Rio and was satisfied with her state for the voyage. The gunports which had no steel covers were blocked up with wooden planks of a heavy Brazilian wood with the strength of teak. As to the last moments of the old battleship, he said that the sea at the time was "very, very heavy. During one of the squalls we could not hold the *Sao Paulo*'s head to wind. When she got broadside to the sea she started to pull us astern. As the tugs went astern they closed. We tried to hold away but were still being dragged in." At this stage the tow-lines went, while the *Dexterous* was still making preparations to slip her hawser. After the break, he was "happy that, lying in the trough, the *Sao Paulo* would be safe. I should," he went on, "have tried to stay nearer to her had I had any anxiety about the ship or those on board her." At daybreak next morning, with nothing in sight but the smashed-up *Dexterous,* there were mountainous seas and almost continuous thunder and lightning. Day and night radar watch was kept as he tried to follow what he considered the probable line of drift of the *Sao Paulo.*

Captain James McDonald, of the *Dexterous,* said that the *Sao Paulo* had been suitably ballasted and prepared for towing. He had lost sight of the *Sao Paulo* about a mile to leeward within a few minutes of his tow-line parting. He ascribed the casualty to exceptionally heavy weather. He had noticed an access hatch open on the foredeck of the battleship on the morning of the day she was lost. The *Sao Paulo* was shipping a lot of water over her bows at the time and, in his opinion, no man could have made his way forward along the deck then to close that hatch. He thought that the vessel had heeled over with a heavy breaking sea running up her side, and the sea perhaps broke into her through the gunports.

Asked whether he thought the open hatch had anything to do with the battleship's loss, Captain McDonald replied that it was a difficult thing to say, but it might have, especially if she developed a list.

Then the rigger left in Rio, Edward de Vos, an able seaman with more than twenty years' experience at sea, gave evidence. He was, he said, the charge hand responsible for the towing gear. That part of it was all right but there were plenty of troubles. The runner crew at one stage walked out of the ship at Rio because of the conditions aboard, but Mr. Painter and Mr. Adams, his mate, persuaded them to return. One thing they did not like, he said in evidence, was the method of closing the side scuttles in the hull. There were about thirty of these in poor shape in the uppermost tier immediately below the weather-deck. There were four companionways on the weather-deck which had no means of closing and, up to the time of leaving Rio, no covers had been provided for these. The chain pipes forward were not covered and the cable locker could be flooded. There were several doorways in the sides of the main deckhouse with no means of being closed. The doors had been removed and no alternative means of securing them had been provided. There were some peaked skylights on the weather-deck which were without their hinge flaps or steel storm shutters. Just before leaving, the *Sao Paulo* had a five-degree list to starboard, which he thought was due to loose water lying about on the starboard side of the main-deck, where it was some fifteen inches deep.

According to Rigger de Vos, neither the runners nor the tugmasters were really satisfied with the manner in which the gunports and ports had been "boxed up." Two old-timers among the runner crew especially expressed dissatisfaction. This pair told the witness that they did not intend to sail in the ship. When Mr. Painter heard of this he said, "What are they worried about? We know we are safe. We have the finest tug in the world with us." The old-timers, still grumbling, were then persuaded to stay. They had not been complaining about the accommodation but the state of the ship, especially the gunports and the scuttles.

Counsel for the Ministry asked Mr. de Vos if he knew anything of the intending passengers who wished to travel by the *Sao Paulo?*

"There was a man, his wife and their child who wanted to get to London but had no fare," the witness related. "The consul suggested that they should go, with the woman doing the cooking and the man helping on deck where he would have been very useful. Bill Painter was a very generous man, willing to help anybody, and I was afraid he would say 'Yes.' I kicked his foot and he knew what I meant. When we were outside I told him, 'You can't do a thing like that. It would be murder.' "

The Judge: "If you thought it was murder to put other people on board, how came it that you wanted to sail in the ship?"

De Vos: "There was the woman with the child. This was a towing job. We had two tugs with us and I knew that if anything happened we should be picked up. That is what made us go in her, and I wanted to get home."

The Bureau Veritas surveyor said it was agreed with Mr. Painter how the open gunports should be closed. He examined the vessel to see whether any other openings in the sides or on the decks required closing. Some doors were repaired and closed, and ventilators, where the frames had been taken out, were welded with metal covers. He had not seen any water lying about anywhere on board. He had recommended that a pump with a capacity of 100 tons an hour should be put in the ship. He was informed before the *Sao Paulo* sailed that this had not been done, but was assured that another pump would be there, in case of emergency. He had then handed over the certificate of seaworthiness.

The cook-steward of the *Dexterous,* having volunteered to give evidence, made some derogatory statements about the officers in that tug, which did not help the court much, if at all. The cook-steward averred that the tugs could have held the tow and blamed the chief engineer in the *Dexterous* for knocking out a pin, which action, he said, preceded the parting of the tow-line. It was obvious that the cook, saddened at the loss of his friends in the runner crew and feeling that his tug might have attempted to save them (though the tugmaster had no reason to imagine that the battleship would go down) was perhaps not a reliable witness. His experience of tug-handling, in gales or in calms, was limited to what he had been able to observe from the galley, and the court was aware of that.

He was the last witness. Counsel then addressed the court, with the same thoroughness and deliberation which had marked all the proceedings during the preceding four days. There were many counsel—for the owners, for the towing company, the rigging company, the Bureau Veritas. Counsel for the British Iron and Steel Corporation (Salvage) Ltd. asked the court to reject the evidence given by De Vos, and not to accept his allegations. At this, some of the seafaring men in the back of the court looked a little hard at counsel. De Vos, they knew, was the man who had been there, the man who, but for God's grace in crippling him on the eve of sailing, would not have been in the court to give evidence at all. And Mr. De Vos, they also knew, had put the crew man's point of view. What degree of hindsight might be in his evidence they, of course, did not know. Neither did the judge. But he could make an intelligent appraisal of that or any other evidence offered before him.

The Ministry, said counsel, was not prepared to settle blame on anybody. From the evidence, he thought the *Sao Paulo* was seaworthy, possibly subject to the covering of the gunports.

Counsel for the towing company said the decision to slip the tow was a right one, in the circumstances. Unless the tow had been slipped it might have meant the certain loss of both tugs, and there was no known reason for anyone then to fear that it was the *Sao Paulo* which would founder.

At this the cook-steward of the *Dexterous,* unable to refrain from comment any longer, shouted from the back of the court, "They murdered them men!", got up and walked quickly out of the room.

The court found that the cause of the loss of the *Sao Paulo* could only remain a matter for conjecture, but it might have been due to the failure of the temporary closings of some of the gunports or other openings. There was no blame attributable to any of those concerned in the preparation for the towage of the vessel nor in the handling of the ship at sea. Evidence about the closing of the deck and side openings was "conflicting and incomplete," but the court was satisfied that the means for closing the gunports were fit and reasonably sufficient, having regard to the fact that the lowest of them was fourteen feet above the waterline. The court was further satisfied that every effort was made to locate the *Sao Paulo* after the tow parted but, in view of all the circumstances, was of the opinion that the *Sao Paulo* sank shortly after the breakaway and probably within an hour. The cause and manner of the sinking could only be a matter of conjecture. The court was satisfied that when the *Sao Paulo* left Rio de Janeiro her draughts and trim were satisfactory and that those about to undertake the tow were reasonably satisfied as to the vessel's stability.

"When the tow broke away she was then out of control and broadside to wind and sea and, no doubt, heavy rolling occurred. It is highly probable that the superstructure soon received damage and there may well have been breaching of one or more gunports. Large quantities of water probably entered the hull not long after the parting."

The theory had been put forward that the rolling period of the 'dead' ship might have coincided with the wave period, as she lay wallowing in the trough during the gale, and that in this manner successive seas increased the roll until the ship rolled right over. The court, though it expressed doubt that such an unusual coincidence could occur, did not discard the theory entirely, but considered that it was far more probable that, far from having a rolling period closely related to the pattern of the sea, the ship was soon in an unstable condition and heeled over until the lee gunports were under water. The wooden coverings might then have been carried away, and the ship flooded.

"In other words," the learned judge read the end of the court's finding, "the loss of stability under the influence of the storm and the inability of the vessel to exert any righting movement, together with the ever-increasing flooding which would accompany such a condition, was the probable cause of the casualty." Nor could the court offer any recommendations which could be embodied in a form to be useful in future similar towages.

The quiet voices ceased and the court rose. The learned judge and the nautical assessors, the quiet men of serious countenance and sombre garb, the line of the strong-faced mariners from the back of the court filed out into the October day, into the leafy square off London's West End which is Carlton House Terrace, past the statue of Captain Robert Falcon Scott, and dispersed about their ways. The matter of the mystery of the *Sao Paulo* had been— well, not perhaps disposed of, but at any rate properly probed, with all its aspects thoroughly ventilated. Except perhaps anything the other runners might have been able to say had they lived, in support of or against the evidence put forward by their shipmate De Vos. Who knows? They were all dead three years by then, gone in an old Brazilian battleship to rest for ever among their brethren of the sea. They had taken their chances, well aware of what they were doing, and they had at any rate prevented a stranded husband, wife, and little child from joining them in their armour-plated grave.

In the last resort, if anything did go seriously wrong, they had reckoned to be picked up by one or other tug. They could not foresee that it might be the tugs themselves which—temporarily at any rate—were in the greatest danger and had all they could do to take care of themselves, while the 20,000-ton battleship, beset and battered in the gale, rolled and floundered until she slipped down like a great tired stone.

PART

3

"BLACK FROST"

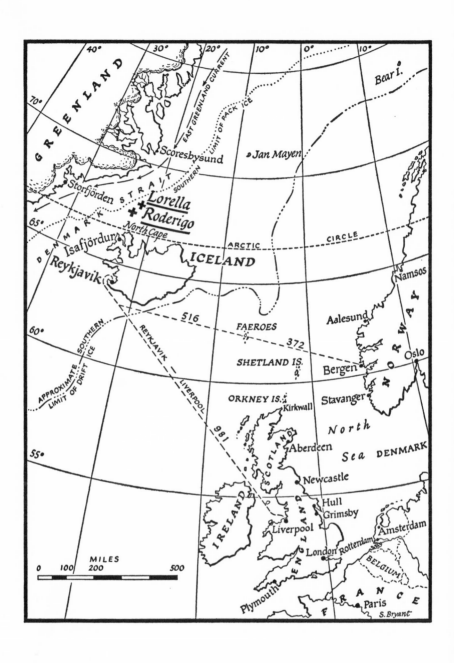

GREENLAND

70°

40°   30°   20°   10°   0°   10°

Bear I.

EAST GREENLAND CURRENT

LIMIT OF PACK ICE

Scoresbysund

Jan Mayen

SOUTHERN

Storfjörden

STRAIT

+ Lorella
+ Roderigo

DENMARK

65°

North Cape

Isafjördur

ARCTIC   CIRCLE

ICELAND

Reykjavik

Namsos

Aalesund

516

FAEROES

NORWAY

60°

372

Bergen

Oslo

REYKJAVIK—

SHETLAND IS.

APPROXIMATE SOUTHERN
LIMIT OF DRIFT ICE

LIVERPOOL

Stavanger

North

981

ORKNEY IS.

Kirkwall

Sea   DENMARK

55°

SCOTLAND

Aberdeen

Newcastle

IRELAND

ENGLAND

Hull
Grimsby

Liverpool

Amsterdam

London Rotterdam

BELGIUM

MILES

0   100   200   500

Plymouth

FRANCE

Paris

S. Bryant

CHAPTER SIX

Mayday

LLOYD'S NOTICE

MISSING VESSELS

The Committee of Lloyd's have directed that the following vessels be posted as Missing:—

"LORELLA," steam trawler of Hull, Official No. 181320, 559 tons gross, sailed from Hull for the Icelandic fishing grounds on the 14th January, 1955, and reported by wireless, in distress, off North Cape, Iceland, on the 26th January.

"RODERIGO," steam trawler of Hull, Official No. 183449, 810 tons gross, sailed from Hull for the Icelandic fishing grounds on the 12th January, 1955, and reported by wireless, in distress, off North Cape, Iceland, on the 26th January.

Lloyd's, London, E.C. 3.
16th February, 1955.

THE *Lorella* was as fine a trawler as sailed out of the great fishing port of Hull. Skipper Steve Blackshaw sometimes wondered what his old father would have thought of her, of all these super-electrified, high-powered 800-tonners which did the distant water fishing in these days. His father had been a fishing skipper before him, but old George Blackshaw had fished in the smacks in the days before steam trawlers came to the ancient port of Hull. Skipper George was admiral of the Great Northern Fishing Fleet—admiral, the senior skipper, the one who controlled, at first, all the smacks of that particular fleet and, later, when they were mechanised, all the steam trawlers. There were no admirals left in 1955—no place for admirals in today's fishing. It was pretty much every man for himself now.

True, as young Skipper Blackshaw reflected, he had every possible aid he could be given. He had a magnificent ship to command, a fine unit in Hull's fleet of 160 Arctic trawlers, which was the largest and the best such fleet in the world. He was proud of that as were all Hull's 3,500 fishermen whether they were skippers, mates, cooks, spare hands or 'deckie-learners.' She had all the navigational and fishing equipment that could be packed into her. Consider the electric depth-recorders, for instance. Young skipper Blackshaw (he was the young skipper but he was forty-eight years old: the old man had died at well past seventy) sometimes wondered how he had ever got on without such gadgets. He remembered the scorn the old man had poured on electric depth-recorders when they were first introduced.

"What's wrong with the lead?" he'd said. "Give me a lead and a lead-line. I know I can trust them."

Nowadays some of the electric gadgets were literally fish-finders. A skipper kept a very watchful eye on the recording graph of his echo-sounder. If he could only read the messages in the various 'blotches' correctly, it would indicate to him when he was on fish, and he could, indeed, stay in his comfortable charthouse and watch a shoal of fish until he was sure they were at a depth where his trawl could scoop them up.

"Seek and ye shall find," said the old man, whose fishing skill was based on a lifetime of hard knocks and hardly-acquired knowledge. But the old man hadn't to fill a 600-ton ship that had cost the best part of £200,000 to build and all of £300 a day to run, every day she was at sea. The old man hadn't been required to go as far as the White Sea or the Barents Sea, or to the ice-littered waters north of Iceland very often. The problems of navigation round Arctic waters in the long winter night were still serious, in spite of radar and everything else. Radar could get out of order, despite the best of care from experts every time the ship was in port. The old man had not to bother with things like that, in the far-off smack days, though they had problems enough of their own and he had had his share of the long voyages, too, when distant Arctic fishing was introduced into the Hull fleet in the first decade of the century. The Hull fishermen were always an enterprising lot, ever since the monks of Meaux Abbey were given a charter to fish in the Humber, back in the dark ages of 1160. The smacks fished the nearer North Sea grounds but, by the mid-1880's, they were being converted to steam and before that, one of the main duties of the admiral had been to direct the movements of the special steamer which the smackmen had clubbed together to buy to collect their fish on the grounds and carry to the big market in London. Before that, after the first steam fishing smack was built in 1870, they were soon fishing off the coast of Norway and then, in 1881, off Iceland and the Faeroe Islands.

The trouble was that they had fished too well. Now they had such magnificent fish-finders as well as trawlers, they too often found themselves excluded from many of the better fishing banks, because the banks were so denuded of fish that fishing had been prohibited there. First Norway, then Iceland had excluded the big British trawlers. They were too good. The charge against them was that they took too much fish too often, and the constant scraping of the sea bed by their great trawls did the feeding grounds no good. The poor fish stood too little chance against them. So nowadays the *Lorella* and her sisters had to go a long way and remain well offshore, outside the newfangled idea of 'territorial waters'—out of sight of the coast of Iceland, in places, and well away from the coast of Norway. The fishing banks shrunk as the fishing methods improved.

Life was still hard for a fisherman. It was a strain on a skipper to fill his ship with a payload of good fish voyage after voyage, despite the weather, the worrying extension of offshore limits, the high cost of fishery operations and everything else. The recent increase in the cost of fuel oil—his ship, like so many others, burned fuel oil to give steam for her engines—made it even more important for a skipper to fill with good fish, and fast. How was he to keep doing that? The echo-sounder was all very well, but it would not find fish where there were none—and this was perhaps an even more serious disability—it could not distinguish between good fish and poor fish. Skipper Blackshaw, like all other skippers, still had his own good ideas as to where the best fish were. Of course, he was making good money. So were Mate Hunter, Bosun Wildbore, Third Hand Collins, Radioman Hobson and the rest of his crew. They made good money but it cost more and more to live and, if a man really got in the big money, the tax was crippling.

Skipper Blackshaw looked round at his fine ship again, the handsome—even sleek—big ocean-going trawler he commanded. She was a good ship, only eight years old—a postwar job of the best kind, an oil-fired steamer 171 feet long by 29 feet in beam, and 14 feet deep. She was built for long-distance fishing, to Lloyd's highest class. She had radio, radar, everything. The Skipper was particularly pleased to have a radio operator. The radio telephone was a most useful way of keeping in touch with the other ships and of knowing —more or less—what was going on, but with an operator as well, a skipper knew that he could always get in touch with distant ships and stations, if he needed to. The radio was, above all, a wonderful life-saver. Trawlers could still get into trouble, and Skipper Blackshaw was well aware of that—trawlers like the *Hildina*, for instance, which was pulled over when a big sea struck her and her gear was foul on the ground (a rather extraordinary accident, that, but the *Hildina* was a Fleetwood ship: anything might happen to a Fleetwood ship), or the *Kingston Aquamarine,* which got herself stranded on the coast of Norway, or the *Sheldon* and the *Guava,* which were missing. Well, he had radio to summon help if he ever needed it. He had two excellent lifeboats on patent davits, so they did not have to be manhandled over the side. He had flares, line-throwing apparatus, distress rockets, life-jackets for everyone, and all the rest of the life-saving equipment his ship might need. He had a new inflatable rubber dinghy stowed up on the top deck, if that were any use.

And he had a good crew. Thank heavens fishing out of Hull was still an important and a well-manned industry. There was no trouble about crews. It was not like the Merchant Navy, which would not be fully manned at all were it not for the National Service Act, which exempted seamen. Fishing and merchant seafaring were different things. Merchant ships might have their manning problems, but the fishermen followed a calling which was traditional, passed from father to son. They were paid well and the conditions of work, though still hard, were wonderfully good compared with those his father had known or even those he had known himself, not so many years ago. All hands still had to work very hard when the ship was on fish, but there was no more of that old stuff of "come on deck, stay on deck" until the fishing was over, with the men asleep on their feet by the time they'd had thirty-six hours of it. Now, no matter how good the fishing might be, a fourth of them were entitled to be below. The *Lorella* was well manned with twenty men aboard—skipper, mate, bosun, third hand, deck hand, six spare hands (the word 'spare' was a technical term to distinguish them from more senior fishermen: there was nothing spare about them, really), two 'deckie-learners' (deckhand-learners, boys learning the combined business of fishing and seafaring), two engineers, two cooks, two trimmers (another technical term deriving from the coal-fired days: these were really enginemen), and a radioman who came in on the fishing, too, for he looked after the cod-liver oil plant and that kept him busy. . . . Aye, it was a good crew.

The ice for preserving his fish was all aboard, shot into its stowages by the usual shoot from the quayside ice plants. Fuel, food, fresh water, stores and everything else needed for a month (if she were out that long: more usually a winter voyage lasted anything from three to four weeks) were all aboard. Chief engineer Neil—a good name for a chief—had the 900-h.p. engine in first-rate order, and the *Lorella* was ready to undock on the tide and sail down the broad brown river to sea. The date was January 14, 1955. Radar, radio, echo-sounders, compasses, electric logs and all the rest of the useful and expensive instruments were in as first-class order as the best of maintenance engineers and experts could keep them. The ship herself, always well kept up, looked fine, even alongside the fish docks in the depths of winter. There was an able, sturdy look about the sweep of her decks and a sea-kindliness in the noble hull which Skipper Blackshaw found pleasing. Aye, she'd do—she'd do, even for January passages to the fishing grounds between the north coast of Iceland and the frozen pack-ice off Greenland. He looked along the dock. It was time to go.

"Let go for'ard!" he shouted to the mate.

"Let go it is!" came the answering hail.

A few engine movements, and the ship slipped away easily from the quay as she had done so many time before, slipped down the dark dock waters to the lock gates and, twenty minutes or so later, was locked out into the stream. It was cold, blustery weather, but the ship was snug inside and secure out. Here again, she would have seemed like a dream to old man Blackshaw. The crew's accommodation was in cabins, and the interior of the superstructure was so arranged that there was access to galley, mess-room, quarters, and engine-room, without going outside.

If the big river was cold and blustery, the North Sea was more so—much more so—as the *Lorella* steamed past Spurn Head and turned towards the north, to make her way up the whole of the east coast of England and Scotland, past the Orkneys, Shetlands, and Faeroes towards Iceland—the proximity of Iceland, not the island itself, for the new fishing limits kept her well away from the coast. It was a long way to go for fish, but she could be on the grounds in three and a half days provided the weather did not remain too bad. She was on the fishing grounds off Iceland's north coast in something under four days, and Skipper Blackshaw began to fish on the bank about thirty miles off the North Cape. It was a good place for fish, but a bad place for weather. It was not so bitterly cold as a landsman might expect, for a faint flow of the mighty Gulf Stream was perceptible even there, bringing if not warm, at any rate some less cold water from the Gulf of Mexico east and north towards Norway. If a seaman didn't know for fact that some influence of the Gulf Stream was felt there, it would be useless to tell him. The place was cold enough. Westerly and south-westerly winds, though often severe in strength, were not so cold. It was the easterly and northerly winds which really had the breath of frozen hell in them.

Though the weather was bad, Skipper Blackshaw and his men managed to get in some fishing, between January 18 and January 23. But on the 23rd the wind set in from the east-north-east, which was a foul direction. It brought snow squalls and bad visibility and, as time passed and the wind did not ease, it brought up quite a big sea too. The *Lorella* could fish no longer. The conditions were too bad. Instead of easing off, the wind freshened first to a gale and then to a hard gale, still from the east-north-east and north-east, and the *Lorella* had to 'dodge'—to steam into the wind and sea at easy speed, just keeping steerage way, virtually hove-to, waiting for a chance to fish again. The *Lorella*'s radar became defective, which was a pity. A ship needed her radar if she were going to seek shelter in one of Iceland's bays. By that time the visibility was often down to nil and the snow was driving horizontally. It was thoroughly nasty weather, even for the month of January, north of Iceland.

There were plenty of other Hull and several Grimsby ships in the same predicament—maybe as many as fifteen or twenty of them, for the grounds north of Iceland were a favourite January haunt. The place might be difficult but the alternatives—the White Sea, the Barents Sea, round Spitzbergen, off Bear Island, the Newfoundland Banks: what places the cod chose to live!—were worse. Skipper Blackshaw heard many Hull ships on his radio. His practice was to keep the radio tuned into the trawlerman's band and listen avidly (either himself or through his well-trained operator) for any scrap of news which would indicate how the others were doing or where there were good fish. Not that they gave away much. There still were fishing 'secrets,' in spite of echo-sounders and all the rest, but at any rate a skipper would have ample news of the weather and how the ships were getting on with that if not with fishing, if he listened long enough.

The big Hull trawler *Roderigo,* a magnificent 800-tonner built as the *Princess Elizabeth* and launched with fanfare only five years earlier, the sturdy *Kingston Garnet,* the *Kingston Zircon* and some others of the Kingston fleet, the *Imperialist, Lancella, Macbeth, Eskimo, Conan Doyle,* the Grimsby ship *Grimsby Manor* and a great many more were all in the same gale. Some of them went in for shelter. The *Kingston Garnet,* the *Roderigo* and the *Lorella* stayed out. There was no warning that the gale might worsen, or that it would be unduly long continued. Sooner or later, it ought to ease. It was as safe or safer to 'dodge' out the storm with sea room rather than—in the *Lorella*'s case—to go groping in towards a dangerous lee shore, obscured behind heavy snow squalls, and try to find the entrance of some bay, without the ship's radar working. What if she missed the entrance? Ships had done that. No, Skipper

Blackshaw kept the sea. He would be better off when the wind eased for being on the fishing grounds.

The gale continued to blow, day after day. The wind continued in the north-east. The *Lorella,* in time, drew out of the zone where the weak waters of the Gulf Stream kept the sea temperature at least a little from the freezing. It began to freeze—a little at first and then hard, really hard. The spray breaking over her began to stick, forming an armour of ice. The snow in the snow squalls stuck, too, and froze on the ice, and into the corners of the decks, behind the fish hatches and everywhere it could, nor did the swish of the sea across the decks suffice any longer to wash it away, as it had been doing.

At three o'clock on the afternoon of the 25th of January, Skipper Blackshaw had his operator send a radio to the owners in Hull, reporting that he had been dodging, then, in a north-easterly gale for sixty hours, which is a long time for a full-powered ship to have to dodge, even in January off Iceland. He did not say so but in that time, too, the *Lorella* had gradually drawn further and further from the land, nearer and nearer the place where the winter pack from the frozen Arctic stretched down to rim the sea, and the nearer he came to that pack-ice the colder was the temperature, the heavier was the ice forming on his vessel.

There were many places for the ice to form. It clung to every wire stay, thickening them until the forestay was as thick as a telegraph pole; it clung to the ratlines, the steel steps in the rigging; it froze round the steel mainmast and all its fittings, round the fish-working lights, round the bridge, along the steel bulwarks, on the boats. It froze into the boats and froze the boats and their davits solid. All this time, whenever they could, the *Lorella's* crew were out on deck chipping and hacking at the ice, despite the really terrible conditions. But they could not safely work on deck, and they could not get at the worst of the ice. They could not go aloft. It was impossible. The ship had a hot-water pumping system which could be connected up to the deck-washing pipe-lines. They put hot water through this but it froze in the pipes. Even if they had been able to use the hot water freely from these points, much of the water would have frozen as it emerged.

So the long night of the 25th of January passed. No one in the *Lorella* was alarmed, then. Surely the weather must change, the wind drop, the temperature rise! Yet the wild gale continued to howl from the north-north-east, and she continued to dodge along into it, freezing herself up the more with each passing hour, getting more to the north, nearer the ice, and becoming sluggish on the helm with the extra burden of more and more ice ever thickening on her. The wind was still blowing a strong gale with squalls to near-hurricane force, nasty long squalls with a scream of vicious snow tearing at the ship. And the snow clung, too, wherever it could, and packed itself in, froze, and continued to cling.

No longer was the *Lorella* steering and behaving as a good ship should.

Skipper Blackshaw was glad now that the *Roderigo* was not far away. The *Roderigo* was a 'chummy' ship of his, the two skippers being friends. Together, a day or so earlier, they had heard the *Kingston Garnet* reporting that he was in trouble with a trawl wire round his propeller. The tough and supremely competent skipper of the *Kingston Garnet* could be relied upon to perform whatever prodigy of seamanship was necessary to clear his propeller and save his ship, even in those ferocious conditions and, indeed, even if he heard the last trump sounding in his lee ear, but the two skippers of the *Lorella* and *Roderigo* kept an eye and an ear open, in case they could assist if the *Garnet* really got into distress. At the time, they had no idea that they were heading into the direst distress themselves. The *Garnet* got himself out of his difficulties, but the ice had knocked his aerial down and he could not tell them.

On the 26th, the two ships were close together, still both dodging to the north, the *Lorella* a little further to the north than the other, and a little more heavily iced. Though they were comparatively close together the two ships could rarely see one another. They were in communication by means of their radio telephones. All the other ships could hear, even those safely at anchor in shelter in various Icelandic fjords. (The event showed that these were the wise ones.) The *Lorella* was behaving more and more sluggishly in the sea now, showing a tendency to fall off and get the wind on either bow. When that happened, Skipper Blackshaw had to ring down for full ahead on his engine, and drive his ship into it until she had full steerage way again. But each time he rang down full ahead the sprays and the driving seas clouded over her the more heavily, and green water broke on deck. Wherever the water touched, it left ice. And that made his ship the more sluggish, which made her the more inclined to fall off, to get into the dangerous trough of the sea, and that made him ring again, more and more often, for full ahead, and that iced his ship the more. . . . She began to list, heavily. All hands had been hacking at the ice every chance they had, with axe and crowbar and anything that came to hand. But at full ahead they could not go anywhere on deck. . . . Soon they could not go on deck at all.

Skipper Blackshaw looked at the sea, listened to the howling of the gale. Could he bring her round? *Could* she run before it safely, even if she did come round? With their deep draught aft and their low sterns, trawlers were more vulnerable when running before the gale with a big following sea. They lay-to through anything, but they might not run. They could fill their decks and suffer fatal damage. If he continued to head into wind and sea he would continue to ice up and, if that went on long enough and the weather did not ease nor the temperature lift, there was only one end. The temperature had little chance of rising in a northerly wind, with the ship approaching nearer and nearer the edge of the pack-ice. He knew that. But could he turn?

Well, he could try. She *might* come round. Skipper Blackshaw told his mate what he was going to do, and warned the chief down below. For a while, he watched for a lull. At last, after a very bad squall had passed, there seemed to be no more squalls coming for the moment. The sea was running like angry, foam-streaked mountains, hissing and snarling. Well, he could not help that. She came round or she didn't come round. The skipper rang the engines to Stop. He wanted her bows to fall off, and he hoped that then she would blow around as a trawler normally would.

Her bows blew off but she did not come round. She fell into the trough and rolled there as if she would roll right over, the weight of ice pinning her down and down! Roll! It was alarming. She rolled as if she would throw the main engines off their bed and fling her funnel overboard, as if she would dislodge the galley stove and all its equipment. Full ahead! The Skipper rang at once. This was no use. Full ahead! She must come up to the wind again. She would never come round and run now, even if—had she come round—she *could* have run.

Slowly, shuddering, gushing the cold sea from every icy scupper-hole, she came—slowly, so slowly, as if she were tired. She came in time—a long terrifying time—but she came with a heavier list. The ice was holding her down. Still the ever-freshening gale howled and shrieked with new notes in the ice-thickened rigging, and still the sprays flung themselves at bridge, superstructure, masts, everywhere, adding always to the weight of ice. Even in that wind, under those conditions, the men of the *Lorella* got out on deck and on the superstructure, and hacked and cut at the ice. It was no use. As fast as they knocked some away, more formed. They could get at very little of its total bulk. It was hopeless.

The *Lorella* began to list a little more—just a little, at first, but unmistakably.

Skipper Blackshaw picked up the microphone. It was quiet inside the wheel-house, despite the howling gale outside.

"Lorella calling *Roderigo,"* he began. *"Lorella* calling *Roderigo.* Been dodging full speed and half-speed all night to keep her up. Getting serious now. It is getting serious now. Been trying to get her round but no go. I am going over, and I cannot get back."

A cable or two away the *Roderigo* was little if any better off. Skipper Coverdale, too, had found himself forced into the position of standing on too long, of taking more and more ice and being unable to clear it, or to turn his ship and run from the frozen area. His decks were a mass of ice. His stays, rigging, mast, masthead lights, superstructure—everything not constantly swept by the heavy seas—were masses of ice. His boats were frozen solid in their chocks, and the falls were blocks of ice. His ship, too, was getting sluggish—dangerously sluggish in the sea. He, too, had to give increasing spurts of full ahead to keep manageable way on her, and the more he did that the more she covered herself with the fatal, freezing sprays.

"Roderigo to *Lorella,"* he answered. "Bad here, too. Boat decks solid with frozen snow. Lads been digging it out since breakfast. Terrible lot on bridge top and they are going up there if possible. I cannot get her round."

"Same here, George, and the whale-back is a solid mess," the other trawlers heard Skipper Blackshaw say to his friend George Coverdale. "Same here, George," in a quiet voice. Then there was silence for a while. That was about mid-afternoon on the 26th of January.

Not long after that, still in Skipper Blackshaw's quiet voice, the *Lorella* was heard to say, "I am going over now. Going over," the voice repeated, as if the speaker were going over to a comfortable home. Then once more, "Going over. Mayday! Mayday! Mayday!"

And then silence.

The *Roderigo* relayed the *Lorella*'s distress signal—the spoken word 'Mayday' (selected because it is unmistakable) is the voice-radio SOS—and gave a position about 90 miles north of the North Cape of Iceland. But the *Roderigo* was in a desperate situation herself. She could not have approached any nearer to the *Lorella* than she was, and she was quite helpless. Her boats were frozen up, as the *Lorella*'s were. She was all but uncontrollable, as the *Lorella* also had been. What could she do to save her capsizing fellow-fishermen, pressed down into the freezing sea by the ever-increasing weight of the relentless ice?

Within four hours of the time that last message was heard from the *Lorella,* the *Roderigo* was going over, too. For the second time that day the other trawlers listened to the quiet voice of one of their fellow-skippers announcing his own, his crew's and his ship's doom—listened helplessly, miles away, pinned down themselves by the gale and the ice that would also so easily destroy them.

It was at 7 P.M. that the *Roderigo* was heard for the last time. "I am going over," said Skipper Coverdale. "I am going over now. I cannot abandon ship. Mayday! Mayday! Mayday!"

Then there was silence from the *Roderigo,* too.

There has been silence from both the *Lorella* and the *Roderigo* from that day to this. Nothing was found of either of them—nothing but an inflatable dinghy, inflated and empty, found adrift on the sea about ninety miles from the position where they probably went down.

In due course, though their fates could be surmised all too clearly, both became overdue vessels, then vessels for inquiry. And then, when the allotted time had run, they were posted missing at Lloyd's. Though the crews of twenty ships had heard them go to their deaths no one had seen them, and their names were added to the long, long list of fine ships and old ships, big ships and small ships which are missing in the depths of the sea.

CHAPTER SEVEN

Dodging to Death

THE loss of the *Lorella* and *Roderigo* was a shock to the trawler-men of Hull, though these are seafarers well accustomed to tragedy. It was the way they went that was so shocking—two of the best trawlers, two excellent and highly experienced distant-water skippers, forty fine fishermen. If they could go like that, then others could expect the same fate sooner or later: but there had not been a tragedy from the port quite like this ever before. Two ships just iced up and iced over, going on being more and more iced up until they lost all stability, caught in a vicious circle, compelled to stand on to the north getting more and more iced. . . . It was frightful, and it was also frightening. Were the methods used in such ships for clearing themselves of ice really satisfactory? If not, what could be done about it?

Other seamen besides trawlermen were interested in the matter. Why, some asked who had no special knowledge of the difficulties, could the two trawlers not have hove-to in the sea, with a sea anchor if necessary, or to a bit of a mizzen set to keep them head-to-sea? Then the crew could have gone safely on deck and rid the ships of ice, even with the primitive means of hacking at it with a few axes. Why, indeed? Couldn't the modern trawler be properly hove-to? Did she have to 'dodge'—to keep under way? Was this, then, yet another tragedy of the power age? The old-time trawlers could heave-to well enough: were they safer in this respect than the new ships, despite the new ships' size, their power, their electronic gadgets and their enormous cost? How was it that, after eighty years of Arctic fishing, the year 1955 should see the first such tragedy as this? Old fishermen could not remember anything like it.

At first, some put it down to an icing condition loosely referred to as 'black frost.' The *Lorella* and the *Roderigo* were lost, according to this theory, because they were *suddenly* iced up in a grim cloud of black frost which, apparently, had rolled at them across the sea. But what was this 'black frost'? The newspapers took up this story, which seemed (to them) both dramatic and reasonably convincing. Black frost, however, is an icing condition of calm, a cloud of frost-smoke such as the sea gives off when the temperature is well below freezing and it is calm enough for the whole surface of the sea to begin to freeze. The *Lorella* and *Roderigo* had gone down in a gale of wind. It was obvious to anyone who knew anything at all of ice navigation and of the Arctic seas—or Antarctic—that black frost had had nothing to do with their tragedy. Frost-smoke accompanies icing conditions, of course, but since it can rise only in periods of good weather, it can very easily be coped with. No, this was something else, something much worse. It was not a freak accident: perhaps it could happen again.

To find out everything that could be found out and to prevent if possible such a tragedy striking the port again, the Ministry of Transport convened a Court of Formal Investigation which sat in the Council Chamber of the city of Hull for three days on August 8, 9 and 10, 1955. Again the familiar scene was enacted—the gathering of counsel, judge, assessors, witnesses, in an ornate room, with the row of mariners in the back—trawler skippers this time, weather-beaten men in blue suits. The chandeliers, the marble, the dark wooden walls, the named seats of the aldermen in Hull's Guildhall, all seemed remote from the waters north of Iceland and the harsh business of distant water fishing. But the fish dock was a short bus ride away and other docks were near the Guildhall's front door. The brown Humber itself was close by, bearing its daily run of the big trawlermen outwards and inwards and its deepwater and coasting ships, going and coming to and from the seven seas. Hull is very conscious of its close connection with the sea and the importance of its fishing industry.

The inquiry was conducted by a wreck commissioner, a Queen's counsel long experienced in maritime cases, assisted by three assessors (none of whom, however, was an ice expert: experts in ice navigation are rare in Britain, yet icing of ships was the crux of this matter). Counsel for the Ministry of Transport outlined the facts—all the known facts of both ships and their voyages. There was no accusation of any kind, he made quite clear, against the seaworthiness, maintenance, manning or anything else to do with either ship. The lost ships were good trawlers, well handled by good skippers and well run by good owners. At the time the ships were lost the wind was blowing from the north-east at Force 11 to 12, which is hurricane force. One inflatable rubber dinghy had been picked up about a week after the ships were presumed to have gone down. It was found some 95 miles from the place where the ships were, as far as this position was known. The question might be asked, why had these trawlers not run for shelter, as other trawlers had done? But it was perfectly right for a skipper to make his own decision about that. The *Lorella*'s radar had broken down, and it might well be more dangerous to seek shelter, with its accompanying risk of wreck, than to keep the sea, where there was plenty of room. The skippers had no reason to fear either an exceptionally severe and long-continued gale (for there was no evidence that such a condition had been forecast in the English language) or unusually severe icing conditions. They could have coped with either condition of itself, but not with both together, and they were not to foresee that. When it was known that the trawlers were in difficulties, aircraft searched the area but could find nothing. Other trawlers did their best to go to their aid, including some which were themselves sheltering at the time.

But no trawler could get near the *Lorella* or *Roderigo* without herself sharing their fate, and several had come near to doing this. It was a most tragic thing for them to listen to their fellow skippers, hearing the quiet voices of Skipper Coverdale and Skipper Blackshaw as their ships, caught in the deathly clutch of the fatal ice, heeled further and further over, became more and more difficult to manoeuvre, and more and more ice formed on them. "Listing heavily to starboard and going over. Ninety miles northeast of North Cape. Unable to abandon ship. NE 11/12 and freezing hard." "Taking heavy water now: having difficulty in manoeuvring." "Going over to starboard." These were among the actual messages sent out by the lost ships and logged by the trawler *Lancella* and the *Imperialist* as they were trying to steam towards them. The *Lancella* did her best to reach the area but was badly iced herself, and had to turn and get out of it while she was still stable. She did all she could.

Owners, builders, surveyors, marine superintendents, all spoke of the excellence of the lost ships and the lost men. Each trawler had an outfit of axes to cut away ice, and they also had hot water and steam systems, though it appeared that the hot water would have to be used through the ordinary pipeline for washing down (which would freeze). Neither skipper was the sort of man who would knowingly take a serious risk. The vessels had plenty of reserve stability, as trawlers have. Both were excellent sea vessels, praised by skippers and crews alike. Their crews remained with them voyage after voyage, with little alteration. But there was some haziness about the availability of steam for fighting icing conditions. It was clear from what was said that fighting really severe icing was something unexpected. The *Lorella* was said to have two means of using steam on deck—if anyone could get on deck to direct it. Icing was accepted as a normal risk, but not severe and continuous icing in a gale of wind. Other trawlers in the same general area successfully dodged out the storm, but they were not as far north as the lost ships, and they did not suffer anything like the same degree of icing. The *Roderigo*, it transpired, had eight axes, sharpened every trip. Experiments had been made with de-icing pastes as used in aircraft, but this method had not proved of much use in ships. Neither had electrical de-icing, but the court was told that experiments were continuing.

The weather expert from the Air Ministry demolished the 'black frost' theory. He knew no such term, he said, though trawlermen used the expression to mean a freezing dark fog. What brought the two ships down, in his opinion, was frozen spray. There were four possibilities—collision with floating ice; freezing up solidly through Arctic frost-smoke; freezing up from freezing drizzle; and, the fourth, freezing up from the spray and seas driving over the vessels. The first three were ruled out. Collision with floating ice was not possible where the ships were, in winter: ice floes drift in spring and summer when ice melts. Arctic sea-smoke—or frost-smoke—was dispersed by the wind. There was a gale at the time and had been for several days. Freezing drizzle caused small-scale ice, and could be dismissed. There was a very much more rapid fall of temperature north of Iceland than elsewhere, and the more northerly the ships were, the more rapid the rate of icing became.

The court listened intently as the weather expert explained that each degree of latitude to the north there meant an average drop of three degrees in temperature. At an air temperature of 22 degrees, the rate of freezing would be nearly twice as great as it would be a degree or two further to the south. The icing conditions on the 26th of January were very bad. The sun rose at 0938 and set at 1444, giving a very short period of day. Visibility was bad— less than half a mile at the best, and down to zero in the numerous snow squalls. The wind in the area was east to north-east at first, full-gale strength, and it later became north to north-east at Force

10 and 11, with squalls to hurricane strength. The area where the trawlers was lost was not covered by the B.B.C. weather forecasts, but by the forecasts issued by the Icelandic Meteorological Service. It was unusual for north to north-east gales to last so long. Records showed that there were perhaps three such cases a year, though the gales might not be as severe as that blowing when the *Lorella* and *Roderigo* were lost. The last similar gale blew in early April, 1952, when five Norwegian sealers were lost. Aircraft of the United States Air Force, the weather expert continued, had made a number of runs over the area when the trawlers were in trouble. They found severe icing conditions and also very severe turbulence.

Leaving a shivering picture of a ghastly day of almost continuous snow squalls and dreadful high seas, with the two ships—big enough in the fish dock but pitifully small up there—caught in the appalling circumstance of having always to go more and more northerly where conditions were worse, the man from the Air Ministry sat down, and the court was quiet for a moment while the images he had evoked sank into its collective mind. Then the skippers took the stand—many skippers. The skipper of the *Lancella,* fleet sister of the lost *Lorella,* told how the gale and the icing conditions forced him to turn back before he could reach the latitude where the stricken ships were. This was obviously a man much moved by the tragedy of his experience. He could feel his ship becoming more and more difficult to handle, he said. She became sluggish on the helm, listing with the weight of ice, becoming dangerously 'dead' on the roll. When he turned —and it was obvious that he did this only just in time—he was in the fury of a Force 11 north-north-east gale and the icing conditions were extreme. He did not say so but, had he gone on, there would have been three ships missing. There was nothing he could do but get out of it and, at the last moment, he barely managed to do that. Further to the east he found the icing conditions to be not so bad.

[122]

The skipper of the trawler *Conan Doyle,* a man with thirty-seven years' experience in distant water trawlers, was waiting for a chance to fish off the North Cape of Iceland at the same time. He heard the two iced-up trawlers on the air and he made towards them, but he, too, could not carry on, though the icing conditions had not been so bad nearer to the land. He thought the *Lorella* was at least 40 miles more northerly than he was—probably further. He found that the icing conditions worsened very quickly, within a period of four hours. The ice was from spray and the sea. It was not 'black frost.'

"There was a terrific sea running," said the skipper. "I turned the ship and ran before it, because of the icing. Other times I have been able to chop the ice away, but not this time. The weather was too bad. I took a long chance, turning round in that sort of sea, but it was the only thing to do. It was very difficult. If the *Conan Doyle* had been iced up a bit more she would have gone over. I thought turning was the less of two evils. The ship suffered damage running before the sea, but we got out of it."

The veteran skipper of the *Kingston Garnet* said the ice brought his aerials down. He reckoned he had eighty or a hundred tons of ice on his ship before he turned. The ice was frozen spray and packed snow. The wheel-house was covered with six or eight inches of solid ice in a layer caked round it. They had to open the windows and hack at the ice with anything that came to hand—marline spikes, chisels, engine tools. The men could not go on deck to hack the ice or they would have been washed overboard. He was worried about his ship's stability but he had to 'keep dodging.' It was the less of two evils. He was luckier where he was—the wind allowed him to dodge in a more easterly direction, and the icing did not become fatal.

No one asked the old skipper how he had got the wire from round his ship's propeller. That happened a day or two before the 26th, but it must have been a prodigious feat of good seamanship.

What would he have done if he had not managed to free his ship's motive power? He could not have 'dodged' then. He would have had to lie hove-to in the sea the best way he could. Skipper Trolle, of the *Kingston Garnet,* was one of the most experienced distant-water skippers sailing out of Hull. It might have helped the court if he had been asked further about these things. If the *Lorella* and the *Roderigo* could have been made to lie-to, without appreciable headway, and put out oil to windward to stop the spray and sea from driving over them, then their crews might have dealt with the ice and the ships need not have been lost. Perhaps it was significant that the *Kingston Garnet* had kept dodging herself. Maybe the modern trawler will not lie safely in a very bad sea and high wind. No one mentioned the old practice of putting out a film of oil and lying to a sea anchor. A film of oil is of no use if it only quietens the sea behind the ship, as it would if a vessel were dodging, but if she can drift in her own 'slick,' it will save her.

All the skippers agreed that the conditions were unusually bad. Only old skippers, now retired from the sea, could recall the like. Ex-Skipper J. H. Ellis, for example—now a trawler manager ashore —told the court of an occasion some thirty years earlier when he was in the steam trawler *St. Brelade* which was badly iced up. The conditions must have been similar to those of the end of January, 1955. He recalled that three ships were lost then, one each from Hull, Iceland, and Germany. The wind increased very quickly to gale force and kept on blowing. He tried to run before it, but his ship took too much water when running. So he dodged. A shift of coal in the bunkers did not help things, but the crew got that trimmed again. (The *Lorella* and *Roderigo* were spared at least that hazard. They both burned oil fuel.) While he dodged, the wind shifted to the north—it had been east—with very bad icing. The rigging soon became a solid mass of ice, and the ice was caking hard and heavily everywhere. Had the wind continued at its original violence his ship would not have survived but, fortunately for her, the wind eased and the sea went down, and the crew were able to get at the ice and hack a lot off before it had quite robbed the ship of her stability.

It was his experience, said this witness, that even a difference of 20 miles between trawlers' positions, in the north of Iceland, might mean very marked changes in the icing conditions. Sometimes there was a clear line of demarcation between just freezing and severe freezing, and no man could tell where the line was until he had crossed it. The *St. Brelade,* like most trawlers, lay better heading into the sea than running before wind and sea, but some ships ran better than others. The trouble with running was that ships yaw, and trawlers have a lot of deck to flood with a pooping sea. They did themselves damage, and they could fall into the trough. A seaman had better control of his ship, lying head to sea. The ideal was just to keep the ship up head-to-sea with minimum engine movement, so she was yielding to the sea and not fighting it, and meeting wind and sea bows-on. That was what 'dodging' really was. But when a ship's upper works were iced up she became sluggish and she would fall away, the wind catching one bow or the other, and the mass of ice in her fore rigging, in time, acted like a sail, which further blew her head around. Then the only thing to do was to keep more way on the ship in order to keep her bows up, but that meant more sprays, more seas breaking over, more ice.

The Judge: "Is there no answer to such a condition?"

Ex-Skipper Ellis: "I know of none. Either the wind moderates or the temperature rises. Or . . ."

Counsel for the Ministry: "What about hot water? Or steam?"

Ex-Skipper Ellis: "When you want hot water you can't use it. When you can use it you don't need it. Men couldn't get on deck to use steam pipes. They would have to be directed by remote control. There is no present answer to that."

The Judge: "Do you know of any other ships lost in such conditions?"

Ex-Skipper Ellis: "I do not know another case in the past thirty years."

The Judge: "My colleagues have suggested that a small mizzen might be useful, for ships to lie hove-to. What does the witness think of that?"

Ex-Skipper Ellis: "It might help under some conditions. But any sail would blow out in a Force 10 wind. None of the Hull ships use mizzens now. The mizzen has gone out."

Skipper Balls, of the trawler *Grimsby Town*—not a Hull vessel —said the ice had thickened his forestay until it was seven or eight feet round. Twice he had had his crew chopping ice away for six hours at a time. When he headed for the position given by the *Roderigo,* he could not chop the ice away and it was very much worse.

The Judge: "What about the chances of lying-to under a mizzen?"

The Skipper: "We used to do that. We don't have a mizzen now. You can't set one because of the boats. There is no way to set a mizzen in these modern trawlers."

The skipper of another Grimsby trawler, the *York City,* said that he, too, had taken the last chance and turned his ship to run when he found the icing conditions becoming impossible. "When you are going to Davy Jones' locker if you keep on, you might as well try to turn," he said. He added that he had only just got away with it. He had never seen such serious icing in twenty-five years of distant-water fishing, all of it in the far north.

"I got her round by stopping and letting the wind blow her bows off, because the ice for'ard was like a sail," said this skipper. "It was a last resort. If she went over she went over. I knew that turning with critical stability might capsize the ship. I also knew that not turning would soon give me no stability at all. She went over on her beam ends but she came up again. It took about six minutes. Then she righted herself and paid off, and I got some way on her. I could put men on deck when I was before the wind."

The skippers of the *Kingston Zircon,* the *Brutus,* the *Stafnes,* the *Imperialist,* followed one another with similar evidence. Large men, small men, all with quiet voices, they spoke of the freezing hell of Denmark Straits as just one more risk of the trade, one more factor against them in the constant fight to get a 'fill of fish' and make a living from the enemy sea. Now and again, the judge had to ask one of the skippers to speak more loudly so as to be heard in the large domed room. An old Norwegian skipper, one of the veterans who helped introduce some of the remoter Arctic grounds to Hull, told how he had dodged out a similar frozen gale fifty years ago, to a buoy for sea anchor. Two ships were lost that time, he recalled, but he lay to his buoy all right. In all his fishing experience, which began in 1907, he had only once known all three conditions—very heavy gale, very heavy freezing and very heavy snow—together in such a way as when the *Lorella* and *Roderigo* went down. The bigger the trawler the bigger the area to catch the spray, he added.

When the skippers had had their say, and a stability expert had given his calculated view that 55 tons of ice added to the superstructure of the *Lorella* would be enough to cause her to capsize in a beam wind of 75 knots, and full details were given of the search instituted and all that had been done, and the Ministry's and the court's sympathy was extended to the relatives of those lost, the inquiry was over. It had done what it could, but it had no real answers. Skipper after skipper had been asked if he could put forward any suggestions to cope with the problems that were too much for the *Lorella* and her consort, but they could only shake their heads. The whole problem, said counsel, was being looked into most thoroughly by the Hull trawler owners, but they had not been able to find any full answer yet.

A full answer? There is no full answer to the wiles of the demon sea, with or without freezing ice for ally. The court, when it issued its official findings after due deliberation, gave no full answers either. The two trawlers, it found, were lost through severe icing in very heavy weather. The skippers had no reason to foresee such rapid development of heavy icing with persistent gales. The other trawlers in the area, the United States Air Force and the Icelandic authorities were thanked for all they did to aid the rescue work. But with regard to the all-important matter of putting forward suggestions to prevent a similar calamity, the court regretted that it had been able to produce no useful ideas. It was glad to note that the trawler owners were themselves studying the problem and doing their utmost to ensure additional safety for their vessels and the gallant crews who manned them.

It is to be hoped that the trawler owners do find some answers whether in the form of a re-introduced lying-to sail, or a stout weather-cloth that could be lashed in the mizzen rigging, or an alteration of design which would enable a modern trawler to run better—this would be difficult, for the trawler hull-form has been derived from many years of hard experience—or adequate de-icing equipment which would not be impossible to install or maintain. There is also the matter, yet once again, of the adequacy—or inadequacy—of the standard lifeboat, though this is not for the trawler owners themselves to decide. They provide the boats which the Ministry, in its wisdom, requires, but it is horribly obvious that iced-up boats with iced-up falls are of use to no one. What could any of those rescuing trawlers have done, had they been able to approach the *Lorella* or the *Roderigo* before those ships capsized? The rescuers' boats were blocks of ice, too.

That they would have done—or tried—*something* goes without saying, for the trawlermen have the hearts of lions. There was the case of the timber steamer *Fred Borchard,* for example, which foundered off the coast of Norway in the autumn of 1951 in a dreadful fury of the sea, littered with great balks of timber broken from the *Borchard*'s decks. A little trawler, by name the *Boston Fury,* steamed among these balks in that wild gale and literally fished twenty-seven of the twenty-nine men in the *Borchard*'s crew out of the sea, though the *Boston Fury* could launch no boats. Boats would be smashed up by the timber. But what about men? She put her men in the water, gale or no gale, and they swam among those murdering balks, which were crashing, rolling and plunging in the violent turmoil of the sea. They got lines to the twenty-seven men, and they saved them. Men said afterwards that only fishermen could have carried out a rescue like that. The *Borchard* went down north of the Arctic Circle, too, and the month was October.

Steve Blackshaw in the *Lorella* knew that George Coverdale in the *Roderigo* would somehow come to the rescue of his men if things went from bad to worse and she really did go over. But when, because of the mercilessness of the frozen gale, that time so quickly came, George Coverdale, poor man, was in no state to assist anyone. He could not manoeuvre his vessel sufficiently well even to approach the *Lorella* and, within a matter of hours, he had slipped below the surface of the sea, too. No one could get near him. The gale continued to scream and the spray and sea and snow continued to turn to ice until the last moment came and the ship, plunging sluggishly in the furiously high sea, slipped on her side straight under—down to her death, with all her electronic aids and her splendid equipment, her noble hull descended from a long, long line of the most seaworthy of all vessels, her crew of twenty. Young Ted Beaumont, aged fifteen, on his first voyage to sea, with the ink scarce dry on his net-mender's certificate from the Nautical School, and Mate Andreasen, as good a mate as sailed from Hull, Radioman George Leadley, and Bob Seddon who had eight children,

[129]

aged thirteen down to one, and all the rest. . . . Gone, no more to steam home again up the wide brown river, bringing a cargo of fish for the homes of Britain, fish from the Arctic to be displayed on slabs in the fishmongers' shops and bought so heedlessly, with never a thought of the real cost of bringing it.

4

THE FIVE SEALERS

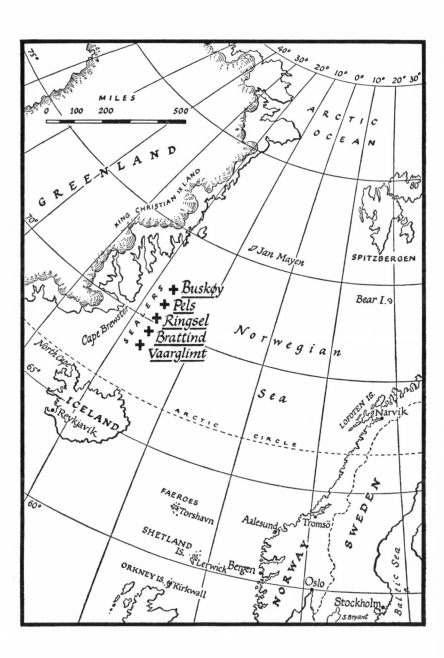

CHAPTER EIGHT

Off Jan Mayen

LLOYD'S NOTICE

THE NORWEGIAN SEALING VESSELS FEARED LOST OFF GREENLAND

Oslo, Apr. 11.—The Norwegian Legation at Reykjavik cabled to-day that search is being made in the Arctic Ocean, between Greenland and Iceland, for Norwegian sealing ships reported missing. It is not yet certain whether there are five ships with a total crew of 100 or the three ships **RINGSAEL, VAARGLIMT** and **BUSKØ** with a total crew of 60.—(See issues of Apr. 12.)

Oslo, Apr. 12.—Hopes for the five Norwegian sealing ships missing in the Arctic for 10 days with 77 persons on board are dwindling. A blizzard to-day kept search aircraft grounded.

St. John's, NF., Apr. 12.—Seventeen 'planes from Iceland failed again to-day to find any trace of five Norwegian seal hunting vessels reported missing in Greenland waters.

THERE are many hard ways to make a living, and some of the hardest are at sea. Human beings do not take 'naturally' to the water, despite assertions to the contrary on the part of some novelists. In periods of full economy, it is always difficult to man ships in countries where other employment offers—in Britain, for example, and in the United States of America. Seamen, on the whole, tend to come from lands which are either harsh or seriously overpopulated, and nationality has nothing to do with it. Men of one nation do not, because of the mere fact of nationality, show more aptitude for the sea than those of other nations. If men are forced to follow the sea for a living, they do so and, having done that for centuries, they establish a tradition of good seafaring. Wherever the rocky high land has pushed the fertile fields into the sea or round the rim of the sea and no sustenance or employment offers for younger sons, there will the menfolk follow the sea, as in the rugged peninsulas of North Wales, the Western Isles of Scotland, much of the Finistère peninsula in Western France and, above all, in Norway.

Down much of Norway's lovely Western coast where the great fjords bite deep into the high and stony land, the mountains overhang the deep waters of the Atlantic itself. The green fields are so small the sparse summer hay is hung on a few short fences to be dried, which takes some time. Here the men turn 'naturally' to the sea, for there is no better alternative. As if to make amends for the sterility of so much of the mountainous and sea-girt land, the coastal waters are the spawning grounds of myriads of fish, splendid food-fish such as the herring, the sardine and the cod. The fish resources of Norwegian coastal and the nearer Arctic waters are immense and endless, though they have been exploited for countless centuries. These are the breeding grounds of seamen, and the Norsemen have roamed the seas from the dawn of modern history. Thousands of them remain fishermen. Thousands more man a large proportion of the oil-tankers and the dry-cargo carriers of the world, not only under their own Norwegian flag. Others hunt whales, for they were the pioneers in modern whaling, with the Svend Foyn gun and the great floating factory-ship with its fleet of 'chasers.' That industry has spread to the Antarctic this past half-century, but it was first developed off Arctic Norway.

Others are sealers—seal-hunters—for the seal is also a source of wealth, even though the Arctic seal is not a true fur-bearer. Compared with the numbers who follow other branches of seafaring, the sealers are a small group—less than 1,400. Theirs is a very special profession, and a most dangerous one. While the fur seal was abundant, the Arctic harp and hooded seals were not considered of much value. Only their babies have fur coats, and the fur begins to change into a hard hair coat when the seals are a few days old. Adult seals offer blubber to be rendered into oil and hide, which is of value in making such things as wallets, handbags and fine gloves. It costs a good deal of money to treat the hides. Over-exploitation almost wiped out the world's herds of fur seals well before the turn of the twentieth century, and so the other varieties have been hunted since.

In Norway, this hunt is regulated. Only Norwegians, Russians and Canadians take part in modern sealing on any large scale, anywhere, but the Canadians have few sealing ships today. Full employment in Newfoundland has made fishing and seafaring less attractive professions there, when other better-paying work can be had and a man can be with his family.

The principal ports which are headquarters for the sealing industry in Norway are Tromsø, in the far north, and Aalesund, which is on a small island about a hundred miles north of Bergen. The majority of the sealing ships and the great majority of the men come from little villages and islands round them, not from the big ports themselves. Aalesund has been sending sealing ships to the Arctic since 1898, beginning with small sailing schooners and ketches of 20 or 30 tons—handy little vessels which, for all their lack of size, were strong in the ice and magnificent in the great seas. A special kind of ice-protected ship had to be developed for sealing. Such ships must be small, to turn swiftly in the ice-lanes and avoid the more dangerous icebergs and the jagged-sided, crushing floes. They must be superbly strong to withstand the pressure of the ice-floes, when the pack-ice jumps and grinds in the spring gales. They have to go into the ice because the herds of seals are to be found there, when the little whitecoat and blueback babies are born. They have to accept all the risks of ice navigation at a particularly bad time of the year, for the valuable seals are born about the time of the spring equinox and are vulnerable only when they are on the sea ice. And so the sealing ships have round hulls, like glass bowls, not the regular boxlike hulls of other ships. When the ice grinds in on it, the round hull yields and is forced up instead of inwards— up, to ride in safety, not crushed and sunk. The ships must also be able to ride out the most severe storms, and they must have good endurance, to keep the sea if necessary for three months or more at a time. Both Tromsø and Aalesund have developed this type of ship magnificently, though they have lost a good many in the process.

Sails were inadequate power for ice navigation and the sealers were among the first ships to use auxiliary motors. Today they use both sails and motors, but they are in fact full-powered motor-ships. The sails are to steady them and for lying-to in gales. The sealer is recognised as the ice-navigating ship par excellence and, for this reason, many such ships have been used for Polar exploration— ships like Shackleton's *Quest*, the big *Norsel*, the Halifax sealer *Theron*, and Riiser-Larsen's *Norvegia*. In the 1950's, both Tromsø and Aalesund have developed a class of super-sealer, fine steel vessels of over 400 tons (which is big for a sealer) like the *Norsel* and the *Polaris*, built in 1951. The *Polaris* is 151 feet long by 27.9 feet beam and 14.8 feet deep, with lookout control from the steel crow's-nest on the mainmast, and ice fins on the hull, a variable-pitch propeller, radar, a refrigerated hold and two-berth cabins for the crew of thirty-three, which is a large crew for a Norwegian sealer. The

Polarbjorn, Polarsel, Polarstar, Jopeter, and *Isflora* are similar ships, the most modern type of polar vessel.

In the 1950's, Aalesund is the centre for a sealing fleet of thirty ships, registering nearly 6,000 tons between them and employing over 600 men. These ships, like the Tromsø and Finnmark vessels, go to the main breeding grounds for the Arctic seals, which are on the ice off the northern end of Newfoundland, and north of the island of Jan Mayen, in that section of the Arctic Ocean which the sealers know as the "western ice." They used to go also to the White Sea grounds, but the Russians have not permitted that in recent years. The Norwegian fleet of 80 sealers in 1951 brought home 373,661 seal pelts, from harps and bluebacks, hooded seals, walrus (few of these) and other types, and 269 polar bears, of which 33 were living bears. All this 6,000 tons of pelts was worth, landed in Norway, the best part of three-quarters of a million pounds. In addition, the ships brought back another 6,000 tons of seal blubber, which makes a special kind of oil. To do this, most of them made two voyages, the first at the time of the spring equinox to get the baby seals, and the second in May for the adults. The rest of the year, except for the harshest winter months, the little ships are employed mainly in the Greenland and the coastal fisheries.

Sealing, then, is still big business.

Torsten Brandal * knew all these things and a great many more about sealing, seal-hunters and sealing ships, even at the age of sixteen. Torsten Brandal was born in 1936 in the village of Brandal on Hareidland, an island near Aalesund. From the windows of his pretty wooden house he could look into the grandeur of the great Store Fjord, where there was room for even the largest Atlantic liners to cruise with ease. As a child, he watched the liners, wonder-

* Torsten Brandal is an imaginary character.

ing that so many persons could possibly have so little to employ them that they came so far in such enormous ships, merely to look at mountains and fjords. He could not know how much they appreciated such sights, for they were with him always. Across the blue water, a short ferry trip away, was Aalesund, the big town and major port of the district of Møre. On the run across he could see the island of Giske where, according to tradition, the famous Viking Ganger Rolf had lived before Harald Hårfagre had driven that wild spirit out, to take his fellow-Vikings and his ships beyond the sea and conquer Normandy. Ganger Rolf was a shadowy figure to the youthful Torsten, even though there was an outsize bronze of him in Aalesund's best park—a statue of a wild-looking character with thighs like a bullock's, long moustachios, and a fierce countenance. If Ganger Rolf from little Giske had conquered so much, he wondered sometimes how it was that Norway had no 'empire,' as had other lands. Slowly he learned that Norway's empire was the sea. All the fit men from Brandal served that empire—almost all the fit young men from the whole of Hareidland, and many who were not so young.

Torsten Brandal waited impatiently for the time when he, too, could take his place with them. He haunted the wooden wharf by Martin Karlsen's blubber and seal-skin treating factory, where the little whalers came in from the bottlenose chase and landed their bloody blubber and big bottlenose heads, which looked like large greasy bells. The bottlenose whale was hunted in the proper season by small motor-ships out of Aalesund and nearby villages, which converted themselves for the whaling by the simple process of shipping an old oil drum for lookout-post on the main, and a platform for a small-size Svend Foyn gun up in the bows, with a tray of rope forerunner coiled down before it and a business-like harpoon protruding from the stocky barrel. All the boys thought it must be wonderful to fire these harpoons and watch the manila line snake through the air. Torsten knew that some youngsters who had followed this calling later became famous harpooners in the Antarctic fleets under the British and Norwegian flags, and earned fabulous sums by shooting great blue whales by the hundred, in the Antarctic summers.

But this life was not for him. The Brandals were sealers. They might be bottlenose men on occasion, for a ship could not go sealing the whole year round. But they were sealers primarily—icemen, pilots of the polar seas, students of the habits of the herds of the Greenland and the other Arctic seals. Martin Karlsen's wharf knew many of these sealing ships—the old-timers like the little *Pels* and the *Eskimo,* and splendid new ships of the latest class like the *Isflora* and later—in 1948—the wonderful *Polarstar* which was built in Glasgow at a cost of over two million Norwegian crowns—$300,000 in American money. Torsten was only twelve when the *Polarstar* first came to Martin Karlsen's wharf, and he ran out to see her steaming up the fjord, because she was the first steel sealer in Norway. Everyone on Hareidland was pleased with her. She seemed like a liner to him, lying there beside the little wharf, a sleek grey ship, compact and powerful.

Even the marvels of the whale-oil and seal-pelt treating plant in the factory could not distract him as he gazed at the grey hull of the *Polarstar.* Usually, he loved to watch the electric machines spinning while they stripped the bits of blubber still clinging to the seal pelts, and the apparatus which cleaned the skins off, mixing them with sawdust and turning out a fine product which looked to Torsten as if it were fit for a queen to wear, just as it was. The piles of seal pelts in the corners, the big barrels of treated skins (each barrel worth the best part of £500 when it reached London or Paris, and some fabulous sum when—no longer barrelled—the skins it contained left there as coats and coat-trimmings), all the fascinating paraphernalia of the little factory round which he had played so often meant nothing when the *Polarstar* came in. It was Torsten's ambition to command a ship like the *Polarstar* some day —the sooner the better.

A fine Greenland fisherman named the *Fangst* was also lying at the wharf, with ensign flying to indicate that it was sailing day for the Greenland grounds, and children were playing beneath her whaleback forecastle-head. The *Fangst* was a Norwegian type, too, developed down the centuries. Some large fair men were carrying provisions aboard the *Fangst*—two or three crates of bottled milk, a big can of fresh cream such as the butter factories use, sacks of flour, sugar, coffee beans, crates of eggs. While the large men passed the provisions aboard with the help of the happy, healthy children, another man, with a face like Ganger Rolf and moustachios almost half as long (which was a tremendous length), leapt aboard. All the children were helping to get the ship ready, looking forward to the day when they, too, would be going to sea themselves in some *Fangst* or *Polarstar*. Little girls looked on enviously, knowing this life was not for them.

The *Fangst* being ready, sailed, and the *Polarstar,* having discharged her thousands of pelts, moved over to Aalesund to fit out for a run to Newfoundland, where her 20,000 cubic feet of refrigerated hold was chartered for the carriage of deep-freeze fish from St. John's to Boston. The *Polarstar* was more than just a first-class sealing vessel. She was a high-speed refrigerated cargo-carrier—a little 'reefer'—besides. She could be a fisherman, too, when that employment was all that offered, and she could be easily converted for charter as an expedition ship, carrying scientists to North Greenland or to the Antarctic Continent, if any groups of scientists ever managed to accumulate the large sum necessary to charter her. There was a considerable investment in her, compared with the old schooners, and she would have to earn what she could all the year round.

Young Torsten had heard his father talking of these things with the other captains from Brandal and from Hareid, with Peter Liavaag, captain of the *Buskøy,* or with Knut Johansen of the *Isflora,* whose home was by Aalesund. Torsten loved to visit there and play with the Johansen children, especially in the room with the polar bear skin on the floor and a painting of the ancient sealer *Hercules the First* on the wall. He knew that Captain Johansen's father had died with the old *Hercules* and he knew, too, that that was a risk of the trade. Brandals had died at the sealing, too. Every season when the sealers sailed, the women of Hareidland were lonely, and sad, though they tried not to be, and tried to tell themselves that they were 'used to it.' It was their men's way of life and the women must accept it.

Torsten regretted the newfangled decision which made children stay longer and longer at school, wasting their time (in his opinion), delaying the time when they could go to sea and be *alive.* He longed for the great day when he could put at least one foot on the ladder which led to command of an ice-navigating ship, a sealer like the *Jopeter* or the *Polarstar,* and he could divide his year between the seal hunt off Jan Mayen and off Newfoundland, fishing the Greenland Banks, or spending half a year as a refrigerated ship in trade somewhere, and taking important land parties off on distant Antarctic expeditions for diversion.

Then at last it came, a blustery, cold and snowing day in March, 1952. His ship—she was his father's choice—was the 160-ton *Buskøy* of Vartdal, sailing out of Aalesund with a crew from Hareidland. The *Buskøy* was no *Polarstar* for she was built in 1926, but he loved her because, though he was only a deckboy in her, she was his ship—all of her, the short fore-deck for working the seals, the great high mainmast with its look-out barrel right at the top, the squat little funnel emerging from the sturdy deckhouse aft—to him all these were the stuff of red-blooded living, of a man's life the way it should be lived. Even the number on the strengthened bow —M-17-VD—seemed adventurous to him, though he knew that it only meant: "Møre ship No. 17, registered in Vartdal." With a new Norwegian ensign at both mastheads, the old *Buskøy* looked brave and fine, despite her twenty-five years of hard knocks and hard wandering, and her nett register tonnage of a bare 61 tons.

At that, she was more than twice the tonnage of the *Pels* and about half the age, though the boys in the *Pels* liked their little ship very well, too. What she lacked in size, they said, she made up in strength. As for her age of forty-one years or more, well, she had had the longer time to learn the ways of the sea and the ice, and was the more seasoned warrior. There were other ships in the Møre fleet sailing out of Aalesund that were not much larger than the *Pels,* and there were many from Tromsø which were much the same size. A small ship may live in ice which crushes a larger vessel, and a small sealer may make faster voyages than a large sealer, too, and so get several trips in during the short Arctic season.

He knew everyone aboard the *Buskøy.* Several of the crew of nineteen men were his cousins. Three were about his own age. The oldest man aboard, apart from the captain, was twenty-nine. The snow lay heavy on all the hills round Aalesund as the little ship pulled away from the wharf, her diesel going "plompf-plompf-plompf" and the exhaust frosting away in the clear cold air. The plump little wooden fishermen were "plompf-plompf-plompfing" off to sea all round her, the steady sound of their well-kept diesel engines breaking the stillness of the day. A wave or two to his younger brothers, and the *Buskøy* was gone. There was no fuss, no ceremony. Departures for the sea were commonplace in Aalesund.

The *Buskøy* headed past Giske towards the sea, passing a Faeroese trawler hurrying south to market, with her flag flying, and a big iron-ore man coming down the inside way from Narvik with his heavy load, intent on staying within the shelter of the land as far south as he could and using up fuel to get his draught up a bit before facing the open North Atlantic, and its wild storms.

Very soon the *Buskøy* was outside, for there was no inside way to Jan Mayen. Within half an hour of leaving she was feeling the full motion of the ocean, as she headed north-east towards the ice. She lurched and rolled like a drifting buoy and did not behave like a ship at all, and her motion was horrible. Torsten was accustomed to boats from babyhood and had been out in all kinds of fishing vessels. He thought he was used to the motion of ships in the sea, but this was very different. He became most horribly seasick, for the first time in his life. He was not the only member of the crew in that state.

"Set the sails!" ordered the captain, and they pulled up the stiff gaff-and-boom mainsail on the high mainmast forward, and set the jib-headed mizzen on the short mast behind the funnel. That steadied her considerably, but she still rolled like a ball. She was heavily laden with stores and food and fuel for three months but, though she really rolled abominably, she did not ship any water. She was a lively sea-boat, and how the cook managed ever to produce any cooked food from his heaving, jumping galley Torsten did not understand. But he cooked good meals, and, after a day or two, Torsten was mighty interested in them.

As the ship progressed towards the north in company with some others of the fleet, whose masts and sails were often all they could see of them in the big seas, there was a sort of subdued but growing excitement aboard, about the hunt. All the talk was of seals and ice. Soon the captain climbed to the high crow's-nest, the protected lookout barrel on the main. It was a long, reeling climb up there. Torsten had done it many, many times in port, but at sea with the ship rolling and pitching and lurching, it was different! He was glad it was the captain's job. It was not really the captain's job, but it was so important to find the seal herds in the ice that the captain would not allow anyone else to do it.

Torsten learned that the official opening day for the hunt was to be on March 23, at seven o'clock in the morning, but the *Buskøy*, like all the other sealers, tried to be on the grounds about a week before the day, in order that Captain Liavaag could locate the herds and be ready for the hunt at the first possible moment. The seals came out on the ice in spring for the cows to calve, and it was just at that time that the sealers hunted them. The winter pack-ice had broken then, at any rate at its outer edges, and as the sun came further and further north with each passing day and the Arctic days grew longer and longer, the pack-ice melted more and more and it became easier to enter and to find a way among the floes. The *Buskøy* had to go among the floes to catch the seals, but she had to be very carefully handled to prevent the small icebergs and floes from damaging her. It was all right in fine weather, but in March there could be very bad weather indeed, as well as in April. Torsten was aware that over a hundred sealing vessels had been lost from Norway alone over the preceding twenty-five years. The men did not talk about such things, but he knew. They all knew.

While Captain Peter kept his vigil from the crow's-nest, the ship's radio was tuned in and turned up to maximum strength on the sealers' wave-band, listening for news from the other ships. Like fishermen, the sealers did not part with good news gladly but, like some fishermen, too, some of them talked a lot and the others listened. Captain Peter could detect by an inflection of voice whether such-and-such a captain was in sight of seals, and how things were with him. He knew them all so well. Karsten Brandal his mate—Torsten often played at home with his five little children —knew them just as well and, whenever the captain could not listen because he was too high aloft, Mate Brandal listened for him. So did the whole crew every chance they could get, though they were busy preparing the ship for her cargo.

How slowly the days passed before the official opening! Day after day, more and more seal-hunters came on the air, from Tromsø and from Nordland and from Finnmark, as well as from Møre and Romsdal. The first of the pack-ice they met was a sea full of scattered 'pans'—mushy floes which the greenheart bows of the *Buskøy* could smash through readily. Seals would not calve on such ice. They steamed on. Then the great ice-blink came in sight, soon to fill the northern and the western air—the reflection of thousands upon thousands of square miles of ice jammed in all along the coast of Greenland and up into the Arctic Sea. Then the *Buskøy* was in the ice—not brashy pans but the real thing, millions of acres of giant floes. Torsten looked at this silent, menacing, frozen world with some awe. He had seen ice before, but this was different. The great white silent world closed in all round them, and Torsten hoped the ship would be able to find a way out again.

She bashed her way into the ice, making for a place where Captain Peter reckoned the seals would be. Sometimes her solid bows opened up lanes for her, and she slipped along fairly easily: sometimes she had to stop a while for the ice to 'work,' as the floes got bigger and thicker. They all listened to the radio carefully for news of the weather, too, for the station on Jan Mayen sent out special reports for the sealers. What they were at could be dangerous, steaming into the winter pack so early in the year: a gale of wind could set that ice to dancing, and it could be a dance of death for the little ships. It was all very well while the weather was settled, for then the ice kept the sea down, but a real gale of wind would drive such a sea in among the floes that they would crack and jump and leap about like the horribly dangerous ice-islands they really were. Then the sea would be like some enormous lily pond in an earthquake with frozen rocks instead of lily leaves flung about upon its surface, and the ship jumping among them like a matchbox at their mercy.

So they listened to the weather reports very carefully indeed, and they also watched where they went, and guarded above all the rudder and the propeller from ice damage. Many of those floes had jagged edges sticking out down below to damage the ship. Captain Peter and Mate Brandal watched the ice with experienced eyes, conning the helmsman at the wheel with shouted orders from the crow's-nest, to steer this way or that, dodging the bad ice, brushing through the rotten floes, following the leads. Sometimes they saw seals swimming in the open leads where the sea ran like a river—at first, single seals and small groups, and then herds.

At sunset on the 22nd, the *Buskøy* was close to a great herd of seals which had hauled themselves up on the ice-floes for the night. Captain Peter nosed his ship into a sort of dock among the floes, stopped the diesel, which had been turning slowly, and stayed there, to wait for seven o'clock in the morning. The Jan Mayen station promised good weather.

That night Torsten could not sleep. He thought he heard children crying out there on the silent ice and it bothered him—plaintive, human cries, like small babies crying for their mothers.

"It's the seals, Torsten! You get used to them. Get some rest now, lad. It will be a big day tomorrow," the older hands told him.

He was astonished that baby seals could cry like that. They sounded much too human, and he did not like it.

In the morning, all hands were out at six, guns ready and knives sharpened, though the season did not begin for an hour. Sharp at seven o'clock, all hands but the cook leapt on the ice and got among the herd. There were hundreds of seals—seals everywhere! Little white babies, born during the night and suckling their mothers, big bull seals roaring. These were harp seals and the babies were the valuable whitecoats. The slaughter began immediately. Mother seals scurried for the safety of the open leads, pushing their babies with them if they could, trying to protect them, but the babies, not understanding what was going on, cried and protested, and were loth to go. Delay was fatal. The eighteen men from the *Buskøy* could show no mercy. The slightest tap with a club was enough to dispatch a little seal. Torsten was horrified, at first, when the poor little things rolled and looked pathetically at him with their soft big eyes. He had to suppress that. He clubbed and

[146]

clubbed, with the rest, and soon found himself leaping from floe to floe, jumping sometimes over long open leads to get to the bigger floes where he could see more and more seals, until at last the older men shouted at him, "Not too far, Torsten! Not too far! You will be lost!"

Sometimes he saw the mother seals, after sliding off the edge of a floe where their babies were, swim to the floe edge again and look over, watching him. It seemed like murder but he soon forgot about that and concentrated on the job.

In a little while the adult seals were all gone, and baby seals—creamy-white little babies with beautiful soft coats—lay still by the hundred. They dragged them together in heaps, rigged up tackles and lines from the ship and hove the carcasses aboard with the winch, working as quickly as they could both to get the seals aboard before the ice shifted and to be able to skin them while the bodies were still warm. While a gang of men rigged the lines and hove seals aboard, others were already butchering among the floes, removing the valuable pelts skillfully with their long knives, taking care neither to damage the sealskins nor to cut their fingers. There was an occupational risk called 'speck-finger' which Torsten knew about—a sort of horrible poisoning of the finger from some infection in the blubber which men did not understand. Speck-finger was something to be avoided.

They shot some of the adult seals, too, and hauled these aboard. That day they took 479 whitecoats, which was a splendid start for the season. Torsten was secretly pleased to note in the morning that the great herd of seals had gone into the inner fastness of the pack where neither the *Buskøy* nor any other sealer could follow them. That day, it blew up from east, which was a bad direction, and a turbulent swell underran the floes, causing them to grind and jostle about the ship as if they were angry with her. Captain Peter worked the *Buskøy* to the most open patch he could find, and stayed there.

[147]

Then the weather eased again and the hunt was on—well into the pack, as far as they dared, always after more and more herds of seals.

Most of the seals were harps, but there were some hooded herds, too, with lovely little gunmetal-coloured babies. The *Buskøy* took 320 of these. They were larger than the whitecoats and harder to handle, but their bodies slipped and slithered across the ice, drawn by lines to the *Buskøy*'s fore-deck. The men were busy all day, hunting and dragging and skinning. They saved all the blubber and put that in the hold, and they ate the seal livers and the cook made a special stew from the flippers. Seal meat was not the tastiest of meat, but the seal-men thought the flipper stews were tasty and nourishing, and seal liver was a feast for kings.

Torsten felt a little better about his job when he noticed, one day of bad weather, when they dared not land on the floes, that many baby seals fell off the rolling floes and were drowned. They had not learned how to swim, then. Their mothers could not save them. When he saw that, he did not feel so bad about killing them for their skins.

"Don't worry about the seals," said Mate Brandal. "They are our livelihood, and there are plenty of them. The Government looks after them. We can never take so many that we shall affect the stocks, even though there are eighty ships here this year."

Maybe they would not affect the 'stocks,' thought Torsten, but death was just as tragic for each individual seal they shot or clubbed. If he slipped between the floes he supposed his going would not affect the Norwegian 'stocks,' either, but it would be very unpleasant for him.

The days passed and the *Buskøy* continued to hunt, sometimes with success and sometimes not. Bad weather often held her up. It was a bad season for weather but a good season for seals, and the older men said it was curious how often they met those conditions.

Then early in April, the weather really worsened seriously, and it seemed that they were in for a blow. At the time, they had been doing very well and did not need many more seals. The *Busk∅y* was then one of a group of seven or eight ships, with twenty or so more in the general area. Near her were the *Pels,* the *Ringsel* and the *Brattind*—two small fellows from the Troms∅ area—the *Vaarglimt,* another small sealer from Balsfjord, and the *Flems∅y, Ungsel, Arild, Selfisk* and others.

One of the ships from M∅re, the *Vestis,* had got herself into serious trouble in the ice the very first day of the season, and was crushed and sunk—'screwed down,' the sealers called it. Her crew were all saved. They had been able to land on the ice and were picked up by other ships, where they lent a hand with the sealing. The *Vestis* carried eighteen men. The *Vestis,* like the others, could withstand the ordinary pressure of the ice, but when big floes and icebergs of all sorts of shapes and sizes began to screw in on her, her hull could not stand it. No ship's could—not even the *Jopeter* or the other very modern steel ships. If they got in the ice bad enough they could all be screwed down—ground inwards and so damaged that they sank, like punctured sardine cans.

On the 4th of April, the Jan Mayen weather station spoke of a gale coming from the east. Some ships, being near good seals, decided that they could stay in the ice, on the principle that being far enough in, the storm should not reach and damage them there. Others, fearing easterly and north-easterly gales above all other storms, and being at the ice edge, decided to make their way out of the ice at once and get sea room in the open sea while they could do so. The *Busk∅y* and the group round her stayed where they were. They thought they were all right there. The ice where they were was in deep water. There should be no heavy breaking seas to imperil them.

Very soon after the warning the gale itself came. It got up quickly, and it was a dreadful gale, blowing and screaming. Within an hour the air was full not only of the howling wind and the flying snow which it swept up from the ice-floes, but of the distress calls of little ships, caught now as they had been catching the baby seals a day or two earlier. The storm came too quickly and too violently, and they were in a bad place when the very heavy gale blew the loose ice at the edge back into the firmer ice, breaking it up. Though they had thought they would be safe, from previous experience, they were wrong. All round the *Buskøy* the giant floes began to work horribly, crashing and grinding together in a fearsome manner, while the sea broke through between more and more of them and set them to a wild and exceedingly dangerous dancing. Even when they were still they were dangerous enough. In the *Buskøy*, they heard the *Ungsel* and the *Arild* speak of damage, and heard them say that they were out of the ice and would run for Siglufjord in Iceland to seek shelter. The *Arild* had lost a man overboard. Then the *Selfisk* reported that she, too, was badly damaged and was trying to make for Isafjord. The little *Pels,* the Tromsø ships *Brattind* and *Ringsel,* and the Balsfjord ship *Vaarglimt* were all in serious trouble.

"We are trying to get out of the ice!" was the burden of their messages. "We are trying to get clear of the floes!"

So was the *Buskøy,* then. But it was already too late, where she was. The gale brought poor visibility with driving snow, and the grey sea swirled and leapt, breaking among the floes and tossing them like chips and bits of cork. They were no corks. Time and time again, great blocks of ice crashed into the ship, causing her to shake and tremble, and Torsten wondered that she could stand such terrible blows and yet survive. Once, in a clearing, he saw another Møre sealer—he thought she was the *Pels,* though he had only a brief glimpse—just as a giant floe seemed to rise up and pitch itself at her fore-deck and, while he watched, the high mainmast broke like a weak pine tree in a gale, and collapsed back upon the ship, which took a heavy roll towards him just at that moment, so that he could see some of the crew running from the falling mast and a figure on the bridge, staring upwards. Then the snow, driving horizontally, shut in again and he saw the *Pels* no more. Nor was she heard again on the radio.

The first day of the gale passed and the *Buskøy* was still fighting, though damaged now. There was something wrong with the rudder. They all hoped for a let-up in the gale, for a chance to get out of the ice into which the wind was forcing them, without respite. But there was no easing. All night the gale screamed, now from north-east with squalls of redoubled violence and duration, forcing them back. The diesel worked and coughed as it had never coughed before, but the ship could make no appreciable headway. Sometimes she made a little, only to lose again. The smashing ice, the poor visibility, the crushing weight of the wild wind tearing at her —these things were too much, and the *Buskøy* remained afloat and upright with the greatest difficulty. She was beginning to ice up, too. The flying snow was packing on her, wherever it could, and the spray freezing. The weight of the ice was beginning to hold her down. She was sluggish in her movements—and the rudder, they feared, was hanging on one pintle. It would not last long like that.

Dawn on the 5th brought no respite. Instead there was a worsening. They heard the *Vaarglimt* say that she was being pressed over on the ice and could not get clear—they heard that, and then silence. There were no more messages from the *Vaarglimt,* or the *Pels.* They heard the *Brattind* replying to another Tromsø ship. She said she was over 45 degrees and going further, and she could not get back. They had tried to set a bit of close-reefed sail, but the canvas blew out. No canvas would stand the ferocity of the gale, which was sending its squalls at them now at hurricane strength, and the ice-needles and snow particles flew through the air stinging like a million jet-propelled and armoured bees.

Aboard the *Buskøy,* no one had slept since the gale began. Captain Peter and Mate Brandal looked anxious now—very anxious.

This was the worst gale they had known for many years, and these were the worst possible conditions for a sealer to be caught in, forced in the ice by a violent and long-continued north-easterly gale. Wherever she went there was more ice, more gale. Would the weather not ease? Jan Mayen spoke only of continuing gales. Was there no hope for them, then? Was all the skillful strength which good shipwrights had built into the stout hull futile, in these conditions? All the centuries of ice-navigation wasted, when it came to a fight at the ice edge against the relentless force of a hard and continuing gale?

Torsten saw, about mid-morning, something black fly through the maddened air. It might have been an oilskin coat. For a frightful moment he thought there was a man inside it. Then he saw other dark objects. He knew what they were—hatches, small hatches from a sealing ship. If a ship's hatches went, she was finished. He wondered what ship they came from. The *Brattind? Vaarglimt? Ringsel?*

Early in the afternoon when she was within appreciable distance of getting out, the *Buskøy*'s rudder at last came off, knocked away by a grinding floe. Then she was quite helpless. She was already listed seriously and staying over, even though she was also rolling and pitching and lurching. Her aerials were blown away. She could no longer communicate. She drove now back further into the maddened ice, listing more and more towards it. For a wild second, the sun poked a white finger through a temporary clearing to light her to her doom. She came again among the driven ice, and this time it was final.

The jagged floes ground into her one long and dreadful moment, piercing and rending. Then they ground over her. Her masts fell in on her as she went down, and nothing remained to show the place where she had been. Nothing of the *Buskøy,* or of Captain Peter, Mate Karsten Brandal, deckboy Torsten, or any of them.

The *Buskøy,* the *Brattind,* the *Pels,* the *Vaarglimt,* and the *Ringsel* all failed to survive that storm. The gale blew for two more full days. Ships which had not sheltered in fjords along the coast of Iceland, or had not ice-free sea room to heave-to, died, and their crews died with them. No man could survive on the ice in weather like that. United States Air Force rescue planes, Icelandic and Norwegian planes, Norwegian and Icelandic fishing craft and other sealers all searched for days and weeks. They found nothing. There was a report, for a day or two, that the *Brattind* had arrived in harbour somewhere, but it was cruelly wrong. The families of the *Brattind's* crew had their hopes raised briefly only to be cast down again, and stay down. The *Arild, Ungsel,* and *Selfisk* did manage to reach safety, though all were badly damaged.

Even as late as the 12th of April, seventeen big aircraft were still searching from air fields in Iceland. In May, the sealer *Nordland,* bound out again to the Greenland ice after adult seals, found a new oaken ladder and a broken oar in the drift ice, which may have come from the *Buskøy.* The *Polarsel* found a cargo hatch.

These were all the things which were ever found from the five missing sealers, and their crews of seventy-seven men. Nor was there any form of official inquiry. What good could that do? The risks of the trade were known.

There was a curious incident when the *Buskøy* was lost, of which I learned when I visited Aalesund. The motorman of the sealer was 42-year-old Elling Myklebust, of Vartdal, a man with five small children ranging in age from 11 years to four. His wife was Signy. She told how Elling came to call on her when his ship went down. "The children were in a bustle from early in the morning until late at night," she said. "Now they were sound asleep, lying there with round cheeks, straggling hair and the mouth slightly open. The bedclothes were wrapped around them. Silence reigned upstairs.

I was going to steal half-an-hour to enjoy all by myself. . . . Then all of a sudden it seemed as if Elling came into the hallway. Whether I felt it or heard it I am unable to say. All I know is that it just was so. The whole room was filled with a strange peace, like reconciliation after a struggle. First I looked round quickly to see if anything had moved. No, there was nothing to be observed. But as I opened the outer door, I was met by an uncomfortable and sad, dead silence. Inside there was peace. . . . My thoughts seemed to work no longer. I had received peace and had given peace, and was only glad. . . . In the morning, they told me." This was on the night when the *Buskøy* was lost.

Widow Myklebust now runs a telephone exchange on her island, and by means of that employment, together with her income from the seamen's and national insurance and a subscription from the Norwegian Red Cross, she hopes to be able to send all five children through the grammar school.

PART

5

PASSENGER SHIP

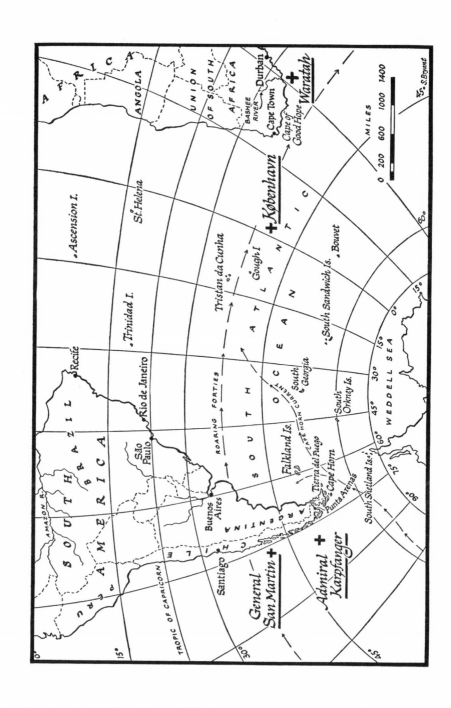

AFRICA

ANGOLA

UNION OF SOUTH AFRICA

BASHEE RIVER

Durban

Cape Town

Cape of Good Hope

Waratah

Ascension I.

St. Helena

Tristan da Cunha

Gough I.

København

SOUTH ATLANTIC OCEAN

South Sandwich Is.

Bouvet

South Georgia

Trinidad I.

Recife

Rio de Janeiro

São Paulo

ROARING FORTIES

CAPE HORN CURRENT

Falkland Is.

South Orkney Is.

WEDDELL SEA

AMAZON R.

SOUTH AMERICA

BRAZIL

PERU

CHILE

ARGENTINA

Buenos Aires

Santiago

TROPIC OF CAPRICORN

Tierra del Fuego

Cape Horn

Punta Arenas

South Shetland Is.

General San Martin

Admiral Karpfanger

45°S.Bryant

MILES

0   200   600   1000   1400

60°

15°

0°

15°

30°

45°

60°

15°

90°

0°

15°

30°

CHAPTER NINE

The Mystery of the *Waratah*

FORTUNATELY, it is most unusual for a passenger vessel ever to appear on the list of the missing, or even the overdue. When a vessel carrying passengers does go missing, she generally turns out to be some little thing bound on what should have been a short passage somewhere among the South Sea Islands or in some other of the remoter areas of the world, which, for some reason, failed to arrive. There have been at least two cases of this happening in the past two years, which is not to infer by any means that South Seas trading vessels—they are generally not passenger vessels in any strict sense of that term—are less seaworthy than others. They are often small auxiliary schooners or little motor-ships, built of wood and sometimes run a long, long time. They lift what offers, from island to island, including passengers, for whom there is rarely any proper accommodation, in the ordinary sense of that word. Just how they may be loaded when they finally leave the last island and head for their main port is—very often—the master's business, and no one else's. They become accustomed to a continuity of fair weather for most of the year at any rate, and the bad weather seasons are reasonably well defined. Sometimes they are required to transport dangerous cargoes, such as gasoline in drums, and the amount of care given to the proper supervision of safety precautions may be inadequate.

And yet, if such a vessel becomes missing and nothing is ever found, the mystery of her precise fate is the deeper because of the very fact that she was wooden and was carrying a lot of miscellaneous deck cargo not—perhaps—as well lashed down as it might be in a Cape Horner, and that there are plenty of reefs and navigational dangers to account for shipwrecks round the South Sea Islands. They are not shipwrecked, or some of the evidence would remain. They cannot disintegrate, or something would drift away. They do not blow up, or charred pieces of wood would be found, probably in abundance. In these days, ships are missed very quickly when they fail to arrive, especially such vessels as these, making short passages. Air search can be laid on quickly and thoroughly, nor do the searching aircraft in these areas have much bad weather or poor visibility to contend with. It is a remote island indeed which has not at least a head man who can be communicated with: wreckage would be found and reported. Radio makes news of missing vessels immediately known, even in the remotest atoll.

Yet no trace was ever found of, and nothing was ever heard from, the 240-ton French motor-vessel *Monique,* of Noumea, which has been missing on a passage from Mare in the Loyalty Islands towards Noumea in New Caledonia since the 31st of July, 1953. The passage is a short one and should not have taken long. The *Monique* was not an old ship. She was a composite ship—wooden planking on steel frames—built in 1945 for the Islands trade. She carried a radio telephone. She had a crew of 19, and 101 passengers, on her last passage, as well as a full cargo which included all that could be safely stowed on deck. Her master was Charles Ohlen, an experienced man, and there were twenty other Europeans aboard the vessel. Her last message, sent out late on the day she sailed, reported that all was well, and confirmed that the vessel would reach Noumea about midday the next day. Nothing further was heard and the *Monique* did not arrive. She could not be communicated with. She disappeared, with her 101 passengers, her crew of 19, her deck cargo and everything else.

Exhaustive air search, radio broadcasts to all the islands, search by canoe, launch, schooner and four-engined aircraft all yielded nothing. The air search was continued until the 8th of August, during which over 30,000 square miles were covered. There were children in the ship, as well as a French police inspector, several Catholic sisters and a group of scientists. Later, three barrels were found, washed up on the beach of a small island south of New Caledonia. They had no particular markings, but they might have been from the *Monique*. No one could say with certainty. Nothing else was found. One of the principal chiefs of the island of Mare alleged that the *Monique* was heavily laden and had a list when she sailed. He said that even the lifeboats were full of goods and cargo, and the decks were so obstructed with cargo and people that it was difficult to move.

That is as may be. At any rate there has been time enough for the mystery of the *Monique* to be cleared up if it is ever to be, but no solution has been put forward. She must have foundered. That seems obvious. But why no survivors? And why no wreckage?

Then there was the little inter-island trader *Joyita,* of Honolulu, which in October, 1955, was making an ordinary two-day passage between Samoa and Tokelau, and failed to arrive. The *Joyita* was 70 tons and carried a certain number of passengers, variously stated at the time as between 9 and 25. Again urgent and far-reaching search was made by air and sea, covering an area of more than 100,000 square miles. The search for the *Joyita* went on for weeks but nothing was found, at the time. She was a well-built and well-kept ship, commanded by an experienced master mariner. She had exceptionally good radio equipment. No storm was reported anywhere near the area where she was lost. She sent out no distress message. The mystery was deepened by the discovery of her hull adrift off the Fijis, weeks later. Her crew and her passengers had gone and no trace of them has been found. Why did they abandon their ship? An exhaustive inquiry failed to find any answer to this, and the fate of the *Joyita*'s people is one of the great mysteries of the sea.

The *Monique* and the *Joyita* were small ships and not strictly passenger vessels, though certified to carry a certain number of passengers. The steamer *Sir Harvey Adamson,* of Glasgow, 1,030 tons, was in a different category. She was indeed a passenger vessel, a steel steamer classed 100 A 1 at Lloyd's and belonging to a great passenger-carrying line, the British India Steam Navigation Company, which seamen call the B.I. The *Sir Harvey Adamson* carried a crew of 64, under Captain Weaver, and 215 passengers, when she sailed from Rangoon on the 17th of April, 1947, bound in the first instance towards the island of Tavoy, the northernmost island in the Mergui Archipelago off the coast of Lower Burma. Like the *Monique*'s this was a commonplace passage which presented no difficulties. The *Sir Harvey Adamson* did not arrive at Tavoy and, despite exhaustive search by sea and air, nothing was ever seen again either of her or any of the 279 persons who had been aboard, though there was life-saving equipment for all of them and the ship was an efficient up-to-date unit of a remarkably fine and well-run fleet.

In her case, the most probable explanation was that she had gone up on a war-time mine, whereof there were many in the area. The Andaman Sea and the approaches to the Straits of Malacca were heavily mined during the Second World War, and these are large areas to clear. The ship was lost not long after the end of the Second World War. The weather at the time of her loss was bad, but by no means bad enough to account for any accident to a well-found ship. But, if she were mined in a vital place and went down quickly, the bad weather would give little chance of survival to her people. Since she was at sea in the bad weather season, her boats and deck gear were well secured.

An official inquiry was held at Rangoon in July, after she was lost. District Magistrate U Ba Thwe conducted the inquiry, and he had the expert assistance of four assessors. They went into every aspect of the case. The vessel and her equipment were in perfect order. Why was there no identifiable wreckage? Why no SOS? Why did no boats get away? Why were no bodies ever found? No one living knew the answers to these questions. The District Magistrate could conclude only that the ship had had the misfortune to strike a mine. That does, indeed, seem the most probable explanation. The people would be below. The loss of life in this vessel was the largest recorded from a missing vessel for many years.

The smallest number is one—Captain Joshua Slocum, in his famous circumnavigating sloop *Spray,* missing since he sailed on a second voyage in 1909. The *Spray* was a tiny thing though adequate for that fine old sea-dog, and she could easily have been knocked down by some big ship in the steamer lanes which would never, indeed, know that she had struck anything. There was a theory put forward by some that the old captain chose to disappear, to sail off to some spot he knew and finish his days in peace. He was sixty-six. These theories allege that he did not get along with Mrs. Slocum very well and, in at least some support of that, it is odd that the old sailor, who had a wife and family, had chosen for years to make his home in a bit of a sloop only 36 feet long and to sail the vessel, alone, round the world.

It would surely be odder if, having made a great success of that, the old captain should deliberately choose to go missing.

"Have you seen anything of the *Waratah?*"
"What ship did you say?"
"The *Waratah.* Lund's Blue Anchor liner. Have you seen anything of her?"
"No, pilot. I've seen no *Waratah.*"
The master of the barque looked bewildered, until the pilot explained that there had been no news of the big passenger liner,

homeward bound from Australia to London, since she sailed from Durban on the 26th of July, and that was then several months ago. The barque had run across from Rio and might have sighted something. The year was 1909, the place the anchorage off Semaphore, in St. Vincent's Gulf, South Australia. All such sailing vessels arriving there or at any other port in Australia for months afterwards were similarly questioned as soon as they came in. These were the years before wireless and, if they had news, they could not have communicated it.

But none of them—and over a hundred square-riggers arrived at Australian ports between August and December, 1909,—had any news. No sailing-ship, wandering her lonely wind-swept route in the Roaring Forties, and no steamship, making a Great Circle run from the Cape toward Australia, had seen anything of the big black *Waratah,* or any of her boats, or as much as the skeleton of any of the 92 passengers who had sailed with her. In the best part of the half-century which has passed since then, the mystery of the loss of the *Waratah* has never been conclusively cleared up, and stories to account for her disappearance still come forward. Hers is regarded as the greatest sea mystery since the curious affair of the *Mary Celeste,* and it is almost as much written about.

The *Waratah* was a passenger- and cargo-liner built at Whiteinch, Scotland, in 1908, by Barclay Curle and Company, for the Australian trade. She was 465 feet long with a beam of 59.45 feet, and a depth of 35.05 feet. Her registered gross tonnage was 9,339.07 and her net register tonnage 6,004 though—in the manner which passenger liners frequently have—she was advertised as being of 16,000 tons. Large advertised tonnages attract passengers, but registered tonnages pay dues. Her five steel boilers provided steam to drive her reciprocal compound quadruple-expansion vertical-inverted engines, which could develop 5,400 indicated horse power, giving her a service speed of 13 knots—quite a reasonable speed for a passenger-and-cargo liner of those days. Her owners were the Blue Anchor Line, for whom the registered managers were Messrs. W., F.W. and A.E. Lund. The contract price for the ship was £139,900, with the builders agreeing to pay a penalty of £50 for each day delivery might be delayed beyond the contracted date. Her specifications were said to be based on those of the steamer *Geelong*, a successful vessel in the owners' line.

She was built by Lloyd's rules for +100 A 1 spar-deck class, but she was a larger ship than had been contemplated when those rules were drawn up. She had three complete steel decks, the lower, main, and spar decks. The crew lived in a raised forecastle in the old style, and this raised forecastle was for'ard of a well-deck—an open deck—73 feet long, with bulwarks 4 feet 2 inches in height. There were three washports each side in these bulwarks, to shed water from seas which broke on to the well-deck. There were coaling-ports in the ship's sides. She had seven watertight bulkheads, and nine tanks in the double bottom.

The *Waratah* carried 16 lifeboats for 787 people (she was designed to carry migrants outwards, when they offered) and she had, in addition, another boat which could carry 29 persons, as well as 3 rafts which could take 105 persons between them. Her life-saving equipment included 930 lifebelts and the usual distress flares, signals and lights but, in common with all other ordinary ocean-going ships of those days, she did not carry wireless. She was a thoroughly up-to-date vessel, despite this. She was fitted with a patent distilling apparatus which could provide 5,500 gallons of fresh water every 24 hours. Her permanent bunker capacity was 2,010 tons of coal, with reserve bunkers of 1,820 tons so, even if she were adrift for a long time, she should be able to provide herself with fresh water.

The specification for the *Waratah* read, "The vessel to be able to stand or shift without any ballast and to be designed, if possible, to go to sea with permanent coal and water ballast only." The builders had added the "if possible" in this clause, because they said they could not guarantee that the vessel would be able to do these things in the circumstances of all her other requirements. In the correspondence which passed between Lunds and the builders over this, the owners insisted when they accepted the "if possible" qualification, that the stability of the *Waratah* should be "greater than that of the *Geelong*," a vessel regarding whose stability there had been no question. The owners wanted to be able to shift their ship as economically as possible, if it were ever necessary when she was in the completely discharged state, and they did not want to have to buy solid ballast. The builders, however, were afraid that the owners were asking too much.

It was finally agreed that the stability of the new ship would be as great as, or greater than, that of the *Geelong*. Captain J. E. Ilbery, who had commanded the *Geelong,* was sent to supervise the later stages of the *Waratah*'s building and appointed to command the ship from the stocks. Captain Ilbery was a highly experienced master mariner and was commodore master of the Blue Anchor Line, with which he had sailed since 1868—forty years.

The *Waratah* was duly delivered to her owners on the 23rd of October, 1908, and Captain Ilbery brought her round from the Clyde to London. She struck some bad weather on this run— October is a bad month—and, regardless of what was said long afterwards at the official inquiry into her loss, there was no complaint at the time as to her general behaviour. "The vessel behaved splendidly," said Mr. F. W. Lund, who made the passage and could hardly be expected to say anything else. "She rolled very little and had only a slight list when broadside on to a gale." She was in a gale off Dungeness and had to wait there for over an hour until a pilot could board her. According to some others who were aboard, she rolled quite badly and showed a nasty inclination to 'stick'— that is, instead of recovering quickly from each roll, sometimes she just seemed to list, and stay over.

Whether Captain Ilbery had any misgivings or not will never be known now but, at any rate—very naturally—he expressed no public opinion. He was getting on in years and he hoped the *Waratah* would be his last ship. He intended only to stay with her as long as it was essential, and then to retire. A passenger certificate was duly issued, apparently without question, and the *Waratah* was certified to carry 128 first-class, 160 third-class passengers and a crew of 144, a total of 432 persons. She was also examined and certified as a migrant-carrier. The ship went on the loading berth in the London docks, for Adelaide, Melbourne and Sydney, and sailed on her maiden voyage on the 5th of November, 1908. She was carrying 67 cabin passengers and 689 immigrants in dormitory accommodation (which would be converted and used for cargo on the homeward run), and she had a crew of 154, which included some extra stewards to look after the immigrants. These extra stewards were probably working a passage to Australia. She was very full, and the immigrants were not exactly comfortable.

There was no really bad weather on the run out, once she was out of the English Channel, and the ship behaved reasonably well. But almost at once there began to be circulated rumours that the *Waratah* was 'top-heavy'—a ship to avoid. Most of these rumours did not come to light then, perhaps unfortunately, but afterwards they did, when the ship was missing. It would appear that Captain Ilbery was not entirely satisfied with the ship's behaviour, and he found her to be a hard ship to load. One reason why this may have been so was that the builders (who may have had their own difficulties working out the data) did not furnish the ship with adequate stability information before she sailed on her first voyage, and their recommendations for her trim did not reach the captain until it was too late to act upon them. In the meantime, he was finding out for himself, which is not the best way to stow a tender large vessel, especially when he had to load a varied cargo of such different densities and weights as wool bales and a quantity of lead concentrates. When such things have to be stowed in a vessel's hold at a range of three ports, for probable discharge 13,000 miles away at a similar range of ports, some pretty problems are presented to ship's officers, not only in the realm of stability. When a ship has difficulties with stability, it takes time to learn how best to distribute the weights of a large general cargo in her several holds in order that she will behave well in the sea, or—perhaps—even with safety. The large cargo passenger liner with a full mixed cargo is a very complex structure to be safely water-borne in all states of the sea, as she uses up her fuel and water in the course of a long voyage.

At any rate the *Waratah* completed her maiden voyage without publicly reported difficulties. Afterwards, some passengers and some members of the crew said they thought the ship was top-heavy. Pilots found her a fine ship to handle but were inclined to take the view that she was very 'tender.' She would roll, some said, and stay over on the least provocation. There was one slight mishap, and that was a bit of a fire in one of the coal bunkers. This was dealt with promptly and caused no damage and, indeed, was considered so unimportant that Captain Ilbery did not even report it.

Before her second voyage, which was to be on the same round as the first, the *Waratah* was dry-docked and surveyed by Lloyd's surveyor. This time she sailed from London on the 27th of April, 1909, with only 22 cabin passengers, 193 in the steerage, and a crew of 119, which included two women. She was carrying 3,456 tons of coal bunkers when she left. Again she was lucky with the weather and struck no real blow the whole way to Australia. In Australia, she loaded a general cargo of about 6,500 tons, which included a parcel of nearly 1,000 tons of lead concentrates. This heavy stuff was taken on at her last loading port, which was Port Adelaide. She also had wheat, oats, flour, hides, tallow and skins—a regular Australian cargo. At Durban, which was her first homeward port of call, she discharged some 240 tons of cargo, and topped up her coal bunkers. She sailed from Durban at 8:15 P.M. on the 26th of July, bound for Cape Town and thence to London.

It was winter off the Cape, and this time she did strike bad weather—very bad weather. She was sighted the following day, close-to, by a cargo steamer, the *Clan MacIntyre,* which was bound in the same direction. When she sailed from Durban there was nothing wrong with the *Waratah.* She had no list. The port captain, the pilot who piloted her out, the tugmaster of the tug *Richard King* which pulled her off the wharf, all agreed that the ship gave no outward sign of having anything wrong whatever, nor did she seem to them to act like an unduly tender ship. The captain of the *Clan MacIntyre,* who had a very good look at her (and was the last man on earth to do so from outside the ship) said "she appeared to me neither to have a list nor to be rolling excessively, but to be proceeding in an exceedingly steady manner," and his chief officer supported this.

It was fine, clear weather when the *Waratah* overhauled the *Clan MacIntyre* and went about her way. The following day the weather deteriorated rapidly, as it knows so well how to do off that well-named old 'Cape of Storms.'

"We experienced a great storm—I had never met with anything as bad on this coast during my thirteen years in the trade," said the *Clan MacIntyre*'s captain. "The wind seemed to tear the water up and was of quite exceptional fierceness and power, rising at times fully to hurricane force. There was a tremendous sea." At times the *Clan MacIntyre* went backwards, but she was not damaged and she came through the storm. The strong Agulhas Current was against the wind and, on the banks off the coast there, the result is a thoroughly nasty and sometimes dangerous cross sea.

The *Waratah* was also sighted by at least one other steamer, a tramp called the *Harlow,* which, like the *Clan MacIntyre,* had no great difficulty in coming through the storm. But the *Waratah* did not arrive at Cape Town when she was expected, on the 29th. Nor did she arrive on the next day, or the next. A thorough local search was quickly begun for her but nothing was found. Then three H.M. ships, a salvage vessel and the specially chartered ship *Sabine,*

[167]

searched for her as far away as the Crozets and St. Paul Island. All ships passing through the area were asked to keep a lookout for the *Waratah,* her boats or survivors. Ports as far away as Australia, Chile, and Peru were watched for the arrival of square-riggers which had 'run their easting down' and so passed through the zone where the *Waratah* might have been lost. Many such ships arrived, but none knew anything of the missing steamer. Though there were plenty of pessimists from the start who were sure the ship had rolled over (for this was the man-in-the-street's view), at first it was thought that the *Waratah* might have had a mechanical breakdown or have lost her propeller, and be drifting.

This hopeful theory was lent substance by the fact that some other fair-sized ships had done just that, in the wild Southern Ocean that sweeps between South Africa and the south of Australia. These included the New Zealand Shipping Company's steamer *Waikato.* The *Waikato* was a fine strong steamship of some 5,000 tons, built in 1892. On a passage from London towards Australia in 1899, her tail shaft had broken when she was about 180 miles south of Cape Agulhas. This was on the 8th of June, and the *Waikato* drifted powerless for the following fourteen weeks before being finally picked up by a steamer called the *Asloun,* which towed her into Fremantle, Western Australia. She reached that port on the 9th of October, four months after first being in trouble. The *Waikato* had been sighted by several sailing-ships, one of which attempted to take her in tow, and she had a bit of sail which she set to help herself. She belonged to the days when steamships still carried yards on the fore and booms on the other masts. The *Waikato,* too, was short of food, and all the hungry crew were able to find in the cargo were some sardines, cocoa, macaroni, cod-liver oil and a patent babies' food. They burned the cod-liver oil as flares, burning a flare every fifteen minutes every night, but no ship ever saw one.

However, the *Waikato* was saved, and at first there was hope that the *Waratah,* having perhaps suffered somewhat the same sort of accident, might also be found afloat and towed in from sea. But a thorough search, which included the whole of the area covered by the *Waikato* in her drift, brought nothing to light. The weeks and the months passed by, and there never was news again of the *Waratah*.

Before then, the rumours had started. There were plenty of them, not all groundless. First there was the curious case of Mr. Sawyer. Mr. Claude G. Sawyer, a company director, had booked passage by the *Waratah* to travel from Sydney to Cape Town with the option of continuing thence to London. Mr. Sawyer soon formed a poor opinion of his chosen vessel. She had, he said, a deplorable habit of rolling with a sickening motion, as if the ship were uncertain what her next move might be and was tired of trying to remain upright. She had, again according to Mr. Sawyer, a bad list leaving Melbourne (which the Port Philip Bay pilot had not noticed). She had a slow roll, and bad. When she rolled she would often remain a long time on her side, and recover all too slowly. Then she would come up again with a jerk. Several passengers had had falls because of this jerk. He heard the third officer—he said afterwards—express the opinion that the ship was top-heavy, and that he would leave her if to leave her did not mean that he must also leave the company, and hence his prospects. Then, a few nights before the ship reached Durban, Mr. Sawyer had a horrible dream. He beheld a man in bloodstained armour, calling for him, and the man had a long sword. Three times Mr. Sawyer dreamed this dream. The third time was too much. Mr. Sawyer stamped down the gangway at Durban with his bags, and refused to go any further in the ship, though this meant forfeiting some of his passage money. The officers and the other passengers laughed at him. Mr. Sawyer stuck to his guns. The *Waratah* could sail without him, and he hoped she would get where she was going.

It was clear that the dreams were the direct result of his disagreeable impressions of the ship and simply pointed to him the resolution he had already formed. But they made a wonderful story when the ship was overdue, and the nightmares of Mr. Sawyer were telegraphed round the world. Even sceptical seamen had to admit that, at any rate, there must have been something odd about the *Waratah* to produce such a state of mind in a man who, after all, was an experienced traveller and not by any means an hysterical person. The *Waratah* was the thirteenth ocean steamer in which Mr. Sawyer had travelled a long distance. And there was corroborative evidence that the *Waratah had* rolled somewhat violently and in an unusual manner immediately after passing through Port Philip Heads, after leaving Melbourne. The pilot had left her then, having seen her safely through the Rip. Others who left the ship at Durban (their passages being completed there) said the same thing. But some others were so pleased with the ship that they booked passages back to Australia in her.

Then the clairvoyants took a hand. A woman named Morris, living in a place called King William's Town, who at the time knew nothing at all about the *Waratah,* was reported to have had a vision of the ship on the night she sailed from Durban. She saw the ship "riding heavily in a storm. It was night, and the *Waratah* was three miles off the normal course. She struck an uncharted rock, was caught broadside by a huge sea, heeled over and plunged down funnel-first in a matter of seconds." How anyone, clairvoyant or otherwise, could detect that the ship was a precise three miles off course no one has said, and the report seemed to indicate that there might be a future for clairvoyants in the painless detection of 'uncharted' rocks. However, the clairvoyant's was a good story, too. There began to be further stories about strange children swept up on the beach from some wreck at sea—doubtless the *Waratah*—and being cared for by a coastal tribe, and about long-haired bodies in the sea. There had been fourteen children in the missing ship, five of whom had come aboard with their mother at Durban, despite the vision of Mr. Sawyer.

The clairvoyants and the visionaries, the rumour-mongers and the long-shore experts who watched the ship go out from Durban with a heavy list, unnoticed either by her pilot or tugmaster, were good copy for the press, though they contributed nothing to solve the mystery of the vessel's disappearance. Mr. Sawyer's vision was not evidence unless perhaps of his own state of mind, though it turned out to be a piece of good luck for him. But among the real experts and in informed seafaring circles in general, there were disquieting rumours about the *Waratah* which could not so easily be passed over. Friends who knew Captain Ilbery and Chief Officer Owen, officials who had dealings with them and with the ship, members of the ship's company who had left after the first voyage for one reason or another—there were quite a few of these—and passengers of experience who had travelled in her during the *Waratah*'s brief life, told stories and reported incidents which served to throw doubt on the ship's seaworthiness, especially her stability. In the aggregate, these could not be ignored, nor did all the stories deal in hind-sight, by any means. The theory was fairly generally put forward that the *Waratah,* a vessel of doubtful stability and perhaps improperly loaded, had developed an excessive list and capsized in her first real storm.

But in fact, had she? What *had* happened to cause her so completely to disappear? After it was quite certain that, *Waikato* or no *Waikato,* the *Waratah* could be afloat no longer anywhere, a Court of Formal Investigation was convened to go thoroughly into every aspect of the matter and to look particularly into the problem of her stability.

CHAPTER TEN

The Inquiry

THE formal investigation into the circumstances attending the loss of the British steamer *Waratah* was held at the Caxton Hall, Westminster, on the 15th, 16th, 17th, 19th, and 20th of December, 1910, and continued into January and February, 1911. It was conducted by John Dickinson, Esq., an experienced magistrate, assisted by four assessors, who included an admiral and a professor who was also a naval architect. All the information which could be assembled about the *Waratah* was assembled, but there were serious gaps. There was, for instance, no cargo plan showing just how the cargo had been stowed on the last voyage. Apparently the only cargo plan was held by the chief officer in the ship and was lost with him. Nor was sufficient evidence as to the ship's stability put before the court. There was no direct evidence at all, as there could not be, of her last voyage, and the indirect evidence was conflicting. Some of it, at least, seemed also evasive.

The court was concerned almost from the beginning with that matter of stability, and the owners were equally concerned—apparently—that no matter what other cause (if any) might be blamed for the tragedy, the alleged top-heaviness of their vessel should not be. This was the natural attitude for them to take. Obviously it was a serious thing if ship owners in the passenger business were so careless as to order, and to send to sea, an unseaworthy vessel. Quite early, the statements by Mr. F. W. Lund about the ship's behaviour on the way round from the builders' yard were challenged. According to Mr. Henry, who was third officer at the time, the *Waratah* had given him a scare when she was broadside to the wind and sea off Dungeness, because he thought she was going to roll over. But Mr. Henry was dead, and his evidence came in the form of a deposition from a Mr. Latimer, in Sydney, reporting what the former third officer was alleged to have said. Mr. Lund's was direct evidence. Not having sailed in his ship from Durban, he was not dead. And Mr. Lund called many prominent 'experts' who declared that the *Waratah* was perfectly stable and a properly designed vessel.

According to some members of the crew, the behaviour of the *Waratah* on her first outward voyage was satisfactory. According to others, it was not. She had a very easy roll and no abnormal list at any time, said a former deck officer, Mr. Harry McKay Bennett. "She neither pitched nor rolled anything out of the ordinary," said Mr. John F. Ryan, fourth engineer on that first voyage, who left when promoted to be third engineer in another vessel.

"I have made three voyages to Australia round the Cape," said Mr. Worthington Church, a passenger on the *Waratah*'s maiden voyage. "I thought she was very top-heavy. I had a conversation with Captain Ilbery, who said he was not altogether satisfied with the ship."

Passenger Leslie Augustus Burton Wade said the vessel rolled so much, so curiously and so unpredictably all the way from the Cape to Sydney that the 'fiddles' were on the tables the whole time, the fiddles being a sort of small fence which is put up round tables aboard ships in heavy weather when otherwise the dishes might roll off. But a Mr. Morley Johnson, who was also a passenger outwards on the maiden voyage, told the court that the "behaviour of the vessel was in general quite equal to that of any vessel I have been in. Her rolling was not unusual. No person ever expressed to me any doubt of the ship's stability."

Other passengers supported this view. As for the fiddles on the tables, it would be odd if they were not kept handy, in that stormy stretch of the ocean where, gales or no gales (and the *Waratah* was lucky with her weather there), such a big sea runs that ships must be expected to roll and roll heavily, whether they are stiff or tender, stable or unstable. Some passengers supported this; others spoke in favour of Mr. Worthington Church's view. The truth seemed to be that the *Waratah,* not striking any particularly bad weather on that voyage, had not behaved too badly as far as the passengers were concerned, but there was little doubt that she had seriously worried her master.

It was significant that no report from Captain Ilbery on the ship's behaviour, nor as much as a mention of the subject, was put before the court. It would appear that all references to the subject had been carefully suppressed. The owners put Captain Ilbery's letters in, or some of them, but in not a single letter was the ship's behaviour even mentioned. The court, suspicious that there must be good reason for withholding the master's views on a topic so vital, re-marked that it was very odd. The letters went into all sorts of triv-ialities, but at no time did this experienced shipmaster give his owners any information on the subject upon which, beyond all oth-ers, they were entitled and would expect to be informed. This was especially the case because the *Waratah* was a new type of ship for them, and they contemplated using her specification as the basis for another vessel.

Again and again, the owners were questioned on this point. "The court is quite unable to understand how silence could have been preserved on such an important and interesting subject as the *Waratah*'s stability and behaviour at sea," said the judge, adding that it was contrary to the whole practice of the sea to treat such matters with indifference. From this, the court inferred that the owners were holding back something—that they had, indeed, delib-erately suppressed Captain Ilbery's report because they considered it reflected on them as shipowners. This inference was strengthened, in the court's view, by correspondence which had passed between the owners and the builders. After the vessel had been loaded with full cargo for the first time, the owners asked for a conference with the builders, and it was rather obvious that they must have had good reason for seeking this. But no evidence was produced of anything Captain Ilbery might have had to say either on the general subject of stability or the particular reason for seeking what must have been a stability conference. In a letter to the builders, Lunds had said: "From what our representatives report, it seems clear that the *Waratah* has not the same stability as the *Geelong*."

In another letter, dated the 4th of April, 1909, the owners said: "We have consulted Captain Ilbery and he has been able to convince us that this vessel has not the same stability as the *Geelong* and, considering that he was present during the construction of both vessels and has commanded them both, he is in a perfect position to judge this and all other matters." (What 'other matters'? These did not come out.) It was the *Waratah*'s stability *in port* that they were worried over, said the owners—her stability when working cargo and bunkering, not her stability at sea. The court remained unconvinced, and said so. But it got no further information, though it openly expressed the view that it was not being told the full story. The owners said that they were fighting for their demurrage at the time—that £50 a day penalty if the ship was not delivered by the contracted date, as she was not—and, they added, the complaints about stability were 'bluff.'

Then, asked the court, was this demurrage paid?

But the owners could not say. The inference from this was very plain. The matter was pointed by the evidence of one of the passengers who joined the ship in Australia for her first passage homewards. This was not the ordinary type of passenger at all, but an expert on stability—the professor of physics at the University of Leeds, Professor William Bragg, a Fellow of the Royal Society. Professor Bragg said that the behaviour of the *Waratah* alarmed him. In his opinion, the vessel was in neutral equilibrium. He had, he said, asked the captain for her stability curves, but the captain said he had not been furnished with this information. There was no such data aboard.

"I was very alarmed," said the Professor. "My impression was that the metacentre was just slightly below the ship's centre of gravity when she was upright, then as she heeled over to either side she came to a position of equilibrium." And she hung there for an appreciable length of time. In other words, it seemed that it was Act of God that she had not gone over on that voyage, for she had not sufficient righting moment * to bring her back when she rolled. If this were the case, it was no wonder that Captain Ilbery was worried.

Such evidence as this could not be sneered away. The owners produced more experts who declared the ship to be beyond fault. There were plenty of passengers who swore, upon oath, that they had failed to observe any shortcomings. Why should they notice such things, of which they had no knowledge?

"I was never in a better ship nor had a better voyage," declared one David Tweedle, who claimed to have made sixteen various ocean voyages but was described in court as "a personal friend of the owners." Coal-trimmer William Marshall said he did not like the way the *Waratah* rolled and was anxious to get out of her, which he did. Seaman Nicholas declared that when he was signing on the ship's articles, the chief officer, Mr. Owen, said to him, "If you can get anything else, take it, because this ship will be a coffin for somebody." He remembered the advice and left in Sydney. Carpenter's mate Pinel said he considered the ship "a bit top-heavy." Various stewards declared that "she always had a list." Some of the able seamen from the first voyage described her as "dead on the roll"—that neutral equilibrium again which the pro-

* The "righting moment" is the force which restores a stable ship back to the upright when she rolls.

[176]

fessor had noted. She rolled and she stayed over longer than a good ship should, they said.

Edward Dischler, an able-bodied seaman with long experience of deepsea ships, including service in fourteen such vessels in the North Atlantic and Australian trades, told the court that the *Waratah* when rolling "went right over on one side and did not seem to be able to recover herself, but stayed there quite an appreciable time. . . . She was the unsteadiest ship I ever voyaged in." The ship's surgeon from the first voyage said much the same thing, complaining of a heavy list and sudden jerk which had upset him in his bath one morning. He left the *Waratah,* too. He did not care for being rolled out of his bath.

Then Mr. Sawyer, whose vivid dreams had been so useful to him and to the newspaper men covering the story, gave evidence. He gave his evidence in a perfectly straightforward manner and did not appear to be a neurotic person. But it became obvious that, although he did not care for the *Waratah*'s rolling, it was her pitching that had bothered him most. He had no knowledge of "neutral equilibrium" or of the real meaning of that "dead roll." He was frightened by the wrong thing. He feared the ship would dig into a big head sea, pitching, and not come up again. Another passenger gave what might have been supporting evidence about the pitching. This was Mr. George S. Richardson, described as the chief mechanical engineer of the Geelong Harbour Trust. He had, he admitted, said in Mr. Sawyer's hearing one day, after some rather bad rolls and jerks, and stops and starts thrown in with a bit of pitching and trembling, "One of these days she will dip her nose down too far and not come up again." This was said as a joke. He did not believe the statement and would not have recalled it at all if the ship had not afterwards disappeared.

But pitch under? This was a new angle. Any ship will pitch in a big sea, and shudder and tremble a bit, too, with the shock of the seas, and some hard-driven vessels have damaged themselves in this way. But pitch on under? It was hardly likely. If Mr. Sawyer, already troubled deeply by what seemed to him was unnatural behaviour on the part of the *Waratah* when she rolled, began to be concerned also that she might pitch herself under (as he obviously was concerned) then it was no wonder the poor man began to have nightmares. He tried to induce a former ship's officer named Ebsworth, who also had been critical of the ship's curious motion, to leave with him at Durban, but Ebsworth refused.

Day after day the court listened to whatever was offered it as evidence, even about dreams. The master of a ship said to be called the *Talis* wrote that he had seen the *Waratah* and knew what happened to the ship, but though this mysterious individual was sighted once, he quickly disappeared again without giving evidence, and it was then discovered that there was no such ship as the *Talis*. The master of a big steamer called the *Guelph* declared that he might have seen the *Waratah* but was not sure. He had sighted a large passenger vessel and tried to exchange signals, but failed. He thought her name ended in "t-a-h," and that was all he knew. His ship at the time was less than 100 miles from Durban and the *Waratah* must have been a good deal further south.

The captain of the steamer *Harlow* suggested that the *Waratah*'s bunker coal had overheated and she blew up. He said that about 5:30 P.M. on the 27th of July, 1909, when off Cape Hermes, he saw smoke 25 miles astern of his ship, and he took this to be from a fast steamer coming up behind him. Later, at 7:15 P.M., he saw masthead lights and a red light right astern, about 10 to 12 miles away. At 7:50 P.M. he went off the bridge to look at the chart and, when he returned, he saw two quick flashes astern. One of these flashes went a thousand feet into the air. There was no noise. No steamer overtook the *Harlow*. No lights were seen again. But he heard no explosion. The lighthouse keeper ashore had seen no flashes or fire at sea, and also had heard nothing. The chief officer of the *Harlow* added that if the *Waratah* had been afire, she would have sent up rockets. He saw no rockets. She could also have got some boats away, for the weather then was not bad. He said that in his opinion the flashes came from bush fires ashore. The captain of the *Harlow* had neither made any report of the alleged incident at the time nor recorded it in the ship's log. If he attached any importance to what he saw, or thought he saw, he would have reported it at the first opportunity.

Then there were reports of sighting bodies. Two ships reported that they had seen bodies floating in the sea after the *Waratah* was missing. These were the *Insizwa* and the *Tottenham,* steamers, which both reported that they saw bodies on the 11th of August, following the tragedy. But they did not see the bodies in the same place. The *Insizwa* was off the Bashee River and the *Tottenham* was the best part of a hundred miles away, 25 miles or so south of East London. They could not both have seen the same bodies. The captain of the *Insizwa* said he saw four objects which looked like bodies, floating just below the surface, about ten miles off the Bashee River. The weather was bad and he did not stop to investigate. Not all his officers agreed with him about the bodies.

According to some of her officers, the *Tottenham* had passed human bodies in the water the same day. They reported this to their captain at once, but after taking a good look (without stopping, however) he said the objects were not bodies but other things, including whale offal. A large amount of whale offal is set adrift in those waters. The *Clan MacIntyre,* too, had seen the *Waratah* abeam of the Bashee River. Any bodies that came from her must have been further to the south. The court did not accept either story of sighting bodies. The clairvoyants, the public-house theorists, and the rumour-mongers were not called upon to give their 'evidence' and the court, remarking that "where so little is known the range of conjecture is wide" and that it was idle to discuss the many guesses, retired to sift the evidence through and to think things over. Two significant things had emerged from the welter of talk, allegations, depositions, dream recitals, papers, plans, experts' statements and so forth which had cluttered the proceedings for days. These were the Leeds professor's evidence, and the failure of the owners to produce Captain Ilbery's views on the ship's behaviour at sea.

On the 22nd of February, 1911, the court delivered its findings. These were "that the ship was lost in the gale of the 28th of July, 1909, which was of exceptional violence for those waters and was the first great storm she had encountered. The Court is led to this conclusion by the fact that she overhauled the *Clan MacIntyre* which afterwards experienced the gale, was last seen heading in a direction which would take her into a position where she would feel the full force of the storm, and was never afterwards sighted by the *Clan MacIntyre*. Had she been only disabled it is almost certain that she would have been so sighted [for the Clan ship was following in her wake] and, if not, would have been picked up by one of the many ships subsequently on the lookout for her." The total absence of direct evidence and the conflicting evidence of an indirect character made it impossible for the court to say how the ship was lost. It must have been very sudden. But the court "on the whole, inclines to the opinion that she capsized." Why she capsized, the court, however, did not feel that it could say.

It had said enough. The Blue Anchor Line sold its other ships and went out of the passenger-carrying business. The court recommended that there should be further study of the question of stability in ocean-going ships—the same recommendation which was to be made over forty years later in the case of the lost tramp steamer *Hopestar,* and, a decade prior to that, for the *Anglo-Australian,* too.

Looking back on it now, there can be little doubt that the *Waratah*'s was a tragedy of stability. The owners, acting in good faith, gave the builders an extremely difficult specification, with which their naval architects and designers did their best. The result was not good enough, and there was no time to learn how best to load the insufficiently stable vessel before she rolled over in her first severe storm. Somewhere south of the Bashee River the *Waratah* must have rolled over, with worried Captain Ilbery and Chief Officer Owen, who had done their best, too, with poor Mrs. Turner from Durban and her five children aged from three to fourteen years, and all the other passengers and crew. Perhaps in the awful tumult of the dreadful storm, she was flung violently about and then suddenly she lurched and rolled far over, and did not come back. She hung there for a frightful second, swung helpless into the trough of the sea, was struck by a great sea and, as if she were sick of it all, rolled on right over. With a crashing of the five steel boilers breaking from their beds and a roar of steam stifled upon the instant by the inrush of the cold sea, quickly she went on down, before her startled passengers had time to scream. Then the sea boiled over the place where she had been, the impersonal and murderous sea, always waiting to snatch at ships large or small which, for any reason, understood or not understood, connived at or innocent, venture to do battle with the great waters handicapped in any way. There was scope for further examination of the question of stability, indeed! Two hundred and eleven people had died.

The ghost of the *Waratah* takes a long time to die. To this day—at the end of 1955—persons come forward from time to time to acquire a little brief publicity for some 'clue' or other, some new rumour, some old sailor's yarn. Not long ago, I did a broadcast for the British Broadcasting Corporation in London about the case of the *Waratah*. The broadcast was barely finished before a listener was telephoning the B.B.C. to say that he had the 'key' of the mystery. He had, he said, watched the ship go out from Durban in a dangerously loaded state. He was sitting on the beach and he watched her go round the Bluff. "The ship," said this informant, nearly fifty years after the event, "was laden high with yellow timber on its decks, and I remarked to my wife at the time that she looked fearfully top-heavy. I was sure she would roll over."

Whatever else the *Waratah* was carrying, she had no timber high on her decks or anywhere else. What she was carrying was well known. It was how it was stowed that was not fully established. Some years before that, an Irishman was reported to have been found in the British Army who was a 'survivor' from the *Waratah* and, as such, he achieved some brief notoriety. His name was Staunton. There was no such name or anything like that name in either the crew list or the passenger list of the missing vessel and, when this was known, nothing further was heard from this particular 'survivor.' But it is remarkable how well his story was received and how long it was before anyone thought of looking up the official records.

After the broadcast, I heard from several friends of Captain Ilbery and Chief Officer Owen who brought forward again the matter which had worried the court, their reported but unproduced view that all was far from well with the *Waratah*. One correspondent wrote from Lewes in Sussex: "Captain Josiah Ilbery was an intimate friend of my family. We had sailed to Australia with him in the SS *Wilcannia* in 1901 and home again in the *Commonwealth* two years later. After that he frequently visited us. After the maiden trip of the *Waratah* he seemed less cheerful than usual, and one evening he told us that he was not happy about her. Old Mr. Lund, head of the company which owned the Blue Anchor ships, had retired, and his sons when they took his place were intent on making larger profits, so they built this new vessel. Captain Ilbery did not like her and had done his best, but in vain, to get the plans altered before she was built. . . . Even now, I cannot think of the awful last moments of the *Waratah* without horror—awful for the passengers and crew, but perhaps worst of all for the good old man who was responsible for their safety and had done his best."

A former shipping official wrote that he knew, quite well, the father of Chief Engineer Hodder, who died with the *Waratah*. From the first moment the ship became overdue, the old man was certain that she had turned over. In his last conversation before the ship left London, his son had said, "I am not going back in her after this trip. She's top-heavy, father; she's top-heavy."

Old sailors who were at sea off the Cape at the time and spoke of the bad weather, and others who had been all but rolled over off the Cape themselves in perfectly stable vessels; nice old ladies who wanted to believe in the story about a girl-baby being washed ashore in a dying sailor's arms and brought up in some remote district in ignorance of her origin (which was a persistent but baseless *Waratah* rumour); elderly gentlemen who had lost friends and relatives in the ship—many of these wrote to me. But they could add nothing to what was known. There was one report, however, which sounded as if it had something new in it. A year or two ago a South African Air Force aircraft was reported to have flown over the area where the *Waratah* was lost. The pilot, looking down into the sea—it was a remarkably fine day and the sea was perfectly clear—suddenly saw a large ship lying on her side, deep down by a large reef. What evidence there was that this was the *Waratah* was not mentioned, but it was reported to be that vessel, though there have been other ships lost in the area.

However, when the same pilot flew out again to find the ship, this time with a newspaper man aboard, he failed to do so. Nor has anyone else seen the reported wreck since.

6

SAILING-SHIP

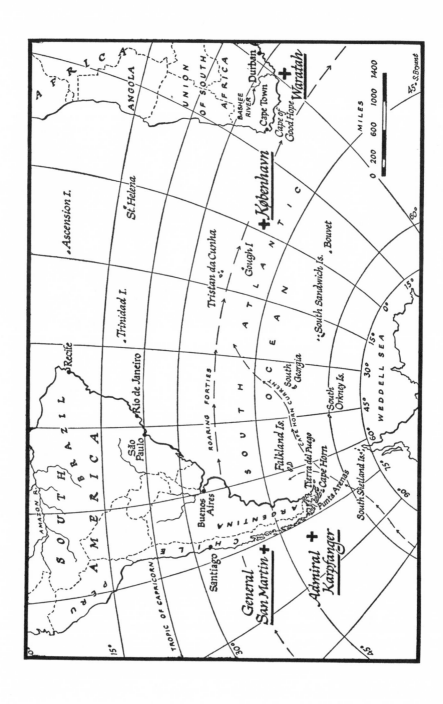

AFRICA

ANGOLA

UNION OF SOUTH AFRICA

BASHEE RIVER

Cape Town

Durban

Cape of Good Hope

✚ Waratah

MILES

0   200   600   1000   1400

45° S.Bryant

Ascension I.

St.Helena.

✚ København

60°

Tristan da Cunha

Gough I.

S O U T H   A T L A N T I C   O C E A N

South Sandwich Is.

Bouvet

15°

Recife

Trinidad I.

Rio de Janeiro

ROARING FORTIES

São Paulo

CAPE HORN CURRENT

South Georgia

South Orkney Is.

WEDDELL SEA

30°

15°

0°

B R A Z I L

AMAZON R.

S O U T H   A M E R I C A

Buenos Aires

ARGENTINA

Falkland Is.

Tierra del Fuego

Cape Horn

Punta Arenas

South Shetland Is.

45°

60°

90°

15°

PERU

CHILE

Santiago

TROPIC OF CAPRICORN

✚ General San Martin

✚ Admiral Karpfanger

30°

45°

Two School Ships

IN the days of sail a good many ships went missing, and the loss of each was accounted as just one more victim of the sea, sometimes mysterious, sometimes not. Old seamen shook their heads, young seamen signed on the articles of other vessels, and the seafaring life continued as before. The *Loch Vennachar,* the shapely *Clan MacPherson,* the beautiful *Engelhorn,* the *Ellisland,* the American four-masted schooner *Omega,* the handsome barquentine *Amelia J.* out of Hobart in Tasmania—barques, barquentines, schooners, four-masted barques, full-rigged ships, each contributed their share to the lists of the lost, and the mystery of their going was rarely cleared. They had no radio. They sailed a lonely road, and they used great storms to blow them on their way. If now and again one was overwhelmed in a storm, that was a risk of the trade. If the ship could not survive, neither would her boats, and no one came back to tell the tale. The boats were often lashed down. The old seafarers rarely learned to swim. If the ship was drowned, so were her people.

And yet it is an odd thing that the two last of the great square-rigged ships to be posted missing were, in many ways, the best ships of all. One had an auxiliary motor. Both had radio. Both were exceptionally well manned. Both were school ships, designed and built as such, and splendidly maintained throughout their careers. One, the more recently lost, was the German training-ship *Admiral Karpfanger,* a four-masted barque of 2,853 tons built of steel as the Belgian training-ship *L'Avenir* in 1908, and a regular Cape Horn trader for thirty years when she was lost. The *L'Avenir* was sold to the late Gustaf Erikson, the Finnish sailing-ship owner, during the depression of the 1930's, and he ran her in the Australian grain trade, where she did very well. When in 1937 the Hamburg-America Line was looking for a suitable sailing school ship to continue sail-training for the line's officers, the former Belgian four-master was the best ship available. She was surveyed and bought, and extensively refitted for her new duties. No money was spared on making her as good a ship as possible and, after this refit in 1937, she was given the classification of 100 A 4 by Germanischer Lloyds. She was renamed *Admiral Karpfanger*—the old sailing-ship men did not like their ships to be renamed: a ship, they held, should keep her christened name, like a person—and off she went to Australia. The outward passage was made without incident. The ship proved herself a good ship, and the cadets soon shook down into a competent and happy crew.

The *Admiral Karpfanger* loaded a full cargo of 42,549 bags of wheat, at the little port of Port Germein, well inside Spencer Gulf in South Australia—a place which, outport though it was, had plenty of stevedores who well understood the stowage of a cargo of grain for a sailing-ship's Cape Horn passage. There were shifting-boards in the hold, built up strongly fore-and-aft, in order that the sacks of grain could not shift and so cause the vessel to take a dangerous list. Everything was in order when, on the 8th of February, 1938, the fine-looking four-master hove up her anchor and stood down the gulf and out to sea, under a cloud of sail. She had a crew of sixty all told, thirty-three of them cadets. The master had orders to report the ship's position by radio to the owners at least once each fortnight, and this he did, though he had written home from Port Germein saying that his generator had been giving some trouble.

On the 1st of March, the *Admiral Karpfanger* reported herself through Norddeich Radio as storming along on 51 degrees south latitude, 172 degrees east longitude, and all well aboard. The position she gave was on the usual square-rigger's track between South Australia and Cape Horn but—and this may be significant— the German sailer was three weeks at sea at the time and her progress had not been as good as it might have been. It was usual for the faster ships (among whose number she belonged) to be past Cape Horn about a month after leaving their loading ports, but the *Admiral Karpfanger* then had still over 3,000 miles to sail. Probably she had been unlucky with her winds. It was summer in the far south, then, and there might have been some weeks of light and baffling winds.

No further messages were sent, though the ship acknowledged a radio signal sent to her on the 12th of March. That was the last ever heard of her. From that day, the *Admiral Karpfanger* disappeared. She should have arrived off Falmouth or Queenstown within 100 or 110 days of leaving Australia—at the most, within 130. But 140, 150 days passed, and she did not come in. Other sailing-ships which had sailed from Spencer Gulf before and after her arrived safely. All reported that they had seen nothing of her. This in itself was by no means strange. It was rare for one of these last square-riggers to sight another on the Cape Horn run. By that time there were only about a dozen such ships left, and though now and again two or three might leave port the same day, they usually sailed alone. There was a chance of speaking another vessel on the Equator, perhaps, or in the calm zone off the Azores after passing through the north-east trades (it is curious how calms brought ships together), but there was nothing at all remarkable in the fact that no other sailing-vessel had sighted the German school ship. But five months passed, and there was still no news—no radio message, no report of a sighting or speaking from any vessel. The big German was then overdue. She came in the reinsurance market, a certain indication that those who had underwritten ship and cargo were worried about her safety. The rate quoted to reinsure her was 80 percent. The other underwriters were worried, too.

So were the owners. It was perhaps understandable that there might have been a radio breakdown aboard their ship, preventing the master from sending the fortnightly reports of his position which his orders called for. But when five months had passed and there was still no news whatever of the ship, it began to be obvious that more than the radio had broken down. All the young cadets for a great steamship line were aboard, thirty-three lads aged from fifteen to eighteen years. Hapag, the owners, ordered their freighter *Leuna,* then loading in Australia, to come home round Cape Horn instead of by her planned route through the Suez Canal, and to keep a thorough lookout for the *Karpfanger,* or her derelict hulk (if she had been dismasted) or her boats, or anything else from her. The *Leuna* did this, searched diligently and saw nothing. The British motor vessel *Durham,* bound from Wellington, New Zealand, towards the United Kingdom by way of Cape Horn, came in with the report that she had sighted icebergs on the route, not far from Cape Horn and in the sailing-ship's track. She had heard no signals from the *Karpfanger* or from any other ship, though she must have been between New Zealand and the Horn at the time the four-masted barque was making that run. Another British merchantman, the *Waiwera,* had rounded the Horn about a week ahead of the *Durham.* She also had seen nothing of any sailing-ship.

The Argentine Government, asked to cooperate, sent its survey-ship *Bahia Blanca* to search thoroughly around the Cape Horn islands, in case the ship had been driven up there and survivors were living ashore. The *Bahia Blanca* made an exhaustive search of both the mainland and the islands and, though she found ancient wreckage from a good many other sailing-ships, she came upon no fresh wreckage, no survivors, and nothing from the *Karpfanger* at all.

In the meantime, on the 21st of September, 1938, when she had been over seven months at sea and was three months overdue, the Committee at Lloyd's finally posted the *Admiral Karpfanger* as a missing vessel. There had been the usual false reports. Some of the Finnish four-masters were wrongly reported as the missing ship. An Air France plane, flying down to South America, flew over a big four-masted barque in ballast somewhere in the north-east trade winds, south of the Cape Verde Islands. Hapag and all other ships were asked to keep a sharp lookout for this vessel or for any other sign of the school ship. But the vessel in the trade winds turned out to be the old *Lawhill,* a well-known four-masted barque then in the Erikson Line, and not at all like the *Karpfanger.* The barque *Winterhude,* a three-master of the Erikson Line not noted for smart passages, began to be more than four months at sea without being reported (though like most Erikson ships, she had no sending radio) and the underwriters, made nervous by the lack of news of the *Admiral Karpfanger,* began to seek reinsurance on the *Winterhude,* too. The last quoted rate on the German was 90 percent, but the *Winterhude,* sailing slowly homewards round the Cape of Good Hope instead of by the more usual Cape Horn route, showed herself briefly off St. Helena and was back in the land of the living again. Reinsurance on her cargo—the ship herself was not insured —did not go beyond 15 percent, and there was no real fear that she was missing. The underwriters perhaps took the view that the German ship had struck the ice which the *Durham* reported, and they were afraid that the *Winterhude* might have done the same thing. But the *Winterhude* was never within some thousands of miles of the place where the icebergs were seen.

Did ice really claim the *Admiral Karpfanger?* No one can say. Ice was a regular hazard of the Cape Horn passage, and that fact was well known to the school ship's master, who was a most experienced man. The four-master was deeply laden, and if she had struck ice which ripped her open, she would have gone down very quickly—too quickly, perhaps, to get an SOS away, particularly if (not being near the time for one of the fortnightly reports) the generator was under overhaul or for some other reason the radio was not ready to function just at that moment. The *Admiral Karpfanger,* having been designed as a school ship to accommodate a considerable number of cadets, was a long-poop vessel, which is to say that she had less vulnerable decks and a little more buoyancy than the average Cape Horner. Her poop-deck reached right along to forward of the mainmast, leaving only a short fore well-deck to hold heavy water. She could therefore run drier and longer in a gale of wind than a big open-decked ship like, for instance, the *Parma.* She ought not to be overwhelmed in the sea.

But her master—understandably and quite properly—might have been driving her a bit hard. It was her maiden voyage as a German ship, and she belonged to a line with a great reputation and a flag which had flown from the greatest Cape Horners in the world, the mighty *Preussen* and *Potosi*. Though they were so few, the surviving Cape Horners then were still making a race of it, in the grain trade home from Australia. They called it the 'Grain Race,' and the victor was not the first ship in (for they usually sailed from different places at different times, as each ship was loaded at whatever outport furnished her with a cargo) but the vessel which made the fastest passage. The *Karpfanger* had as good a chance as any to win the race.

She had done poorly up to the time of her last reported position. Perhaps, whipped along afterwards before some violent westerly gale, the great ship may have been driven too hard and too long and, in some dreadful cataclysm of the awful sea which races unchecked round the whole world down there, have broached-to and, driving the steel masts out of her, have brought down the aerials and pierced her decks and her steel sides at the same instant. Then she would have gone on down, spinning beneath the breaking sea almost before she had time to lose her headway or a boy aboard had a chance to cry aloud. Maybe . . . It can only be maybe. These things should *not* have happened. After all, others of the square-riggers, pressed hard, too, had been broached-to—the *Parma* and the Swedish school ship *C. B. Pedersen,* for example—and they had survived to tell the tale, though the *Pedersen* was partially dismasted and had had to turn and run for Panama. The *Karpfanger,* with that most valuable long, high poop, was less vulnerable by far than either of these. She had an extra deck along most of her length, good high freeboard, and all her hatches save one were six feet higher than the other sailers. So they stood so much the less chance of being stove-in by breaking masts or by the rioting and destructive force of the malevolent sea.

The *Admiral Karpfanger* might have been sailed under, but the probability is slim. It is more likely that she hit ice—some lurking iceberg low and awash in her track by night, breaking surlily in the great sea which would hide its presence until too late. What chance had the running ship really to see a treacherous low berg awash in the water before her? She had no radar. There was no such thing then available. She had no searchlights. If the gale blew she had to run before it, and that was her purpose—to use the wind to blow her on. If she hove-to every night or when the visibility was bad, she would never make a passage. How could she know, then, where the ice was? Or even if there were any? The drift of icebergs in the great area of the South Pacific is not plotted. There is no South Pacific ice patrol, for the sufficient reason that the ocean is too big and too little used by ships. No, a running Cape Horner had to take her chance, and the chances must have been against the big German that voyage.

Afterwards—long afterwards—when the search was no longer actually continued, some wreckage identified as probably from the *Admiral Karpfanger* was found among the Cape Horn islands—wreckage which had not been there when the *Bahia Blanca* made her thorough search. So the inference was that it had drifted there. The wreckage was found on the rocky beach of Windbound Bay, on Navarin Island, which is very near the island the southernmost tip of which is Cape Horn. The wreckage included some timbers with brass fastenings, the outer parts being painted white and the inner faces varnished. One fresh piece of timber had a piece of electric cable such as was used by the Belgian Navy. About the same time, the tug *Galvarino* arrived at Ushuaia and reported the finding of further wreckage among the southern islands. This included some ship's wooden doors with inscriptions on them in German, as well as a piece of a wooden mast or yard, about 21 feet long. After these discoveries, a few other pieces of recent wreckage came ashore—a wooden box marked "Frieretsen Wellington" and the debris of a lifeboat, which came ashore on Wollaston Island, which is also near Cape Horn. Then a battered lifebuoy came up at Aguirre Bay, on the Argentine side of Tierra del Fuego.

What name had been on this broken buoy it was difficult to make out, but it could have been *Admiral Karpfanger*.

If wreckage was washed up from the sea from her, then the missing four-master had somehow been smashed—not overwhelmed merely, but broken open, too. It is possible that she had driven up on some horrible projection of rocks and, fatally injured, slipped off again to founder in deeper water beneath a maelstrom of sea wherein no man could survive. Afterwards, as she came to pieces slowly deep down where she lay, possibly she threw up these bits of wood and the battered boat and lifebuoy, to be picked up by the winds and cast ashore. It is possible that this may have been the order of things. But it is highly improbable that the master of the *Admiral Karpfanger* was so far out in his reckoning that he cast that fine ship on any rocks near Cape Horn. After all, no one cut that dreaded corner close, and he had to be sure only of his latitude and approximate longitude to get round in safety. It is far more probable that the ship struck an iceberg when running heavily in the middle of the night, for the power of an Antarctic 'berg is tremendous and frightening. Even a glancing blow from such an implacable opponent would rip his ship apart in a matter of seconds, leaving only some splintered bits of wood and a broken lifebuoy to drift away.

The case of the five-masted barque *København* is even more inexplicable. At the time of her mysterious and sudden loss, the *København* was only seven years old. She was the largest and finest sailing-vessel in the world. She was not quite the newest, though she was built in 1921 and lost in 1928 or early '29, for the German four-masted barque *Padua* of the Laeisz Line in Hamburg was built in 1926. (The *Padua* was the last pure big sailing-ship—no auxiliary engine—to be built.) The *København* had a good auxiliary diesel. She had long-range radio equipment. She had a splendid crew. She was an unusually strongly built vessel. She had all the boats and life-saving gear she could possibly have needed. She had made half a dozen successful voyages. She was not in any 'race,' when she sailed from Buenos Aires bound for Australia on a December day in 1928, and disappeared off the face of the sea without leaving as much as an identifiable splinter behind her, or the bones of one of her forty-five boys. She disappeared utterly, and nothing was ever found which might have come from her. She was in ballast, riding light, with no cargo. She had ample buoyancy and should, one would think, have been hard to sink, even had she been ripped apart on the horns of an iceberg. She should at least have taken time enough to get an SOS away. Yet there was no SOS —nothing. No signal. No driftwood. No wreckage. No messages in a bottle—nothing but the continued, mocking silence of the bitter and implacable sea.

The *København* was built to be the school ship of the famous Danish East Asiatic Company, which pioneered the modern ocean-going motor-ship. The Danish East Asiatic Company believed in sail-training for the indoctrination of those who were to have the distinction of serving the company as officers in its ships, a proud and competent group which included a prince of Denmark. When its pioneer big motor-ship *Selandia* first successfully demonstrated the value of the diesel engine for the economic, safe and efficient propulsion of ocean-going ships, not long before the outbreak of the First World War, the Danish company planned to build a big school ship with an auxiliary diesel motor—not just a bit of a puffer to push the ship along in calms, but a real auxiliary engine with some power in it, which could help the ship in adverse conditions as well as calms and serve also to provide the cadets with some engine-room experience. The company believed that the big auxiliary sailing-ship was a useful vessel. So, in 1913, the school ship *København* was ordered to be built by Messrs. Ramage and Ferguson, at Leith, in Scotland. However, the ship was not ready before the war began and, when Britain was short of ships, the British

Admiralty took over the hull and made other use of it. It was not until 1921 that a new *København* could be finished, this time a magnificent great steel five-masted barque, for she was too big to carry sail enough to drive her with only the usual four masts.

From the beginning this new *København* was an outstanding ship. No. 242 at her builders' yard—which was also the number of the original hull—she was just over 354 feet long by 49 feet beam and 28 feet 7 inches in depth. Without cargo but with full water ballast, stores and fuel, she displaced 4,219 tons. She could carry 1,245 tons of water ballast, in a large tank. Her gross tonnage was 3,965 and her deadweight capacity was 5,200 tons. Her over-all length was 430 feet, which is enormous for a sailing-ship. Her loaded draught was 24 feet. Her diesel motor, which was placed well aft in the ship, was designed to give her a speed, when loaded, of 6 knots. Instead of having one huge hold as most sailing-ships had, her holds were bulkheaded by means of thwartships watertight steel partitions, so that she was much stronger and should have been much more difficult to sink than the average sailing vessel. The Danes had had one tragedy with a school ship which had no special watertight bulkheads, when the little *Georg Stage* was cut down while anchored in fog, sank and drowned a number of boys. The *Georg Stage* was salved and reconstructed with bulkheads, and the Danes were determined that, if it could possibly be avoided, they would run no more risk of tragedies of that kind.

The ship was not over-rigged. For such an enormous sailer, her spar and sail-plans were not large. She could spread 56,000 square feet of canvas, but her lower yards were only 90 feet long. Even so they weighed nearly 5 tons apiece, and she carried 8 *tons* of sails. Her shapely array of masts and yards was supported by nearly 5 miles of standing rigging, all of it very strong steel wire, and con-trolled by 23 miles of running rigging, most of which was also wire. Standing and running rigging in current use weighed 50 tons, and one of her steel lower-masts weighed 23 tons. The engine was a

Burmeister and Wain 4-cylinder diesel developing 500 b.h.p., driving a two-bladed controllable-pitch bronze propeller which could be feathered in the fore-and-aft line of the vessel and so cause little or no drag. The pitch of the blades could be adjusted to give maximum power under varying conditions. The diesel was designed to run on considerably less than three tons of oil a day, and the ship could carry 204 tons of this fuel, in double-bottom tanks. She also had generators and other auxiliaries, and was electrically lit and warmed. She had ample pumps. She had a poop 112 feet long, as well as a long 'midships house, like a three-island steamer. She had only two comparatively short well-decks to trap the sea. She was steered from a wheel-house on the 'midships superstructure, with an auxiliary steering position aft which could be brought into almost instant use whenever needed. She was built to Lloyd's highest class, using nothing but the best materials, and she complied in all respects with both British and Danish official requirements, both of which were strict and thorough. Her construction was supervised by an experienced Danish officer, the Baron Nils Juel-Brockdorff, who was her first captain.

The *København* was beautifully finished, and her figurehead was especially magnificent. This was carved for the ship in Copenhagen, her name-town and her home port both, and it was a splendid figure of the warrior-priest Absalom, founder of that city. She carried the East Asiatic Company's house-flag emblazoned on the white canvas of her fore lower topsail, in the way that the Black Ball liners and other sailing 'cracks' of the past had once done. The *København* left Leith in September, 1921, and was visited by over 10,000 people before sailing from Copenhagen on her maiden voyage, her visitors including the King and Queen of Denmark. The King's brother was a master in the East Asiatic Line, and both brothers knew a fine square-rigger when they saw one.

No ship could have been better built nor had a better start, and the big *København* gave an excellent account of herself at once. Her first voyage was a circumnavigation which took from October, 1921, until November of the following year, the first leg of which was outwards with general cargo from Newcastle and Antwerp for San Francisco, San Pedro, and Honolulu. From Honolulu she sailed in ballast across the Pacific to Vladivostok where—and at Dalny— she loaded a full cargo of soya-beans and soya-bean oil. This she delivered by the long sailing route west of the Philippines, across the Indian Ocean round Good Hope and up through both Atlantics, to Stettin, in Germany. The whole round voyage took 404 days, and the ship showed herself to be all that was expected of her.

"She steers well, carries her sail well, is easy to manoeuvre and showed herself a splendid sea-vessel under conditions of severe weather," the Baron reported. On the ballast run across the North Pacific he had loaded 700 tons of sand as well as the water in the ballast-tanks, 250 tons of sand for'ard and 450 tons in the after hold. In this trim the ship sailed and handled splendidly. Her crew of sixty included two boatswains, a sailmaker, a carpenter, sixteen experienced able seamen and ten ordinary seamen, as well as twenty of the company's cadets. The Danes were taking no chances, and there were two officers and twenty-four men in each watch. Nor were any of the cadets green hands. All had been to sea under sail before, at least for an indoctrination voyage of six months in the resurrected *Georg Stage,* and most of them in other vessels as well.

As the cadets gained experience and showed themselves to be good young sailormen to the satisfaction of the officers, who were always studying them, the best of them were advanced to act as ordinary, and then, in time, as able seamen, and the number of cadets in the ship's complement was stepped up progressively until it was forty-eight. This did not happen for some years. By the time there were forty-eight cadets, the nine oldest had an average two and one-half years' experience in sailing school ships, the seventeen next oldest had been one year and nine months in such ships, and the twelve youngest had at least seven months' sailing-ship experience.

This was at a time when the Finnish ships of the Erikson Line often went to sea without a real able seaman at all and only the bare minimum of crew of any kind. There were no five-masters in this line (for the *København,* after the former German *Potosi* was lost, was the sole representative of her rig in the world), but there were plenty of big, heavy four-masters such as the former school ship *Herzogin Cecilie* and the heart-breaking big *Olivebank.* The practice was to man these with a minimum of youths who had some prior experience, usually only in Baltic sailing-vessels, and to take as many premium-paying cadets as might be found—usually something between six and twelve a ship. The average watch in these big four-masters consisted of one officer, one petty officer (in bad weather zones only: at all other times the petty officer worked as a 'dayman' and kept no watch) and seven boys, some of whom might be rated able seamen but most not. The average age of the lot was about 17.

There could be no doubt that the *København* was excellently manned, at all times. Her whole complement was always selected most carefully. Only the best boys from the *Georg Stage* were chosen for her, and the selection was a coveted honour.

Baron Nils Juel-Brockdorff handed over command at the end of the first voyage to his former chief mate, Captain Mortensen, who took the ship on her four next voyages, the first from Norresundby to Buenos Aires and back (which occupied in all 159 days, including time in port), the next from Copenhagen to Norresundby to Balboa, thence via Panama Canal to Honolulu and San Francisco, Eureka, Astoria, and Portland (Oregon), thence through the Pacific to Sydney, New South Wales. In Australia, she loaded a full cargo of wheat in bags at Port Germein and Port Victoria (both outports in Spencer Gulf) for Bordeaux. From Bordeaux she went back to Copenhagen, and this whole voyage took 371 days. The next voyage—the *København*'s fourth—was from Copenhagen to Kotka in Finland and Frederikshamn to load timber for Durban, Delagoa Bay, and Beira, thence back to London. This took 220 days, and was followed by a round trip to Bangkok and Singapore with discharge in Hamburg—a voyage of 175 days in all.

During these several voyages the five-master had carried many diverse cargoes—grain, cement, timber and so forth—and she had also sailed in ballast. She had been through all kinds of weather. She had had some sails blow away (which was commonplace in powerful ships), but she had shown herself, to Captain Mortensen's unequivocal satisfaction, to be a splendid sailing-ship from every point of view. Had there been any reason to question anything about her stability, seaworthiness or anything else, her owners were in a position to put things right and would never have continued to send a ship to sea concerning which there was any possible shade of doubt whatever.

Captain Mortensen in due course stepped down—he had been only thirty-seven years old when he took command: the *København* was a ship for a comparatively young man—and Captain H. J. Christensen took over for three long voyages, her sixth, seventh, and eighth. The sixth took almost a year and included a run out through the west winds to Melbourne in Australia (from Danzig), thence to Java, and so back to Copenhagen—long hauls with plenty of hard sailing. The seventh was a round voyage to South Australia for a grain cargo, which she brought back from Port Adelaide to Liverpool, round the Horn. For the eighth voyage, she sailed to Callao from Liverpool and thence loaded at Caleta Coloso for Korsør and Copenhagen. This round voyage took 207 days. She did not usually make use of her engine except in ports and making transits of occasional calm belts, but the fact that she had an auxiliary gave her an advantage over the other sailing-ships. She could use a greater range of ports. The others usually made passages from one port to one port, with bulk cargoes, and offered shippers no facilities for divided loading or unloading. The *København* could do better, and the experiment of building her was a success.

Captain Christensen was the last surviving captain of the five-master. He handed over command to Captain Hans Ferdinand Andersen for the tenth voyage, which was to be her last. Captain Andersen, like the other masters, did not come to the ship 'green' but had been her mate. Command of a five-masted barque then was unique. There had only been five other such vessels in all history, and one five-masted ship. They were all gone. The company followed the policy of bringing up the ship's officers in the ship, just as they brought up the cadets. That was the only way they could have experience of a five-masted square-rigger. Andersen knew the capabilities of the ship in the west winds zone, the 'Roaring Forties,' where she was lost. Captain Christensen was accustomed to run across from somewhere about Tristan da Cunha to the longitude of his desired port in Australia on the approximate latitude of 42 or 43 south, where the big ship got plenty of wind. She could, he said, easily step along at thirteen knots on these ballast runs. It was unnecessary to drive the ship. She sailed extremely well in a fresh wind with the upper topgallant-sails and the royals secured.

Captain Christensen had the ship for two and half years and, when she was so mysteriously lost, naturally his opinion and his experience of her meant a great deal. The *København*, he said, was the 'solidest' ship he had ever been in, or seen. He could not imagine her being dismasted, or suffering indeed any of the more ordinary calamities and accidents of the sea. He had tried out her strength alow and aloft, and he had found her always to respond magnificently. Her last master had been a witness of all this.

The *København*'s last voyage was from Denmark, first, to Buenos Aires again, with full cargo. There was nothing to carry back to Denmark just then and no other employment for the ship but the grain trade from South Australia, and so she was ordered to run across to Spencer Gulf in ballast in order to load grain at an outport there for Falmouth for orders. Captain Andersen wrote that he intended to follow the west winds route which the former master had used—between 42 and 43 south. Running down there, a square-rigger had the advantage of westerly storm after westerly storm, and that was the reason for going so far south. The 'Roaring Forties' road, south of Good Hope and past the sub-Antarctic islands towards Australia, was as old as big sailing-ships themselves. All the outward-bound ships had raced that way for a hundred years and more. There was a risk of ice, of course—of meeting the odd iceberg drifted up from the Antarctic continent. Such icebergs could usually be seen. They were, as a rule, large, tabular 'bergs, anything up to several miles long and often a couple of hundred feet high. They gave warning of their presence (if the visibility was good) by showing a whitish ice-blink in the sky above them, and by bringing a downwards change to the temperature of the sea. Such icebergs were usually met singly, as they had been cast adrift from the Great Ice Barrier or whatever other huge glacier had given them birth. They could be avoided as the land was avoided, and the possibility of coming across a few of them was a risk which had to be accepted. If ships tried to sail in latitudes further north where there was less chance of meeting ice, there very likely would be no wind either. The auxiliary in the *København* was not intended for making ocean passages—on the high seas she was a sailing-ship —but for restricted use in ports and calms. It was not only reasonable that she would go the way she did—there was no practical alternative.

Of course there were storms—beginning usually in the north or the north-west, with rain and the wind crying and rising in squalls, slow at first but gradually quickening in number and intensity. To these the square-rigged ship would swing her great yards so that the sails accepted the strength of the wind from the ship's port beam or abaft the beam and, as the freshening wind drew aft, the yards were squared in, always to get the best force and use from the wind. Often these westerlies howled and raged for days, bringing up a tremendous sea which could race unchecked by anything, for the southern is the water hemisphere, the sea hemisphere where only the spinal column of South America protrudes far south. If the sea rages high down there, it also rages true. The behaviour of these westerly storms is well known and thoroughly predictable to those whose business it is to sail the ships which use them. The gale having blown for a greater or less period out of the west or west-north-west (or sometimes almost continuously from north-west), with a falling glass, sooner or later the barometer will stand and then give a slight upwards flick. Then it is time to watch out! For the great wind will jump at once to south-west or south-south-west and roar harder than ever, bringing for a moment—until it gains undisputed control of all the sea—a confusion in the breaking crests, to run through which in safety the hard-pressed ship must be steered perfectly, and handled with skill. The yards must be quickly swung lest the ship be taken aback—'caught by the lee,' sailors call it, for the wind jumps round the stern instead of in front of the ship, as it often does in other areas. A square-rigged ship may be taken aback in either way.

It is the business of sailing-ship masters to know and understand these things, and that they do. The art of conducting their charges about the sea in safety calls for knowledge of the ocean weather. 'Running the easting down,' as sailing-ship men used to call this part of their voyages, was commonplace stuff, the very essence of voyage-making, and sudden jumps of wind, the risk of being taken a-lee, the risk of sudden great icebergs showing up ahead, the risk of being caught in a violent change of wind with too much sail aloft—these were the risks of the trade, to be watched for and guarded against by every shipmaster, and safely overcome.

Stress of weather should not have claimed the *København,* above all ships. Moreover there were other sailing-ships running their easting down at the same time, and these all made their passages safely. She was a better ship by far than any of these.

On what was to be her last voyage, the *København* sailed from Buenos Aires on the 14th of December, 1928. She carried a crew of sixty all told. One of the cadets had to leave the ship in South America, for personal reasons, and this cadet, who was aboard until midnight on the day before sailing, was later able to give evidence of the careful manner in which the sand-ballast was stowed. The crew included five deck officers, of whom one was also the ship's radio officer, two engineers and an assistant, a carpenter, sailmaker, baker, stewards, cook, and forty-five cadets, of whom the nine most experienced were rated as able seamen. All forty-five of these boys knew the ship well. All the officers and crew were Danes, though one cadet was born in England, one in Germany and another in Sweden. The cadet who survived said that the crew was a harmonious team and the spirit aboard was splendid. This was well known to be the case. The ballast was the same amount the ship had always carried, stowed in the same way—the full water ballast plus about 700 tons of sand. The sand was not just dumped in the fore and after holds. It was carefully secured against movement by planks constructed to form not merely a box to hold it but with shifting-boards down the middle, on the line of the keel, to prevent the sand shifting from one side to the other with the roll of the ship. The upper surface of the sand was also covered with planks and these were jammed down—'tommed' down is the correct expression—with balks of timber from the decks above, the whole designed and put together to prevent any possibility of the ballast taking charge, no matter how much the ship was flung about in the sea. (As ballast had taken charge in a good many ships, sometimes to their ruin.)

The passage across to Australia presented no difficulties, other than perhaps the risk of ice and the occasional gale. It was high summer. The boys looked forward to celebrating Christmas on board, and had taken special fare with them for this purpose. The average age of the boys was about seventeen and one-half. Captain Andersen was thirty-five, Mate Berthelsen thirty-two, Second Mate Jensen twenty-nine, Third Mate Petersen twenty-six. The oldest man aboard was Peter Bornich, the assistant engineer, who was forty-three. Nobody else was over forty. All hands looked forward to a quick run across to Australia, a pleasant interlude loading grain at some sunny outport, then the interesting stimulus of the Grain Race round the Horn to bring them home for the northern summer—two summers in one year, which was very pleasant.

When she was a week out from Buenos Aires the *København* was in radio touch with the Norwegian steamer *William Blumer,* about a thousand miles out from the South American port. The *København* was about a hundred miles to the south'ard of the steamer, and all was well aboard. Captain Andersen had been mate on both the ship's previous west winds runs to Australia and he knew how to sail that road. But after the exchange with the *William Blumer* no more was heard of the *København.* There had been no previous trouble with the ship's radio equipment, but at first, when there were no longer any reports, no great anxiety was felt. There might be some simple reason for a temporary radio breakdown and it was—well, it was almost unthinkable that the fine big ship could be claimed a victim by the sea. The sea may take any ship, of course, but the chances of loss to any ordinary cause in the case of the big steel five-master were—or ought to have been—very, very slim. The run from Buenos Aires to an Australian port should not have taken more than forty-two to fifty days—say, at the most fifty-five days. That time passed and there was no news of the ship. She did not answer any radio station. By mid-February the owners were in touch with all ships which had used the lonely west winds route, including the South Georgia whalers and the few tramp steamers which passed that way. There was no news. As far as they could do so, they checked on weather and ice reports for the area. There were no weather ships down in that part of the watery world which, at that time, was primarily of interest to a few whalers and the few odd sailing-ships still surviving, but there were no reports of exceptional storms. There were, however, reports of icebergs. The British steamer *Horatius* and the German steamer *Heidelberg* had both sighted icebergs on the west winds route, on about 42 and 43 south latitude. There had been ice, too, south of the Cape, on 43 and 44 south. All this was more or less normal.

By March the *København* was overdue—by March 21, seriously overdue. Exhaustive search was set going for her. Along her route towards Australia were several groups of sub-Antarctic islands, lonely places where the gales scream almost the year round and only the albatross and the sea elephant normally find shelter—places like Gough Island, Kerguelen, St. Paul and Amsterdam, uninhabited islands, some of which had castaways' depots placed on them to offer sustenance to shipwrecked sailing-ship crews (of whom there had been many). Several of these islets and islands were far to the south'ard of any route the *København* would intentionally follow; but she might have been dismasted, and be drifting helplessly towards the Antarctic. It was possible that something might be found of her or of her survivors at one of these islands.

Since no ships beyond the odd exploratory vessel or occasional little sealer ever touched at these remote and storm-swept islands, the East Asiatic Company organised a special search. The shipping world was shocked at the idea that so fine a ship was lost with her sixty young men, and there was plenty of help available. The Alfred Holt steamer *Deucalion,* a big cargo-liner ordinarily in the Australian trade, was sent to make a long and thorough search of all these places. She took additional radio equipment and people, and she searched even remote spots like Prince Edward Island and the Crozets. It was without result. The castaways' depots were untouched. There was no wreckage and there were no survivors from the *København* or any other ship, only the cold sea washing over the slimy rocks and dashing at the horrible cliffs. Other ships took up the search, all fruitlessly. The British steamer *City of Auckland* reported that she had heard the *København* using her radio at ten o'clock on the night of December 21, but the most thorough quest for any vessel which had heard the *København* after that, or any strange SOS, was as fruitless as the search for the ship herself.

The *København* had disappeared—utterly. But the East Asiatic Company did not easily give up the search for any trace of her. Sub-Antarctic waters cover a great area and are notoriously difficult and lonely: the dismasted derelict *might* still be afloat, somewhere, somehow. But the whalers both of South Georgia and the South Shetlands had seen nothing of her. The P. and O. liner *Beltana* and a Clan Line steamer searched islands where the *Deucalion* had not time to go. The company sent out a specially chartered ship, the *Mexico,* to search those islands as they had never been searched before, and there were seamen in the *Mexico* who could have recognised even a belaying-pin or a bull-whanger from the lost sailing-ship. It was all fruitless. The *Mexico* not only searched the islands, she ran over the *København*'s probable course, crossed the position from which she had spoken the *William Blumer,* spoke the settlement at Tristan da Cunha. These searching ships, the *Deucalion,* the *Mexico,* and the others, did more than take a cursory look into the few anchorages round the sub-Antarctic islands. They went wherever it was possible to go. They skirted the coasts, blowing on their steam syrens and firing signal-guns. But no castaways had been near any of those bleak islets for years. The *København* was searched for as no sailing-ship had ever been, before or since, but there was no real clue anywhere.

There were the usual false clues, of course, but fewer of these than usual. One only was worth real investigation. A missionary on Tristan da Cunha came up with a strange story that sounded as if it had something in it. The missionary, who had been on Tristan for three years, gave chapter and verse. He said he had seen a five-masted barque, painted black with a prominent white band (the *København*'s hull colours) in distress near the island on the 21st of January, 1929. The ship, he said, appeared to have no crew on board. Perhaps they were all dead. She was drifting under curiously shortened sail, and she seemed to be headed for danger.

According to the missionary there was no doubt about it.

She was five-masted [he said], but her fore or main mast was broken. A huge white band round the hull was the most prominent mark. It was on January 21, 1929, that she passed. The course she was taking was due north and, as she was roughly in the middle of the islands she would in the ordinary course of events have struck our beach where the settlement was. However, when still a long way off, she seemed to be drifting to the eastward. It was at this time that we watched her most. The sea was too rough for our boats, which are made of canvas sewn together, and so we could do nothing but watch her gradually crawl past and run inside the reefs to the west side of the island.

She was certainly in distress. She was using only one small jib, which appeared to be set from the bow to the broken mast, and her stern was very low in the water. It was almost down to the white band round the hull. This was all seen through glasses at a distance of three-and-a-half miles so we could hardly be mistaken. The usual charts of Tristan have no reefs marked on them but this is dangerous as the island is pretty-well reef-bound, especially so where the *København* went in. I estimated that she was within a quarter of a mile of the shore when we last saw her and the reefs stand out a mile and a quarter, so she must have been well inside. We saw her no more after that, and the place where she went in is quite inaccessible.

Several things were afterwards washed up, but I cannot say that these were from the *København*. Dovetailed boards with buff paint on them, boxes about three feet long by eight inches broad by eight inches deep, and then a thirty-foot flat-bottomed boat in September. . . . To me it is a complete mystery. It would have been impossible for the ship to drift free of the reefs again, once having been bound by them. Many questions remain to be answered. Why didn't she drop a lifeboat? Were they all dead? Had she been abandoned before reaching us? To such questions I can only answer that I do not know: but I am convinced that the ship which approached the Tristan beach so strangely was none other than the missing *København*.

This story, when it became known, was at first accepted at its face value, though not in Denmark. There were too many discrepancies about it. The observant missionary had failed even to ask himself the most elementary question, and that simply was, could he count to five? For no five-masted barque passed near Tristan da Cunha that day, or any other day that year. Investigation showed that the Finnish *four*-masted barque *Ponape,* outward-bound towards Australia with a cargo of pine from Sundsvall, did approach Tristan da Cunha on the afternoon of the 21st of January, 1929. The weather was fine; she had a full crew; she had no broken masts and was in no distress or danger whatever; and she at no time was nearer than six miles from any part of the island. Other people saw this ship from Tristan. It was customary, on a fine day, for the square-riggers to catch a glimpse of Tristan before beginning the often poor-visibility run of the west winds towards Australia. It gave them a useful check on their chronometers and showed that they were where they thought they were (a matter of importance to a sailing-ship, or any other ship). They had to run on some six thousand miles from there, and might go for weeks without good observations. . . . Instead of a phantom five-master creeping in on reefs out of the Atlantic mists, a well-found and competently handled four-master had sailed safely past the island, and continued about her business.

The *Ponape* had sighted icebergs, too. But she had seen nothing of the *København,* nor heard anything. What wreckage had come ashore on Tristan was definitely not from the big Dane. It was the ordinary flotsam and jetsam of the sea. Others on the island had sighted the ship, too, but they had recognised her as the four-masted barque she was.

Even this worthless 'clue,' however, was thoroughly followed up. Might there be a ghost of a chance that, after the *Ponape* sailed by, the lost five-master *had* so mysteriously arisen from the depths of the sea and sailed by, too? The British steamer *Halesius* went to the island to investigate. The *Halesius* closed with the inaccessible part of the island where the phantom ship was alleged to have disappeared. There was nothing there whatever—no wreckage, no sign that any ship had ever been wrecked there. Captain Samuels in the *Halesius,* having thoroughly investigated the story at Tristan, continued to Buenos Aires.

Even then the East Asiatic Company did not give up the search. The Norwegian motorship *Lars Riisdahl* was chartered at the Cape to search the remoter beaches of Southwest and South Africa as far as 25 degrees south latitude (there was a story that a lifeboat of skeletons had been found somewhere there: it had, but it was no boat from the *København* and the skeletons had been there for years). The *Lars Riisdahl* found nothing. The same lack of success marked a long search by the Adelaide Steamships Company's SS *Junee,* begun from Australia.

For over a year the company searched and searched again. The Southern Ocean is a vast area to cover and there was no network of shipping usually steaming down there, to call in for help. Between them all, the specially chartered or diverted ships—the *Deucalion, Mexico, Lars Riisdahl, Beltana, Junee, Halesius*—crossed and recrossed the *København*'s probable track a thousand times and looked thoroughly into every rock and islet, island and beach where anything from the big ship might possibly have been found. It was wholly without result. The great ship, which had built up in the few years allowed her a fine reputation for good voyages and for developing manhood in fine boys, was utterly gone.

There remained only the inquiry. But what good could an inquiry do? The excellent reputation of the *København* was well known. What more could be discovered about her or her probable fate? The captains, the builders, the naval architects, the pilots could only offer, each in turn, their tributes to the lost ship's exceptional excellence. The pilots who undocked the ship at Buenos Aires and took her to sea, the cadet who had been aboard until the last moment, added their knowledge and their tributes. *Everything* had been in order, so far as man under God could make it so— draught, trim, crew, stores, route, every conceivable detail of the voyage. The disappearance of the *København* could only remain a dark and inexplicable mystery, and the inquiring court so found. The court was held on the 15th of October, 1929, in Copenhagen, under President Kuhl, with four nautical assessors, Commander Schultz, Captains Egense and Stabell, and Rear-Admiral Cold. All these were experienced sailing-ship men. All knew the *København*.

All known facts were put before the court, painstakingly, with that same thoroughness which had marked the search for possible survivors. The ship had bought 698 tons of ballast at Buenos Aires. She had left that port with a displacement of 5,150 tons, drawing 17 feet 2 inches of water. She was in perfect condition and perfect trim. The ballast was properly secured. The radio could send 1,200 miles. The metacentric height was 3.04 feet. Stability was excellent. There was some criticism that only nine able seamen were in the crew, and these were promoted cadets. But the court found that the ship was well manned (as indeed she was).

After due deliberation, the court could only find what all seamen already knew—that whatever Act of God had taken the fine Danish ship happened so quickly that no SOS could be sent, no boats lowered, not as much as a raft put over the side. What could have caused so sudden and complete an unpredictable calamity? The answer could be provided by conjecture only, but collision with ice was probably the most likely cause. The long sharp horn of some low iceberg lying all but awash in the dark seas could rip the steel ship's bottom open as she sailed by, driven onwards before some strong west wind, and she may well then have gone on down in her stride. Everything was lashed down on deck for the west winds passage. There would be nothing to float away—nothing, that is, but the watch on deck, the two officers and the twenty-four boys. They would not float for long.

So the court found, and the case of the *København* was closed. But the mystery remains. She may have been claimed by the ice— and she may not have been. She might have blown over. The big steel sailing-ship in ballast did not need to be unstable if she were caught badly by the lee in some violent, sudden shift of wind. The great fore-and-aft sail on the aftermost mast (which had been designed as a double spanker but was later altered to a single sail, with the middle gaff removed) perhaps would not come in, for such sails were brutes to handle. Such a sail, set right at the aftermost end of the ship, would have a very serious effect on her manoeuvrability if it could not be taken off when it had to be. A five-masted barque is a long ship, and hard to handle. The wind, flying suddenly across the stern of the ship and catching her sails aback from the lee side, would also blow the spanker over and, in so doing, further tend to force the ship's head to windward, more and more hopelessly aback. Such a crisis could be fatal. The very massiveness of the powerful rig might then help to undo the splendid ship, and her unyielding strength destroy her. There might not be much time to get the spanker off. Caught aback, temporarily unmanageable, the sails with the wind on that side of them where it should never be and they were not designed to be handled, the great ship might list and list until the heeling decks became unlivable—and all this in a matter of seconds only. The wind gives little warning! In a wild madness of screaming wind, flying spray, blown-aback sails thundering against unyielding steel masts and steel stays, the lovely ship may have lurched so violently that at last even the well-secured ballast in the holds broke from its restraining planks and, flung into the ship's lee side, added its weight to the force of the wind to press her down until she went right over. That *could* happen. Such things had happened, in other ships. No time for boats, for radio signals! For this kind of accident would be sudden, and swift, and final, and nothing would drift away. The ship would go down as a whole.

All this, of course, is pure conjecture. But I have seen this sort of accident nearly destroy a large four-masted barque, in the same part of the world.

THE FISHERMEN OF BRITTANY

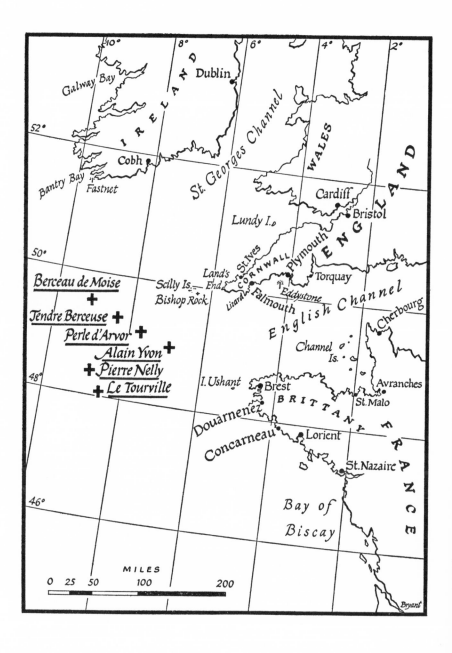

MILES

0   25   50   100   200

CHAPTER TWELVE

Six Ships: Seventy Men

LLOYD'S NOTICE

OVERDUE VESSELS

PIERRE NELLY.—Land's End Radio, Dec. 6.—Following received from Brest–Le-Conquet Radio at 12.21 P.M., G.M.T.: XXX (urgency signal), vessels able to give information of fishing vessel Pierre Nelly, of Concarneau, registered CC 3427, 73 tons, are requested to advise Brest–Le-Conquet Radio. Characteristics of hull: Colour, clear grey lower part, dark grey upper part, two blue masts with white (? yards), cabin clear blue upper part, dark blue lower part.

—Land's End Radio, Dec. 6.—French trawler Pierre Nelly: Following received from Brest–Le-Conquet Radio at 4.22 P.M., G.M.T.: Sighted for the last time on Monday, Nov. 29, position lat. 49 50 N., long. 8 W.

THE mariners of Brittany provide three-fourths of the seamen of modern France. It has been like that, more or less, since Julius Caesar passed that way in 56 B.C. From picturesque little ports such as Concarneau and Douarnenez, Camaret and Etel, Paimpol and Lesconil, and from the larger ports like St. Malo, L'Orient, and Brest, brave men have gone to sea for centuries to man the ships of France, both naval and mercantile. The beautiful big square-riggers

which were France's last Cape Horn fleet were manned and commanded, very largely, by the men of Finistère. The rugged Grand
Banks barquentines, for which the French fishing fleet was once
noteworthy, were manned almost exclusively by Bretons, who
braved the tempests, the fogs and the ice of the notorious Banks
in their small dories. Today the men fish off Greenland, off Iceland,
and off Bear Island, on the Grand Banks and off the White Sea, in
splendid modern trawlers which, though they no longer need launch
dories over the side, still face the sea often at its worst and most
vicious, and wrest their harvest in spite of all the tempests that
can be flung against them.

For many more centuries than they have been going across the
Atlantic to the Grand Banks, the fishermen of Finistère have been
sailing out to fish on the rich banks off their own coast, in that
stormy triangle of furious waters which stretches from the coasts of
Brittany to Fastnet and Cornwall. Since Brittany was known by its
ancient name of Armorica and then, as waves of migrating Britons
came from Wales and the West of England, by the new name of
Lesser Britain, its mariners and its fishermen have been famous for
their skill, their rugged independence and their lion hearts. The
Breton peninsula at France's western extremity juts out into the
wild Atlantic, and the often stormy waters of the English Channel
merge with the even stormier waters of the Bay of Biscay off that
coast. The 'Bay,' as sailors call it, has a deservedly bad name. Those
who go out there in little ships to gather the harvest of the sea
must be brave seamen with brave ships, if they are to survive.

Until a year or two ago, the Biscayan fishing fleets included many
picturesque sailing craft, sturdy yawls with strong and seaworthy
hulls which could stand any punishment (except grinding on rocks),
and a good short rig to help them fight out the gales. Long rods
fixed on the fore-deck, looking like a huge beetle's antennae, added
to their distinctive appearance. They were gaily painted vessels
with powerful lines and, skillfully handled by Breton skippers and

crews, they fished the stormy offshore waters year in, year out. They included lobstermen and crabbers as well as tunnymen, who trailed their lines from the huge rigged-out rods longer than their masts, and they took a good harvest from the rich Sole, Jones, Shamrock and Parsons banks, among others. They also went far afield, to the Irish Sea and the west of Ireland, to the North Sea, to the coast of Portugal. Among these hardworking, hard-driven vessels, none were better handled or better known than the ships of Concarneau and Douarnenez.

Now those old-time ships have mostly gone. A few sail out of the port of Etel, and the hulks of some can be seen up the river by Douarnenez and elsewhere. In their place today is the powered vessel, the sturdy little diesel trawler which fishes from the Breton ports by the hundred. To use the wind for sole power is no longer economic, when markets have to be served on time and all is hurry. But the diesel trawlers and tunnymen face the same conditions. Nothing in the fishing life and nothing in the stormy Bay has changed just because men now go to sea in powered vessels. The prevailing winds of the Bay of Biscay show no tendency to change, and just as many severe gales are experienced. They come on especially from the south-west, as they have always done, with violent squalls, rain, hail and murk. They bring up the same kind of heavy sea they always brought, and they not only drive in their mighty rollers to grind ships upon the rocks all round the lee shore of the Bay but they build up dangerous currents to help take toll of ships, setting inshore always towards danger, never away from it.

A low barometer, heavy cloud banks with lightning to the westward, lovely but threatening sunsets or dawns, often with a big and ominous swell—these still presage the same kind of gales they always have done, and it behooves good mariners to watch out for them and to take shelter in time, if they command ships which require refuge in storms. The collection of navigational dangers round the peninsula of Finistère is as bad a lot as is to be found anywhere facing the watery world—cruel rocks, often jutting far out to sea, and others rising steeply from great depths; iron-bound coasts that are a lee shore in all westerly and south-westerly winds; sets and drifts and currents and tides all making in towards the land, where ferocious rocks wait to rip at the bottoms of good ships; banks and shoals inshore and far offshore to set the breakers rolling and thundering, like an attack of marching wet mountains gone mad— all these are the background of the Breton sea fishing industry, the accepted background, the well-known risk.

In the autumn and winter months especially, the gales blow hard, though inland in the lovely valleys it may be sheltered and even pleasant and warm. Most of the gales begin from south or south-west, which are not cold quarters in the northern hemisphere. The wind usually goes round through west to north-west, often blowing out from there. But there can be no certainty, merely because it does go to north-west, that the gale is through. It can just as easily swing to south-west once more and begin all over again, blowing ferociously for days. A slight rise in the barometer with a shift of wind indicates only that it will blow harder. The old sailors' saying about 'Long notice long last, short notice soon past,' may have originated in the Bay of Biscay, for it is very true that the longer the bad conditions are foretold, the longer will they last and the worse they will be when they come. Bad conditions are very often foretold round the northern waters of the Bay. The gales know no fixed rules, especially near the land. They know only how to try ships and seamen to the utmost.

These were the kind of gales that blew in November and December of 1954—of any year, for that matter. They seem to have been particularly bad in '54. The French, like other seafaring nations, do all they can to make good forecasts available to their fishermen, but the weather stations (apart from the service from ships) are on the lee side of the North Atlantic. A gale may reach the ships before knowledge that it is coming reaches the forecasters, or it may be locally more severe than the indications known ashore would lead the weather experts to foresee. The information sent in from weather-ships must be collated first. Gales do not wait to be collated. They march, and they know how to march furiously and to wreak destruction. The curves of storms are often impossible to predict with accuracy and even the most skillful meteorologist knows that he has much to learn. Ships can still be caught out and, indeed, they often are—sometimes six at a time.

Like, for instance, the six little fishermen of Concarneau and Douarnenez, which went missing in the autumnal gales of 1954.

The *Pierre Nelly* of Concarneau was a stout little ship and strongly built, though she registered only 73 tons. She was six months old when she sailed from her home port on the 17th of November, 1954, bound out on the usual 14-to-15-day fishing voyage to the banks off the south of Ireland. Skipper of the *Pierre Nelly* was Yves Ollivier, whose skipper's certificate was about the same age as his ship. Skipper Ollivier was twenty-five years old, and he had qualified only during the preceding April. He looked at the pleasant scene of pretty Concarneau as he took the diesel trawler and her crew of nine good men—mostly very young, too—from the dock and to sea. He was always fascinated by the contrast between the old and the new, round Concarneau's interesting waterfront. Though he was brought up there, he never tired of admiring the scene. The picturesque old walled town on the fortified island of Ville-Close where the ancient ramparts still stood, all in perfect repair, faced, across the narrow basin of the inner harbour, the most modern fish-handling and auction sheds in the west of France. With their modern architecture and their smooth efficiency, the fish wharves were as interesting in their way as the old town was, with its single main street, the old Rue Vauban, and its narrow lanes of little houses packed so closely together, as if they were anxious to draw support and company from their neighbours. Ville-

Close had a long, long history, and Yves Ollivier knew that. The Bretons there had thrown the marauding English out in 1373: somehow 1373 did not seem so long ago as long as his eyes rested on the ramparts of this medieval town, where there was no jarring note; but with a turn of the head he was immediately back in the mid-twentieth century.

As his sailors let go the few lines and he slipped stern-first from the fish wharf, the stream of Concarneau's morning traffic was passing by—old ladies dressed in black, with wonderful lace caps pinned to their well-kept hair, some high, some low, some with curved flaps like eaves and some straight upright, like starched cylinders, all of best quality lace, handsomely kept and clean and lovely. He knew which village the old ladies came from by those lace caps, each village a different type. Men in peaked sailor's caps, dungarees and clogs walked along the quayside, too, and the morning bustle of the fish market was just drawing to a close. The *Kerguelen,* the *Risquetout,* the *Iris, Sylvia, France Libre,* and *Claude Françoise,* having put out their catches to be sold, were moving along the dock to take in ice and fresh water and diesel oil for another voyage, just as he had done earlier in the morning. The new wharf had all these things conveniently laid on.

Some of the men were carrying huge baskets of fresh-baked bread in wonderful long loaves. Others had crates of wine on their shoulders, or parcels of meat—not much of that. It was foolish to take meat to sea when the Lord provided all the fish you could eat once you were out there. In the far corner of the docks were another eight or ten of the Concarneau fishermen, some under repair, a few laid up, some new and just fitting out. They were a mixed lot—there were hardly two the same. The strong hull of yet another new ship rose from the ways at the wooden shipyard just beyond and she, too, was of yet another type. A few of the ships were steel, but most were wood. Nearly all had a bit of sail bent, if only a small mizzen for lying-to. The more elderly ships had the older type hulls, in clear descent from the sailing craft. Some of the new ships had hulls like big lifeboats—not ship's boats, real lifeboats like those stationed round the coasts to be launched when ships are in grave danger. Some hulls were double-ended, others square-sterned, some almost straight, others with a lovely sheer. Indeed, there was a regular boat show of ships alongside at Concarneau and, across the basin, there were even more, one of them an old-time sailing yawl not now in commission, with a line of fat gulls squatting along her jib-boom, her only crew. The day of such ships was past and well past, thought Skipper Yves, looking about his decks with pride as he backed his ship, turned her quickly and skillfully in the middle of the basin, applied starboard helm and headed at good speed for the waterway that passed the eastern end of Ville-Close and led to sea. As he passed the island he took a quick look through the big water-gates. The inevitable artist was sitting there, well wrapped up against the chill November air, painting away at a bit of canvas on an ancient easel. Skipper Yves reflected that he had never known Concarneau without its quota of artists, though most of them still loved to paint the sailing tunnymen, not the fine new diesel trawlers. They refused to be up-to-date. The artist looked up a second as the *Pierre Nelly* hurried past, her smooth diesel purring and her bow-wave treading back the racing tide. Then he looked back at his canvas at once.

Aha, thought Skipper Yves, he will not be adding this fine ship to his masterpiece! Not at all. Give him one of those clumsy big yawls or a crabbing ketch with lots of sails and a clear deck, and a big tiller for steering, and a horrible liking for being forced upon leeward rocks in a breeze of wind! Those sailing-vessels were all right with lots of sea-room, but the rocks of Finistère were littered with their wrecks after every hard winter gale. It was not like that now! No sir, not like that, with fine powered vessels which could

[223]

keep themselves off rock-bound coasts. . . . Skipper Yves opened the throttle wider, let the diesel open up and give him the thrill of splendid power.

The *Pierre Nelly* raced along. Past the Pointe de Beg-Meil with the pretty beaches of the little seaside resort of Beg-Meil itself, then over the bay and past Lesconil (which sent its own quota of fishermen to sea), round the Pointe de Penmarc'h and thence on a straight course to pass between the Île de Sein and the Pointe de Raz, the little ship made good speed, though she was so small out there in the open waters of the bay. A dark, heavy swell made her roll and heave and plunge too, but she rode the big seas well. The weather was not bad, for the moment, and the forecasts indicated at least a few days of favourable fishing weather. The *Pierre Nelly* and her crew of nine good men sped on, across the mouth of the great Bay of Douarnenez (whence other diesel fishermen were coming out to sea) and onwards to pass the Île d'Oussant well clear, and make for Jones Bank—about eighty miles due west of the Bishop Rock by the Scilly Islands—while the going was good. There she would scoop up fine fat fish from the sea, which would bring a good price at the Concarneau auctions.

Next morning, on the banks, Skipper Yves sent a message by radio telephone. *"Pierre Nelly en route pêche,"* was all he said—the *Pierre Nelly* was on the way to fish. That told nobody anything. The skipper might be young in years but he was an old hand when it came to not giving away information. Let them make of that what they could.

He would have been the most surprised man upon earth or sea if he had known that that was the last message the *Pierre Nelly* would ever send; but it was. For, some time after that, between the 18th of November and the end of the month, the *Pierre Nelly* disappeared.

So did the Concarneau ships *Perle d'Arvor,* 66 tons, with a crew of 9 under Skipper Jean Gestalin, aged 33, which sailed the day before the *Pierre Nelly;* the 57-ton *Berceau de Moïse,* crew 9, Skipper Jean-Marie Cadiou, aged 47, which sailed on the 23rd of November; the 39-ton *Alain Yvon,* crew 9, Skipper Firmin Portal, aged 34, which sailed on the 24th; the 86-ton *Tourville,* crew 10, Skipper Ambroise Signour, aged 23, which sailed on the 25th; and the Douarnenez 53-tonner *Tendre Berceuse,* crew 10, Skipper Le Bot, aged 50, which sailed from her home port on the 20th of

—Brest, Dec. 5.—The deep-sea tug Rhinoceros left here to-day to try to find the **ALAIN YVON**, one of five French trawlers missing since a storm nine days ago. An R.A.F. 'plane reported sighting the **ALAIN YVON** on Friday (Dec. 3). Maritime officials have had high hopes that at least this ship would soon return to her home port. The search for three other trawlers from the Breton port of Concarneau and a fifth from Douarnenez is concentrated on the area between Brittany, Cornwall and south-west Ireland. R.A.F. 'planes have joined 'planes from Lorient in patrolling the area. About 50 men are on board the five missing trawlers. (See issues of Dec. 4 and 6.)
—Land's End Radio, Dec. 10.—Following received from Brest–Le-Conquet Radio at 2.44 P.M., G.M.T.: French trawlers **TENDRE BERCEUSE, PERLE D'ARVOR, ALAIN YVON, BERCEAU DE MOISE, PIERRE NELLY** and **LE TOURVILLE** are now considered definitely lost.

November for a ten-day fishing cruise to Parsons Bank and the Shamrock, which are closer inshore than the Jones Bank.

What destroyed all these ships so utterly and rapidly that they sent no distress messages, left no survivors and—except for the *Pierre Nelly,* whose empty boat drifted ashore on a beach in the Scillies afterwards—left no trace of themselves anywhere? They were not wrecked on Finistère's rocks, as the old sailing fishermen had sometimes been. They had good power to keep themselves off rocks, so long as their diesel engines were in working order. But the broken hulls of none of them ever showed on any rocks or, indeed, were found anywhere. It was obvious, when long search showed no trace of any of the six, that it was not a combination of rocks and storm which had finished them. It must have been the storm alone. They were not smashed up so much by the sea, but *in* the sea—and that, said the old-timers, the good stout sailing-vessels rarely were, for they knew when to yield and when to fight, whichever was the best tactic in a violent gale. The lee shores and the rock pinnacles took them, but the sea did not swallow them as it had taken these six modern diesel fishermen.

And, asked the old-timers, too, what about those very youthful skippers? Two of them, aged twenty-five and twenty-three—may they not have been *too* young, with all their experience in mech-anised ships, never knowing really the ways of the ocean in full storm as one learns in sail? There was a lot of shaking of old heads, and of some heads not so old. Had the too-rapid expansion and mechanisation of Biscayan fishing fleets led, perhaps, to the tolera-tion of some—well, perhaps indifferent building practices, or errors in design? And what about the weather information? These young fellows grew to rely on that, flicking a switch and twiddling a knob to hear the radio. It had not been so good, for really awful storms blew up towards the end of that November and the broadcast warn-ings, said the fishermen, were both late and inadequate. But the sea and the sky had given their local signs to men who could see them.

On the night of the 25th there was a very bad gale, and it was even worse during the following night. There were brief periods of better weather, and the *Alain Yvon* and *Tourville* had gone out during these. Again on the night of the 29th there was a dreadful gale, a full tempest, which came on quickly without, indeed, any real respite from its predecessor. These were typical November Bis-cayan gales and, though severe, they were not exceptionally so. They were bad enough, and a vile sea raged over all the fishing banks and thundered at the black rocks of Finistère, as if God were angry that they had stood there so long and was bent upon destroying them. The little ships were among many which were trying to ride out the storm on or near the fishing banks. Once caught there, there was little else they could have done, though they could have run before the south-west wind towards the shelter of the Irish or the Cornish ports, had they run in time. When the seas grew too big and broke too violently, they dared not run.

They were more vulnerable from aft, running before wind and sea. Unlike the buoyant old ketches and yawls, they did not always lift their counters high enough to the raging seas and—also unlike the sturdy, windswept old yawls—they had many openings in their decks, perhaps vulnerable openings. They had to have air-intakes somewhere to keep the diesels going, and ventilation for the engineers below. There had to be some form of engine-room skylight. Unlike the sailers, too, they had developed big deckhouses, which often grew up high upon the main-deck aft, where the ship sat heavily in the water with the weight of her engines and her fuel. The ships were low 'midships, the better to work their fishing-gear— the nets and trawls with which they took their cargoes from the sea. A big deckhouse might catch a lot of wind in a gale. A glassed-in bridge or a skylight might easily be stove in by a sea sweeping over the low stern; if water got below, the diesel would not work for very long. . . .

After the bad storms, day followed day and none of the five ships from Concarneau or the *Tendre Berceuse* of Douarnenez came back to port again, or put in for shelter anywhere. At first they were not missed. Four of them were last heard using their radio telephones—they all had such equipment, in good order and powerful—on the 26th and, when they were not heard afterwards, it was at first considered that probably their aerials had blown down. Other little ships whose aerials had gone came safely back to port, at the termination of their fishing cruises. There were one or two reports that such and such a ship among the missing six had been seen, when a skipper came back or an aircraft pilot flying in the area reported some swift glimpse of a little fellow struggling in the great sea but did not get time really to identify the ship.

There were many ships. Fishing registration numbers are hard to read, especially from the air. This is particularly the case when— so great is the local tradition of fishing—even the numerals 1 and 4 are painted to look like fish-hooks, and every other numeral which can possibly be given one has a fish-hook flourish somewhere. The sighting reports were false, unfortunately, but who was to know that at the time? Anxious relatives grasped at any hope, eager only for their loved ones to come in from sea.

The search for possible survivors was hampered, as it too often is in the case of fishing vessels, by the fact that the ships were not missed soon enough and, when they were, their last positions were not known. A thorough search by sea and air was rapidly organized when real fears were felt for the vessels and their crews. Royal Air Force aircraft helped, and French naval vessels and rescue tugs searched all the banks. Concarneau sent out a special vessel to aid in the search, which was further hindered by more gales. While the search was in progress, the little fishing vessel *Lilas Blanc* of Guilvinec, which sailed from Lesconil on the 3rd of December, was also lost. Scarcely was the search all over before yet another fisherman was added to the lists of the missing. This last was the 50-tonner *Michel Annick,* of Etel, a converted sailing tunnyman built in 1932 and reconstructed as a powered trawler in 1947.

The *Michel Annick* sailed from Etel on the 3rd of January, 1955, and was seen by another fisherman, the *Claude André,* nine days later. She was never seen again. Perhaps the old sailer resented the loss of her beauty, the heavy engine which had been built into her, and the openings in her decks. If men in their desire for greater 'efficiency' made her more vulnerable, then she would sink, when the chance came, and chances come easily in the Bay of Biscay. Winter fishing voyages are hard on old hulls which are perhaps strained by excessive power in their age.

The five ships from Concarneau and the one from Douarnenez were officially declared lost by the French Maritime Records Administration—l'Inscription Maritime—in Paris on the 9th of December, 1954, and the others in due course afterwards. The losses of so many ships led to an inquiry, not just official investigations into the separate cases but a more general inquiry into all of them. Other such fishermen had been lost since the war, though never in such numbers—the *Korrigan* of Lorient, with her crew of nine; the *Michel le Nobletz* of Douarnenez, with her crew of eighteen; the *Petit Jeannot* of La Rochelle and the *Pierre Ange* of Auray, each with a crew of eight, among others. Might there be something in the views which the old hands were urging, that the methods of construction and design of modern offshore fishing ships ought to be thoroughly examined? And, maybe, some of those very young skippers, unaware of, or unimpressed by, the limitations of their vessels, allowed themselves to be too greatly carried away by their aim to get good fish and risked their ships when they ought not, and so lost them. The loss of the *Tendre Berceuse* of Douarnenez might be accepted as a *'fortune de mer,'* as indeed it was, for the ship was thoroughly sound and no one could say that old Skipper Le Pot was young or inexperienced: but what about the *Tendre Berceuse,* and the new *Pierre Nelly?*

Under the energetic presidency of M. Maurel, Administrator-in-Chief of l'Inscription Maritime, with the experienced MM. Bureau and Drouglazet to assist him, a far-reaching inquiry was begun before the end of January at Concarneau, and carried on subsequently at Douarnenez, Guilvinec, Brest, and Etel. All who had any evidence or ideas to offer were heard, and the inquiry covered every aspect—the weather service, fishing vessels' stability, navigation, the qualifications and experience of skippers, radio communications, search, life-saving and rescue services.

The owners' organization at Concarneau, much concerned with the losses of its fine ships and men, put forward three suggestions —that there should be a better meteorological service in which perhaps the British could be asked to join, so that weather forecasts could go out both in French and English to cover the fishermen at work on the banks off the chops of the Channel; that the fishermen should be required to report their positions periodically so that, if search had to be made for them, it would at least be known approximately where to look; and that consideration should be given to providing an assistance vessel for the special purpose of looking after the big fleet of fishermen operating in the Bay of Biscay and on the western banks. All three were excellent suggestions and M. Maurel's committee recommended their adoption.

But there were other matters. Especially was there that problem of the best hull-form for diesel fishermen, and the best methods of construction. There had been various moves on the part of the Government to assist the building-up of a good postwar fishing fleet, in the way of cheap loans to finance construction and improved marketing facilities and so forth: had these brought the desired result? Or had, perhaps, a few disadvantages also crept in which must now be removed? The construction of offshore fishing vessels is an ancient and complicated skill, and the problems of design are exemplified by the profusion of designs created—not just one, developed by long experience, for each big port or particular stretch of coastline (as was more or less the case in the sailing days), but several, few of which could be the products of much experience at all. Was it not time to select the best and concentrate on those? And yet, fishermen are the most independent of mariners—not only in Brittany. The same problems could be found round the coasts of Britain. The offshore fishing vessel is a very dangerous type of ship to fool with, nor are the fishermen themselves necessarily most qualified to decide the answers to their problems. Local lore can be pigheaded sometimes, and local prejudice more so.

The root of the matter is that the fishing vessel must load her cargo in the sea, summer and winter, generally on shallow banks where gales bring up an exceptionally dangerous sea, short, steep, irregular and breaking. The vessel must provide a stable working-platform to work her gear and the fish; she must be able to accept all sorts of alterations in trim; she must not roll her catch of fish overside before it can be cleaned, yet she cannot have bulwarks really good enough to provide proper security for her crew. She has to be low 'midships though, in fact, she ought also to have as much freeboard—to be as high out of the water—as possible. If she has too much freeboard it is awkward to work her gear. If she has too little, she may be dangerous. She must have deck openings, but they are dangerous, too. Her big deckhouse, her low stern, her roomy open decks, her skylights and her low coamings are all possible points of vulnerability. She is at best a compromise—a compromise between the demands of her needs to fish and to survive. She has to be the right compromise if she is to survive a couple of hundred miles off shore in places like the Bay of Biscay, or off Iceland, in all the winter storms.

M. Maurel's committee was not the first to recommend that the whole matter called for further careful study. The Herring Board in Britain and the International Fishing Boat Congress of the Food and Agriculture Organization—a section of the United Nations Organization—have those matters in hand. It took a long time to evolve the best types of sailing form: after all, there has not been long to find by trial and error the best kind of powered fishing hull.

In France, the problem is being urgently studied. M. Maurel's committee, noting that Britain, Iceland, Germany and Portugal all provide assistance vessels for their fishing fleets, recommended that France should not content herself with the frigates *L'Aventure* and *L'Ailette* but base a special fisheries assistance vessel on Brest. Inflatable life-rafts for fishing crews, greater attention to some aspects of stability, to the use of the sea anchor and oil on the sea and the management generally of small vessels in great seas, more thorough inspection of fishing vessels both building and in use, and some revision of the requirements for offshore fishing skippers' certificates of competence were also recommended.

There is no reason whatever why small vessels, properly designed, built and handled, should not survive the onslaughts of the sea just as well as large vessels. But there can never be any lessening in the constant effort against the sea. Fishermen, like other seamen, must guard against that spirit of carefreeness and sometimes of fatality with which they accept the always present risks of their calling. Too-great familiarity with danger can bring its own serious risks. Sometimes the price is called for, in some horrible Bay of Biscay or North Sea storm and, when it is called for, it must be paid —even to the extent of six little ships, and seventy men.

8

TRAMPS

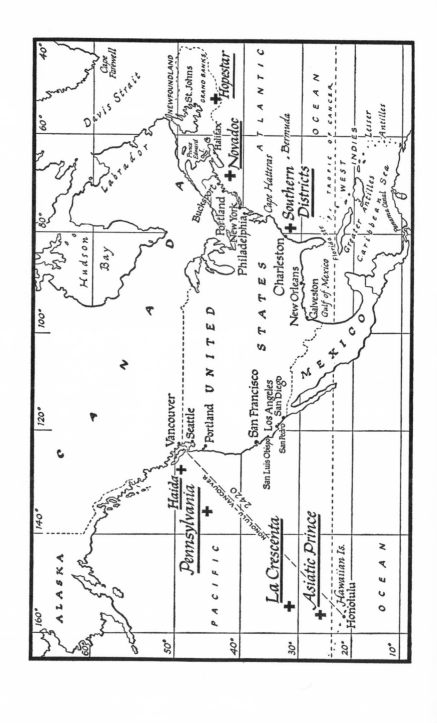

CHAPTER THIRTEEN

The Oil-Tanker

A 'TRAMP' is not a lesser breed of ship, despite the sneer in the name. A tramp is a dry-cargo vessel which carries bulk cargoes—grain, coals, cement, timber, ores and the like—anywhere, usually from one port or one range of ports to another single port. She does not ply for hire on a scheduled run, accepting the cargo shippers care to bring forward for her by a certain date. She is chartered —hired—for a voyage and she may go anywhere, upon no schedule at all. She may leave Europe with a cargo to take outwards—say, a haul of Welsh coals to Djibouti, in French Somaliland, or to Buenos Aires; or sulphate of ammonia in bags from Antwerp for Durban—and the skill of her owners is so to plan her voyages that she finds herself empty and ready for the next cargo in some part of the world where a good-paying cargo is to be found just at the time she is there, with as few as possible other tramps in the vicinity to compete with her. Passages in ballast are ruinous, unless the ship is a special bulk-carrier designed and costed for one-way traffic. The 'tramp' must be a good ship, fit to carry any sort of cargo, either heavy iron ore deep in her holds or stacks of light timber high on her decks, or grain in bulk or in sacks, or anything else that offers, heavy or light, be it cork from Lisbon or ore from Narvik. She is subject to precisely the same amount and kind of regulation and restriction as are other vessels. She must be built to a high standard, classed, insured, inspected, surveyed. In these days, she may fly an odd flag. She might find herself, for example, registered under the Liberian flag but owned by a Greek born in Armenia with Argentinian nationality and offices in New York and London. Whether she be registered as Liberian, Panamanian, Turkish, Dutch, British, Greek or Peruvian, she must be a classed and properly kept-up vessel or she will get no insurable cargoes anywhere and soon find herself held in port either by labour trouble or official restraint, or both. She often flies odd flags because these offer her owners advantages such as low taxation, and high taxation is much more ruinous even than ballast passages can be.

In these days of the mid-1950's, the tendency is for ships to become more and more specialised, and the tramp is a dying type of ocean-going vessel. There are specially built bulk-carriers for almost everything—raw sugar, molasses, iron ore, bulk cement, butane gas, even for Irish stout and Florida orange-juice. The earliest of these bulk-carriers was the oil-tanker, which has been plying the seas since the later days of the nineteenth century. The oil-tanker is often a tramp, too, though here again the modern tendency is against that. Many oil-tankers belong to the great oil companies or are time-chartered to them, which is to say that an expensive tanker is built by a shipping line but, perhaps even before the ship is due for delivery from her builders, some oil company or other hires her at a paying rate for a certain number of consecutive voyages or a period of years. Dry-cargo ships may also be time-chartered, particularly if some cargo-liner firm, building up a new trade or finding an old trade very quickly expanding, wants to make sure of extra bottoms at a time of high building costs and slow deliveries. Then the tramp will become temporarily a 'liner,' a vessel on a 'line'— conducting a regular service. Many modern tramps are just as splendid vessels as any cargo-liner, but their owners, not having built up that kind of business, do not operate a scheduled 'line.'

Just as she was the oldest of the bulk-carriers, the oil-company-owned or the tramp oil-tanker is or ought to be the most unsinkable of vessels. The old sailing-ship's hold was one big space. If the sea broke in anywhere it could overwhelm the lot. The early steamers put bulkheads in their holds to divide the engine-room and the boiler-rooms from the rest of the hold, for obvious reasons. If they were not seriously overloaded and the hulls were properly staunch, they were the more seaworthy because of these extra bulkheads, which were made watertight. As steamers became bigger there were more divisions in their holds, for convenience in loading and un-loading. The normal thing in a fair-sized steamer, tramp or cargo-liner was that she would have at least six or seven watertight bulk-heads. These were all athwartships—across the ship. She had no longitudinal bulk-heads, which would get in the way of her cargo.

But the oil-tanker, being a carrier of liquids, was different. She had to have her hold subdivided in such a way that the liquid she was carrying could slop about to the minimum extent, and expand or contract without seriously disturbing the ship's stability. This meant more compartments, all solidly watertight and gas-tight, too, and it meant longitudinal bulk-heads. As a bulk liquid carrier, with double-bottom fuel-oil tanks and her hold divided into many sep-arate tanks for oil, the properly designed oil-tanker then became virtually unsinkable. She could break in two and both ends would float. (She sometimes does.) Her seaworthiness was further en-hanced by the absence of normal hatches. Since her cargo was pumped in and out of her, she required no great deck-occupying openings, to be pulled apart every time she worked cargo and covered again for sea. She has hatches of the minimum size, steel-covered.

It is true that, since the hull is so seaworthy, an oil-tanker may be permitted to load to a deeper draught than a comparable cargo-carrier would be, and she often rides along practically awash in the sea. But her crew live in spacious quarters in the big after-castle, often in these days in separate cabins under the best of conditions, with a swimming-pool and all kinds of other amenities to divert them in their free time, and the deck officers are grouped amidships in a solidly built house surmounted by the navigating bridge. There is always a stout gangway extending the length of the decks, and no one is ordinarily required to descend to the main-deck in bad weather. This gangway is a very solid construction, carrying important pipelines beneath it.

In the Second World War, a good many tankers survived the most terrific punishment from shell, torpedo, mine and bomb, so long as they were not full of high-octane gas to blow them up. They either went up at once or they took a lot of sinking. In time of peace, a big ocean-going oil-tanker should be the last type of vessel one would ever expect to find on the overdue or missing lists. Yet there is such a vessel missing—missing just as mysteriously and as completely as any of the deep-laden engineless sailing-ships lost on the stormy Cape Horn road or the little fishermen from Concarneau or the sealers from Tromsø. There is only the one big tanker missing, as far as I know, though there are more than enough big tramps in that sad category. The missing tanker is the London-owned 6,000-ton *La Crescenta,* and the inquiries into her disappearance, unlike many such inquiries, uncovered some regrettable facts. The loss of the *La Crescenta* was, indeed, a tragedy of the bad days of shipping which, it is to be hoped, will never come again.

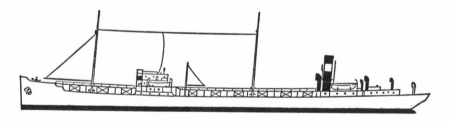

Fɪɢ. 3. Oil-Tanker, old type

The *La Crescenta,* 400 feet long, 5,880 tons, was built by the Furness Ship-building Company, in the north of England, in 1923 to Lloyd's requirements, and was classed 100 A 1 for carrying petroleum in bulk. She was designed originally to be a dry cargo ship for Norwegian owners, but was converted on the stocks. She was a tramp—that is, she went anywhere and carried such oil cargoes as she could find. She did not work for any one oil company on time-charter, or any other basis. Before she was very old or had had a chance to earn back much of the capital invested in her, she was caught in a slump, a serious shipping and trade slump which lasted for several years. She was, indeed, first put into service at a time when shipping had not wholly recovered from the false boom and artificial conditions of the First World War, but it is to be presumed that her owners knew what they were doing. She was an economical ship, carrying 8,500 tons as cheaply as possible. At first she had a crew of forty men all told, and she did reasonably well. But trade conditions continued to worsen. Freight rates, never high in those immediate postwar years, continued to drop. The *La Crescenta* fell on hard times. In this she was far from alone. The years of the 1920's were very hard for British shipping and for British owners and seamen—and not only for Britishers. Pay and conditions at sea were deplorable, and many seafaring men were out of work. A man was lucky to have a ship at all, though he might be required to work his heart out in her, and for a pittance. Officers were little if any better off. It was as bad ashore. Miners, skilled shipbuilders, craftsmen of all kinds were walking the gutters in South Wales and the north of England. Those were the years of apparent hopelessness when men's will to work was sapped, and twenty years of full employment and good conditions, long afterwards, failed to wipe out altogether the memories of these times.

The *La Crescenta* stayed at sea. Her crew was cut down—from forty to thirty-seven, then thirty-five, then thirty. Her deck officers were left in no doubt as to what was required of them—plenty of manual work through the daylight hours, and watch-and-watch on the bridge with no nonsense about an officer being an officer with his responsibility and prime duty the safe conduct of the ship. He had to be an able seaman too. A chipping hammer and the sludge-bucket were more often in his hand than a sextant. If he didn't like it, he could go ashore. There were plenty to take his place. The watch-keeping engineers were expected to perform prodigies of maintenance, too, and the engine-room complement was also cut to the minimum. Every economy that could conceivably be practised no matter how petty or how mean, or how serious, was enforced on the ship, as on so many ships of those days. The owners were at their wits' ends, too. But conditions towards '29 and '30 worsened. Qualified deck and engine-room officers of the merchant service, by the hundred, were walking the streets of all the large seaports, look-ing in vain for a job—any job. The *La Crescenta* became one of the British merchantmen which were run by a deck complement which, though their work was of the hardest, least skillful deck-labouring type, consisted entirely of 'deckhands' who held licenses declaring that they were competent to act as master mariners—deepsea master mariners, of any size ship. Those licenses had been hard to get and now, for the time being, at any rate, they were use-less.

Still it was not enough. The *La Crescenta* lost money and was laid up, and the deckhand master mariners were turned out in the streets. She was left to swing around a buoy in idleness for a year. Then, manned by a total crew of twenty-nine where forty had been few enough, with the master required to keep the second and third mates' daylight watches while they got on with cleaning sludge out of the dirty tanks or labouring about the decks, the *La Crescenta* went again to sea. The master and the chief officer had to help clean out tanks on the ship's ballast passages, too. She was allowed no carpenter for the very real and important maintenance work an ocean-going oil-tanker can be relied upon to supply, to say nothing of ordinary routine care and emergency repairs. There was some trouble with leaky rivets, but these had to be patched up. At the official inquiry into her loss, there was more than a suspicion that other more sinister 'economies' were put into practice, after the *La Crescenta* sailed from the United Kingdom for the last time. Her owners had been officially informed that her load-line could be moved up a little, which would permit the ship to carry more cargo and so earn more money, but to do this they had first to strengthen their ship in several important ways. To do these things cost money. It would increase the capital investment in a property which was earning very little. They refused the offer and did not strengthen the ship, but there was evidence—afterwards, when the *La Crescenta* had disappeared—that they virtually instructed the master to load her down to where the new marks should have been. If he refused, the inference was that they would find another master who would comply with their orders. They did not use these words but, according to the court, their meaning was plain. The master did not refuse. The *La Crescenta* was overloaded. Poor man, what could he do? He wrote home bitterly to his wife, telling her what was happening. He would not, he wrote, overload the ship for anybody. But he did. Maybe he just couldn't face the prospect of going home to his wife without a job. Like Captain Potts of the little *Yewvalley,* maybe he cherished the hope that some day he could run a little chicken-farm and be for ever finished with the sea: as with Captain Potts, too, it was never to be.

The *La Crescenta* sailed for the last time from the United Kingdom on the 13th of January, 1934. The port she left was Dundee. She was seaworthy when she sailed and she was far from overloaded then, for she was in ballast. She went off to tramp oil cargoes about the world, from the Black Sea, from the oil ports of California, from wherever oil was produced to wherever it was refined, wherever the odd, cheaply run ship able to deliver 8,500 tons of oil— maybe about 9,000 tons—was required. There was plenty of work to be done, depression or no depression. The difficulty was to gear down, to run ships cheaply enough to make ends meet on the low rates of freight then offering. Shipping is a fiercely international business. Ships must be as cheaply run as possible. The *La Crescenta*'s master carried with him instructions to "load all you possibly can"—and he knew what that meant. When the tanker sailed from Port San Luis, near San Luis Obispo in California, on the 24th of November, 1934, she carried 441 tons more cargo than she should have done. She was bound for Osaka in Japan, and she was overloaded by the best part of a foot of draught. Calculations made afterwards showed that her excess draught was 10¾ inches. It was the fall of the year in the North Pacific Ocean, and from Port San Luis to Osaka is a long, long way. The idea that bad weather is largely confined to the North Atlantic and that the Pacific is a more kindly ocean is erroneous. There was plenty of bad weather in front of the *La Crescenta* then. In normal circumstances and in her proper trim, it would not have bothered her. But that overloading, together with the fact that she had not been strengthened for it, was fatal.

The tanker, after being in radio communication with other vessels on the 5th of December, including the *Athelviscount,* disappeared. There was bad weather at the time, but it was not all that bad. In no sense could it be claimed to be exceptionally bad weather. No other vessels were lost in the vicinity, nor seriously damaged. When the *La Crescenta* was speaking to the *Athelviscount* earlier on the 5th of December, nothing was amiss. (Her draught would have come up by that time, through the usual daily consumption of the fuel oil necessary to drive her, until her Plimsoll line was submerged by only about half a foot.) The *Athelviscount* called her again that evening and could get no response, nor was anything ever heard again of the *La Crescenta*. There was never again any report of the ship herself at sea, or of any wreckage, boats, or bodies from her.

But there were some ugly stories ashore, ten thousand miles away in Britain. Something of the manner in which the ship was run was known to the seafarers' organizations. They considered that the ship was seriously undermanned and they had reason to suspect that, once away from home waters, she might have been overloaded too. The stories unearthed by the preliminary investigation conducted by the Board of Trade—forerunner of the Ministry of Transport—indicated that there was every justification for a searching inquiry. The *La Crescenta,* though the only tanker, was not the only British tramp which was lost with all hands that autumn. When she went missing, the tramps *Millpool* and *Usworth* had already been lost in the North Atlantic, the *Millpool* with all hands and the *Usworth* with serious loss of life. Shortly afterwards yet a third British tramp also went down in the North Atlantic, taking her whole crew with her. This was the steamer *Blairgowrie.* These three ships were westbound in the North Atlantic, carrying heavy cargoes, as the *La Crescenta* was westbound in the North Pacific. Between them, they killed ninety-seven British seamen. There were serious allegations that all four could not be regarded as properly seaworthy ships. They were alleged to be undermanned, and the *Millpool* and *La Crescenta* were also alleged to be unseaworthy. The cargo-carriers all used the old-fashioned rod-and-chain steering-gear. The *Millpool* was an old ship, built in 1906, but the three others were not old ships.

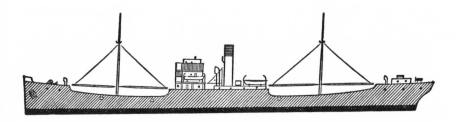

Fig. 4. Tramp steamer, old style

[243]

All four, in a way, were victims of the depression, but the seafarers' organizations observed that the owners, in some cases, recovered greater sums from the underwriters for the loss of the ships than the market value of the vessels, or indeed, the value at which the ships stood in their own books. The *Millpool,* for example, when she was lost, was insured against total loss for £14,000 with an additional £3,500 to cover the freight, but her value on her owners' books was £3,500. It was admitted in court that it was doubtful if she could have been sold for much over £6,000. In those bad times, the dependents of the lost seafarers had to suffer a rigorous and hated 'means test' before the most miserable public assistance was allowed them, and it rankled with the men that there was even a suspicion that the owners could profit from the losses of their vessels. There was considerable disquiet, and the matter was aired in the House of Commons.

For these and other reasons a searching inquiry was ordered by the President of the Board of Trade—then the competent authority —to be held into the losses of all four ships. The inquiry was conducted by Lord Merrivale, former president of the Admiralty Court, in May, 1935. It uncovered some very sad evidence about the states of all four ships, particularly the *Millpool* and *La Crescenta.* But what was even more serious, it disclosed the regrettable fact that the *La Crescenta,* on her last voyages at any rate, had been systematically overloaded "in conscious disregard of the law" and the court took the view that Captain N. S. Upstill, master of the *La Crescenta* and a competent master mariner, had done this at the express orders of the ship's managers in London. Moreover, the ship leaked notoriously. The pathetic letters which the captain had written to his wife were read out in court, insofar as they showed what the conditions had been like aboard—how he had been virtually commanded to overload, how he had had to go down in the ship's tanks himself to help clean out the filthy, heavy sludge, so poorly was she manned, how he had had to help fix leaky rivets, and to keep the junior officers' bridge watches for them while they also worked. Why he had done these things was only too clear. If he had not, someone else would, and jobs were much, much more scarce than masters.

The fact was mentioned in court that there *was* one possible trace of the *La Crescenta*. The last position she was known to be in was 34.51 North latitude, 163.24 West longitude—about halfway on her journey, or a little less—and, about a month after she had last been heard from, another ship steaming through this position noticed a lake of crude oil there, about a couple of square miles in extent. The court regarded this as evidence that the ship had *not* been blown up, through any reason. Had she been blown up, the undisturbed lake of oil would not have marked the spot where she went down a month afterwards. It would have disintegrated. No, all the evidence pointed to the fact that the *La Crescenta* had foundered, overwhelmed by the relentless antagonist she was unfairly handicapped to fight. The court found that the ship's fore-and-aft gangway was of insufficient strength to do its job. Power-lines, the telemotor steering-gear and communication between bridge and engine-room were all involved there. It found also that, in an emergency, there was insufficient crew aboard to cope with an accident, such as the sea smashing in part of the upper-works and sweeping into the engine-room. Records of previous voyages showed that the lost tanker shipped heavy water even in a moderate gale, and she had partially flooded her engine-room at least once before. Her electrical equipment and auxiliary machinery were in poor condition. The vessel was deep in the water, slow to rise in the sea in heavy weather. She had been repeatedly overloaded, said the court, during 1934. There could be little doubt that the *La Crescenta* went missing because her engine-room was flooded and she foundered too quickly for any SOS to be sent, or a boat to be got away. The too-small crew would be trying to cope with whatever damage had been caused her when the ship went down.

The owners were required to pay £3,400 towards the costs of the inquiry, and Lord Merrivale left no doubt as to what he thought of them. She was run by a single-ship company, and this was in the bad old days which all seamen hope are gone. The year 1934 when the *La Crescenta*'s crew were flung into the sea, hostages of the depression, marked the turning-point. If she had survived that year, perhaps she would not have been overloaded again, for freight markets and world business generally began to recover—very slowly at first but unmistakably and then, as the Second World War became inevitable, with a rush. The *La Crescenta* would have earned good dividends, given even a few more years of life, nor would she have been allowed to go again to sea so undermanned.

Such cases as the loss of the *La Crescenta* are rare, and yet, despite good freight markets, despite the most rigid surveillance of tramp and all other shipping, despite manning regulations, vigilant surveyors, strict rules and everything else, there still may be the odd case where an overloaded or otherwise unseaworthy ship may be sent to sea and the fault, really, be difficult to bring home to anyone. There is always the human element. Since the end of the Second World War two fine large British tramps, the *Hopestar* and the *Samkey,* and one American, the converted tank-landing ship *Southern Districts,* have disappeared at sea without as much as an SOS when they went or a scrap of wreckage to be found and, in each case, the subsequent searching inquiry found some circumstances which, though understandable and no one's fault, were— well, not so good. The *Hopestar* was found to be no less than 15 percent below the constructional strength she should have had, and *no one knew about it* or was really to blame: the *Samkey* went to sea imperfectly ballasted and, for that reason, could have rolled over: in the case of the *Southern Districts,* at least three members of the crew had left her just before her last voyage, on the grounds that they did not consider the ship seaworthy enough to go to sea in, though the master and officers obviously had not shared this view.

Of these cases the *Hopestar*'s, on the face of it, was the most inexplicable. The *Hopestar* was a good-looking tramp steamer, of 5,267 tons gross register. She was built of steel, to Lloyd's highest class, by Messrs. Swan Hunter and Wigham Richardson at New-

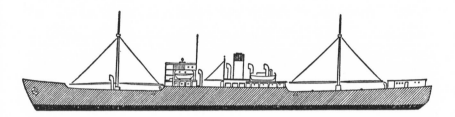

Fig. 5. Modern Tramp—flush-decked with raised forecastle-head

castle-on-Tyne in 1936, and there are no better builders than these. She was a flush-decked steamer with a raised forecastle-head, and her cruiser stern and slightly raked bow gave her a pleasing appearance. She was the normal steel single-screw shelter-deck type of tramp, with machinery amidships. She had seven watertight bulkheads, and a double bottom. The crew lived in a steel house on deck aft, which is the safest place. The main hull was riveted. There was some welding in the watertight bulk-heads, the inner bottom plating, and the shelter-deck. She was 410 feet long, and she had a service speed of 10 knots. Her life-saving gear was all that could be required—boats, buoyant apparatus, rockets, flares, line-throwing guns, everything. She had no less than three separate W/T sets, as well as a battery set for her lifeboats. She had been selected to be an Atlantic weather-reporting ship, sending out reports on the weather as she met it, on a regular schedule to the Air Ministry in London. She was well manned with a full crew of forty men all told, under Captain F. H. Dufton, who had been her chief officer before being promoted. On the face of it, disregarding the unknown factor of that perhaps fatal lack of her full strength, the *Hopestar* was just about the last ship one would expect to disappear into thin air—or deep water. She was, of course, as much subject to the ordinary hazards of the sea as any other apparently well-built and well-found tramp might be—strandings, heavy weather damage, fire aboard and that sort of thing. She escaped these. She had faced those risks for years and had steamed safely right through the Second World War.

And yet the *Hopestar* went missing on just another ordinary North Atlantic voyage. She left the Tyne on the 2nd of November, 1948, bound round the north of Scotland and thence to Philadelphia, by the northern route. She was in ballast. As was to be expected at that time of year, she soon met high winds and heavy seas, but she sent out her normal weather reports as usual and reported by W/T twice weekly to her owners. On the 14th of November, she sent a message to the owners' agents in Philadelphia saying that she had some heavy weather damage in the way of the deep-tank, and requested that Lloyd's surveyors, and ship-repairers, should meet her when she arrived at 10:30 P.M. on the 17th. (The surveyor or surveyors were to survey the damage and so put it on record as being in fact due to heavy weather, which meant that the insurers would pay for it, and the repairers were to do the work.) So the surveyor and the repairers were arranged for, as requested.

But the *Hopestar* did not arrive. She sent out no further signals. Though she was in the shipping lanes, no other vessel sighted her, or her boats, or anything or anybody from her. From the 14th of November, 1948, the *Hopestar* completely disappeared. There were no icebergs in her path. There was bad weather, of course, but she herself—a ship properly qualified to estimate the force of gales and the height of seas—had reported the wind at Force 9, which is a gale but no hurricane, nothing exceptional, just the usual

November nastiness such as all ships and shipmasters must expect from the North Atlantic or the North Pacific in more northerly latitudes.

There was, at first sight, nothing whatever to account for the *Hopestar*'s disappearance. A wartime mine, left drifting on the sea? Could she have been struck by one of these? But wartime mines do not drift about the high seas in anything like the numbers a landsman, aware of the enormity of the defensive fields laid round his country in wartime and of the profusion of aerial mining, might imagine. A live drifting mine in the open waters of the North Atlantic is so rare as almost to be unknown. It was just barely possible that a mine *might* have been in the area and have struck the *Hopestar,* but, if it did, it must have caused an awful disintegration of the ship for her to go down at once without an SOS or a chance to get as much as a raft away. Where had the mine struck her? Why was there no wreckage, after such disintegration? Her people lived aft, her radio operator lived amidships. She had boats both above the deckhouse abaft the funnel and on the bridge superstructure, further forward. Were they all smashed at the same instant? It must have been a terrible mine!

The ship, after all, was in ballast—hard to sink. All those bulkheads would not go at once. There had been, according to the official records, one case and one case only of a vessel being lost by striking a *floating* mine in or near the Atlantic since the end of the war. This was a ship named the *Cydonia* which was mined in the Irish Sea on the 21st of October, 1949. Moored mines which break adrift become harmless, and the *Hopestar* was in deep water where sunken magnetic or acoustic mines could not harm her, assuming that anyone had been so foolish as to waste such mines by sowing them there. No: the assumption was that no wreckage was found from the *Hopestar* because there was no wreckage to drift away and the boats didn't go adrift because they were still lashed in their gripes, stowed for the gale. And they were that way because there was no time, when the last moment of the stricken ship came, to do anything about them.

She might, perhaps, have broken in two and, not being an oiltanker, both parts quickly foundered. If she broke in two amidships there was nothing there to float away. Her radio operator might have been on one section, his equipment on the other. And yet, break in two? Well-built dry-cargo ships should never do that. There had not been a case of such a happening in the North Atlantic for the previous ten years. Why then should the *Hopestar* suddenly decide to break up and founder, in an ordinary gale?

Why, indeed? Her comparative lack of strength was not realised then. The *Hopestar,* after being overdue, was posted a missing vessel at Lloyd's in London on the 31st of December, 1948. But *why* was she missing? The days of 1934–35 were long past then. A quietly methodical but far-reaching preliminary investigation was set on foot. The designs, stability curves, plans of the ship as designed and as built, survey reports, repair bills and everything else about the *Hopestar* were carefully gone over by competent and industrious men—skilled marine surveyors who knew that though there will always be those inexplicable accidents at sea which are put down to Acts of God, there should in these days really be no sea 'mysteries.' If a big ship is lost, no matter how apparently mysteriously, somewhere there is a reason.

While the surveyors and the naval architects got on with their work, other investigators were finding out just what was the reputation of the ship. Could *anyone,* anywhere, throw any light on any possible cause of her loss? Not just conjecture—facts. They found an experienced seaman who had sailed as boatswain in the *Hopestar,* who declared that Captain Dufton lacked confidence in the vessel. (In that case, it was very odd that he remained with her. These were not the bad old days. There was plenty of employment for good ship's officers when the *Hopestar* sailed.) Yet the boatswain reported Captain Dufton as having said, at a Christmas party in 1947, that the *Hopestar* would break up.

"This damn thing is going to break in two some day, and I hope I am not there,"—these were his reported words. More important, there were reports that, on previous North Atlantic winter passages, there had been some 'waviness' in the ship's decks. Waviness may indicate structural weakness. The architects took another careful look at those 'as-built' plans. They discovered that there had been unauthorised alterations made in the hull of the *Hopestar* while she was still on the stocks, alterations which, though known to their surveyor on the spot, had never been reported to Lloyd's in London. They were perfectly proper alterations, but they had weakened the ship, and she should have had some compensating strength built into her to offset their effect. Since it was never officially realised—apparently—that she had been weakened, this strengthening had not been done.

The alterations themselves were relatively simple. While the ship was under construction, somebody—some engineering or marine superintendent, or an engineer standing by the new ship—decided that she would be the more easily worked if she had extra bunker-hatches, just a couple of small hatches cut into her shelter-deck through which good steam coal could be more quickly poured into her, and better trimmed. So the idea was put forward to cut such hatches in, though no such openings were shown on the approved plans. This presented no structural difficulty, and the surveyor representing Lloyd's, apparently regarding such an alteration as a very minor affair, did not report it. But these alterations reduced the strength of the hull of the *Hopestar* because they interfered with her longitudinal structure, breaking the carefully planned skeleton of steel beams and girders which builders in steel had learned down the years would safely carry and accept the stresses of a large metal ship. (A tramp, after all, is very much a large steel box. The box must be strong enough to carry heavy cargoes which may fill it or not fill it, and it must accept all the stresses likely to be put upon it in any condition of sea or wind, or safe loading or trim whatever.) If additional strength had been built into the hull in the way of these new openings (as it certainly would have been asked for had Lloyd's been properly informed), then the *Hopestar* would have been all right.

As it was, she was launched with little more than 90 percent of the conventional strength such a ship should have had, and her owners, taking the understandable view that since Lloyd's had classed her +100 A 1 they knew what they were doing, were not aware of this at all. No one, apparently, had ever worked it out. So the *Hopestar* battled with the sea for the following decade, which included the whole of the Second World War, at only 90 percent of her proper strength, and she suffered no harm. All this goes to show, one would think, how adequate Lloyd's rules must be.

But then the ship, having done so well, was altered again. Again she was weakened, and again the weakening went unnoticed and unreported. And again, it was all very plausible and—apparently —good seamanlike sense. The ship as originally built had two main boilers and a donkey boiler, for economy. She would be a better ship with three main boilers and so, in 1947, the old donkey boiler was removed and a third main boiler put in, in its place. This made her more efficient, but it also caused some further cutting of her steel structure. The work was done on the Tyne, though not by the original builders. Lloyd's representatives were not informed. After these alterations, which would have been all right of themselves, the *Hopestar* was down to 85 percent of her proper strength. This was serious, for the classification of +100 A 1 and the freeboard assigned the ship were in fact not justified by her actual strength.

To find out who was to blame for this unusual condition of

things and to prevent such accidents in future, a Court of Formal Investigation was constituted in London before a judge and three assessors, and the court sat for thirteen days in January, 1950, to sift things through. The *Hopestar* had sailed on her last voyage in perfect trim, with 2,363 tons of ballast properly stowed and secured and 1,175 tons of coal. Her maintenance and general upkeep were satisfactory. Her last-known position was about 150 miles south-east of Sable Island. At no time did the weather she met exceed normal winter North Atlantic conditions. Other ships in the area were not in serious trouble. Her last message, reporting some damage, showed no urgency. She had not altered course towards Halifax, as Captain Dufton could have done had there been any reason for it.

Four possible causes for the *Hopestar*'s disappearance were put to the court: the first, that she broke up because of insufficient strength; the second, that she struck a mine; the third, that she was overwhelmed by heavy seas; and the fourth, that her boilers burst and blew her up. The third, the court held, was "unlikely in the extreme" and ruled it out, and so was the fourth, for the boilers were in good condition. The possibility that she had struck a mine was one which "cannot be altogether dismissed, but the Court is of the opinion that the possibility is a remote one." The court registered the opinion that though it was unlikely in the extreme that the *Hopestar* had struck a floating mine, "it feels that the possibility of this happening cannot be altogether ignored."

But it left little doubt as to its real opinion of what had been the most probable cause of the tragedy. It was the structural weakness of the ship caused by those alterations, both of which had been made in a part of the hull where sagging and hogging strains (bending and breaking movement) were at their highest. If it had been known that the *Hopestar* was in fact only 84.3 percent of the strength laid down in the rules, she would not have been allowed to go to sea. The court added that there had been an error of judg-

[253]

ment on the part of the surveyor who failed to report the original alterations, made worse by the further alterations some ten years later. Under the accepted standards, however, the *Hopestar* was seaworthy for the actual ballast passage on which she was lost, but she was *not* seaworthy for the loaded passage she was chartered to make to the Mediterranean from Philadelphia afterwards. This indicated to the court that there must be something wrong with the accepted standards for such passages, and it suggested that the matter of stresses in big steel ships on ballast voyages was one which ought to be further investigated. The court could not decide definitely that it was unseaworthiness which caused the ship's loss, but the "most probable cause" was deficiency in strength. The court therefore found, after the best part of a fortnight's thorough investigation, that the loss was probably caused by the *Hopestar* breaking in two in bad weather owing to insufficient strength, but added "there is an outside chance that striking a mine caused or contributed thereto."

The first result of all was a tightening in procedure to make sure that such a case did not arise again, and ships which were classed as 100 A 1 were in fact that, in all respects. The next result was a civil case brought against the owners for damages. Forty men had lost their lives, and most of them had left dependents. If the owners had sent an unseaworthy ship to sea and by so doing had caused the loss of those forty men, then they were liable. A test case was brought against them by one of the widows, acting on behalf of herself and her infant son. She claimed that her husband had been lost because the *Hopestar* was unseaworthy and deficient in strength, and the crew had been exposed to danger by the owners' negligence or breach of duty.

This case, too, went on for days. It was not an easy one. The Ministry Court of Inquiry had not in fact ruled that the *Hopestar* was unseaworthy. There was no doubt that the *Hopestar,* at the time of her loss, was deficient in strength. That was accepted, but it was quite another thing to allege and to prove in court that her owners knew of this and, knowing, had deliberately kept the ship at sea. All the evidence was the other way. They knew, or they should have known, of the second alterations and their effect, but it had never been shown at all that they had any reason to suspect that the ship was then already weakened. After all, she had made a good many hard voyages and she had gone right through the war. She was twelve years old when she was lost, and, during those twelve years, nothing had happened to her on previous voyages to give a prudent owner cause for alarm. The repairers who put in the third main boiler had a duty to call the attention of Lloyd's to what they were doing. They had not done so, and in this respect they were at fault. These alterations had been made without the advice of a naval architect, and the learned judge who heard the civil case decided that the owners, though not responsible for the original deficiency in strength, were responsible for the further 7 percent loss which the 1947 alterations caused. But that was not enough to make the ship unseaworthy.

In his delivered judgment, the judge said that he had to consider three main questions. These were as follows:

1. Was the *Hopestar* as safe and seaworthy as reasonable skill and care could make her?
2. If not, were the owners responsible for the consequences of the unseaworthiness?
3. Was the deceased's death a consequence of the unseaworthiness?

If the owners were aware the ship was deficient by 15 percent conventional strength, would they send her to sea? He thought the answer would be "No." A prudent owner would run no risk at all. He (the judge) found that the *Hopestar* was not as safe as she should have been, and the responsibility for that was what he had to consider.

[255]

If the owners or their manager or their superintending engineers were personally negligent, the answer in law would be simple, but he found that in fact none of them was personally responsible. They were each entitled to assume that, as the work was in the hands of the competent builders and had to be done to the satisfaction of Lloyd's Register surveyors, such points would be properly looked after. Was the ship safe at the material time and in the condition in which she was, and what was the cause of the loss? The circumstances of the loss offered so little clue to its nature, it was difficult to exclude any cause however remote it might seem. Several causes had been suggested and two emerged—breaking in two, and loss by striking a mine. Both in peacetime would be very unusual. There was no known case in the preceding ten years of a vessel breaking in two in the Atlantic, and none of a vessel being struck by a mine in the Atlantic since the war.

Though messages were received two or three hours before the casualty probably occurred, there was no evidence of any distress signal. The vessel disappeared completely without leaving any trace of the ship or the crew. Explanation of the loss, said the judge, must account for three factors—the radio silence, the complete disappearance of the ship and the failure of means of escape. If the ship broke in two there would be warning of the break for a period of at least fifteen minutes. It was possible that the main radio and the emergency wireless would be put out of action, and that boats leaving the ship would be lost in heavy weather. "In my opinion," the judge continued, "the breaking in two, unless accompanied by one or more independent incidents, could not satisfactorily account for the loss."

The striking of the ship by a mine offered a more adequate explanation, providing the vessel was struck in a vital part. An explosion amidships might well affect the wireless apparatus and kill or seriously injure some of the officers, thus interfering with safe and effective action to cope with the disaster. He thought that this explanation most satisfactorily covered the circumstances of the loss, though he, too, left no doubt that in fact it seemed improbable. But the owner's alleged negligence was certainly not proved.

And so the widow's case was lost. If a mine took their ship, the owners obviously could not help it. But if in fact there was any possibility that the loss of the ship was due to a mine she became then a ship lost by war risk, and there was machinery for taking proper care of the dependents in such circumstances under the British War Pensions (Mercantile Marine) scheme. The seafarers' organizations took that aspect of the matter up with the Minister and, in due course and after two tribunals had heard all the arguments, the widow who sued the owners was recompensed by the Government, on behalf of the public, and so were all the other widows and dependents left by the forty lost men in the tramp *Hopestar*.

Nor could any thoughtful member of the public, aware of the great debt that Britain owes her mariners year in and year out, war risk or no war risk, mines or no mines, complain about that.

CHAPTER FOURTEEN

Improperly Ballasted

IT is seldom, after a ship is posted missing, that a court of inquiry feels justified in laying down precise reasons for the loss. But in the case of the former Liberty ship *Samkey,* which disappeared somewhere off the Azores while bound in ballast from London towards Cuba in the early winter of 1948, the court which was subsequently convened found that the *"Samkey* was lost with all hands due to a sudden shift of the solid ballast in the 'tween decks during heavy weather." Just that—nothing about a possible mine or blown-up boilers, or breaking in two.

How could a court be so sure in the one case, and uncertain in most others? What was there to go on? There were no witnesses of the *Samkey*'s loss. Nobody survived. Hers was yet another case of the big, well-built, well-found ship going out to sea on a commonplace passage, with all the life-saving equipment an energetic Ministry could require of her, with radio and navigational aids and watertight bulkheads and a double bottom and all the rest of it, yet managing to disappear without sending a signal or leaving a piece of flotsam or jetsam anywhere and remaining a 'mystery of the sea' from that day to this. What made the learned judge and his nautical assessors so sure they knew the answer, at least, to this mystery?

The *Samkey* was a war-built single-screw steel steamer, built under special survey of the American Bureau of Shipping by the Bethlehem-Fairfields Shipyard Inc. at Baltimore, Maryland, in

1943, and she saw her early war service as the *Carl Thusgaard* under the American flag before being transferred to the British and renamed *Samkey*. As the *Samkey,* she was owned by H.M. Government who arranged for her to be managed by the New Zealand Shipping Company, which had plenty of experience in the management of all sorts of ships. Some early Liberty ships—Liberty ships were standard types built in the United States, as far as possible by pre-fabrication, and were designed to be put together as quickly as possible while at the same time being thoroughly seaworthy, reasonably fast and dependable vessels—had given trouble, but these structural and propeller-dropping difficulties had been overcome by the time the *Samkey* was launched. She gave a good account of herself and played her part in wartime Atlantic convoys. She was a good strong ship which could steam 11 knots with a full cargo, on a daily consumption of 30 tons of fuel oil. She was 416 feet long, 57 feet in beam, nearly 35 feet deep, and her gross registered tonnage was 7,219 tons. She had seven watertight bulkheads, all extending to the upper deck. She had three deep tanks to carry water ballast, when steaming without cargo.

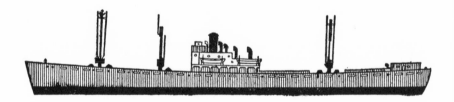

FIG. 6. Liberty Ship

Her crew and officers lived amidships in a steel house surrounding the engine and boiler casing, and the top of this house was a boat deck, on which were four first-class lifeboats, built of steel. Each lifeboat was 24 feet long, and two were powered. The two lifeboats on either side could accommodate 68 persons, and the crew of the *Samkey* when she was lost was 43 men. Since she was primarily a vessel designed to serve in time of war, special consideration had been given to the problem of getting her crew off in a hurry, and all four lifeboats had special quick-release gear. In addition to the lifeboats, she carried 46 special life-jackets of a type which had shown their worth in war, and 8 circular cork lifebuoys, each of which carried her name, the *Samkey* of London. She had three radio transmitters, one of which was an emergency set for the boats, and another could run on batteries, if the main generators broke down.

When she sailed, all these things were in perfect order and so was the ship. She was just recently out of dry-dock when she left London on the morning of the 24th of January, 1948. Everything that could be done to ensure her complete seaworthiness in all respects had been done, and it was to no one's interests to skimp her in any way. She was managed by a great shipping company and belonged to the taxpayers. The war was well over, then, and she had—or should have had—a long career of peaceful employment before her.

But there was one false note in all this, and it was fatal. Liberty ships are designed to be 'stiff,' which is to say, among other things, that they are subject to heavy rolling when empty. There are two sorts of ships, speaking broadly, 'stiff' ships and 'tender' ships. Stiff ships are very stable but they roll violently in a sea-way and, in so doing, can damage themselves. Tender ships roll less and are less stable. A very tender ship may roll over in exceptional circumstances. In order to take some of the stiffness out of Liberty ships not carrying cargo, the practice had grown up during the war of putting solid ballast in their 'tween-decks, that is, high in the ship, to counteract the greater weight down below and so take the stiffness out of them. This solid ballast did in fact make the vessels behave better and more comfortably, but—in some conditions of

[261]

ballasting, at any rate—this was at the expense of stability. A ship, like a person, can't have it both ways.

After some nasty experiences had shown the danger of using unsecured solid ballast in the 'tween-decks of Liberty ships, the Ministry of War Transport sent round a Notice to Shipmasters drawing attention to the danger. This notice mentioned specifically, as types of ballast likely to shift, shale, colliery stone, slag, and sand ballast, the inference being that other types of ballast were at least not so unreliable. Masters were "urged to see that adequate trimming of solid ballast of kinds liable to shift is carried out, and that in any case solid ballast carried in 'tween-decks or on deck is well spread out and trimmed practically level." There was, unfortunately, no instruction that shifting-boards should be employed in order to keep such ballast better under control and, indeed, not just the four types of ballast mentioned were likely to shift, but *all* solid ballast could do so when imperfectly secured.

There had been proof of this, if any further proof was required, when the 'Sam' ship *Sameveron* had a narrow escape from turning over, off the Grand Banks of Newfoundland, in a bit of a blow during the latter part of 1944. The *Sameveron,* which was steaming in ballast, in a convoy, at the time, had loaded about 2,000 tons of Thames ballast—not among the prescribed types—in addition to the water ballast and fuel oil, etc., which the ship carried. The solid ballast was divided about equally between the 'tween-decks and the lower holds. Before he loaded this ballast, the master of the *Sameveron* had made inquiries about its shifting propensities and had been told that it would set almost solid in a ship and, indeed, would probably have to be removed with picks. (This so-called Thames ballast is a mixture of stones of various sizes, mainly small, with sand, usually wet, and its 'angle of repose' is something between 35 and 40 degrees, which is to say that a heap of it with its sides at somewhere about that angle, will 'stay put' and will not slide.)

So the *Sameveron* carried no shifting-boards, although she was on a west-bound winter crossing of the North Atlantic which would take her pretty far to the north. Off the Banks, she struck a severe blow with wind and sea on her beam and, very suddenly one day, the ballast in the 'tween-decks shifted with a run, throwing the ship almost on her beam ends. She lay over at an angle of 55 degrees but, very fortunately, she hung there, and rolled no further. The solid ballast down below did not shift. The weather began to improve, and the *Sameveron*'s crew, forced to take desperate measures, were able to get into the 'tween-decks and shovel the ballast uphill back again, this time with shifting-boards, and save their ship. They were extremely lucky as they well knew, and so should the Ministry have known, but the Ministry apparently failed to heed the lesson, although the incident was fully reported and investigated at the time. No warning notice was sent to other 'Sam' shipmasters or managers and they continued to load Thames ballast in their 'tween-decks, generally without shifting-boards.

The *Samkey* took 1,500 tons of the stuff and stowed it all in her 'tween-decks, without shifting-boards. This Thames ballast was wet and fairly sticky when it was taken aboard, and it looked all right. It was spread fairly evenly, and the ship sailed. She had plenty of fuel oil, fresh water and stores, and her deep-tanks were either full then or filled—according to the master's intentions as discussed with his marine superintendent—as soon as the ship was outside. So long as the ballast did not shift, she was in good trim. Neither the master nor the marine superintendent had heard of the ballast-shifting incident in the *Sameveron,* and so the *Samkey* went cheerfully off to sea, bound for the West Coast of North America by way of the Panama Canal.

She never arrived. She sent out half a dozen position messages, each of which reported all well on board and good progress, though head winds slowed her to eight knots for a while. In addition to these radio messages, the *Samkey* was sighted at sea by the steamer

Innesmoor on the morning of the 29th of January, when she was steaming along upright and in good order. At a quarter to two in the afternoon of the 31st of January, she reported by radio to Horta in the Azores that she was on Latitude 41.48 north, Longitude 24 west, and the wind was strong from the south-west—strong, but not gale force, nor anything like it. No further message was received from the ship and no boats, wreckage, lifebuoys or bodies were ever found from her, though when she was last heard from she was not far from the Azores.

On the 24th of March of the same year, after the usual fruitless advertisement for news and period of being overdue, the *Samkey* was posted missing, and that was that—until the Ministry investigators found out about the Thames ballast, and the absence of shifting-boards. A formal investigation was held with as little delay as possible, lest other ships be lost through the same cause, and the members of the court—a judge, two sea captains and one naval architect to act as his assessors—went into the case thoroughly over a period of four days, sitting in London. The Ministry might have been at fault in failing to publicise the *Sameveron* case, but now it was trying to make amends.

After due deliberation and going thoroughly into every other possible cause, the court—having discovered that the *Samkey* must have passed through some very bad weather with winds of strong gale force, shortly after she had sent her last message—found that the ballast, "uncontrolled as it was, was very likely to shift and probably did so with a run. Such a shift, coupled with two or three big waves and the wind, might well have caused the *Samkey* to have been overwhelmed. . . . A sudden disastrous shift would account for no distress signals having been heard, and for the absence of floating wreckage. . . ." She rolled over as she was, with everything secured for sea, and she took all hands down with her.

The *Sameveron* had been lucky but her sister-ship the *Samkey* was not, and the tragedy was that, had those responsible for the

Samkey's safety that voyage known of what happened to the *Sameveron,* their charge would have had shifting-boards to keep the Thames ballast from moving and she would have been all right. The court recorded its view that her loss was in part due to the failure of the Ministry to circulate information, and recommended that instructions be issued immediately that solid ballast of *any* character should not be carried in the 'tween-decks without suitable precautions, and that the taking of such precautions should be regarded as essential to seaworthiness.

This recommendation was acted upon, and no more 'Sam' ships went missing. But one was too many.

Some years earlier, the stowage of her ballast had been—as far as is known—the undoing of another tramp, and, very curiously, she also was on a west-bound North Atlantic voyage and had reached almost the place where the *Samkey* was later lost. This vessel was the 5,500-ton steamer *Anglo-Australian,* a steel single-screw vessel built for the Nitrate Producer S.S. Company of London, by Short Brothers at Sunderland, in 1927. The *Anglo-Australian* was 426 feet long with a beam of 58 feet and a depth of $28\frac{1}{2}$ feet. She was classed 100A1, and she had the usual seven watertight bulkheads of the fair-sized modern steamer, a double bottom, first-class life-saving equipment, lifeboats, powerful radio, flares, rockets and everything else that could be carried for her own safety and that of her thirty-eight-man crew. She was properly manned by a competent crew. She had been in dry-dock at Cardiff shortly before her last voyage, and her hull was perfectly sound. Her boilers had been surveyed and were in good order.

She, too, was outward bound westwards in ballast across the North Atlantic when she sailed from Cardiff on the 8th of March, 1938, and passed to oblivion. She had aboard the best part of 2,000 tons of coal bunkers and as much solid ballast as she needed, properly secured, with shifting-boards. She was neither 'stiff' nor 'tender'

[265]

and, unless she sprung a leak (which, being usually a slow business for a ship in ballast, would at least allow time to get a signal away) she should never have rolled over. In 1938 there were no mines about, except perhaps some very ancient mines from the First World War and maybe—about the coasts of Spain—a few from the Spanish civil war. From a position among the Azores, the *Anglo-Australian* sent a routine report giving her position, weather and fuel consumption. "Passed Fayal this afternoon," she sent. "Nine knots. Twenty-six tons bunker consumption. Rough weather. All well."

That was the last ever heard of her. She was passing the Azores in the channel south of the island of Flores. There were other ships about. The land was in sight. The weather, it is true, was bad, with winds to fresh gale force and a high sea. But it was not the sort of really exceptional weather which got the *Sao Paulo* into trouble, or took toll of the nine little ships in the narrow seas on January 31, 1953. It was what seamen regard as normal bad weather, the sort of stuff well-found ships must take in their stride. It might slow them down a little but it ought not to damage them, much less overwhelm them. No other ships in the vicinity reported any damage from that blow. The *Anglo-Australian,* being in ballast, was the better able to withstand the force of any breaking sea. The heavy-laden ship might pitch her bows in and is much more vulnerable to the sea's onslaught. The ballasted ship rides high, and the sea cannot ordinarily reach her decks to cause much damage.

But the *Anglo-Australian* disappeared as utterly as the island of Atlantis—no wreckage, no bodies, no message in a bottle ever came from her. What happened? Was there something mysterious in the vicinity of the Azores (as the ancients seemed to think) which caused the undoing of good ships? Or had her boilers blown up? Had she collided with some submerged object, or a drifting derelict, and foundered? Had a drifting mine from the coast of Spain somehow managed to reach the area and get in front of her, to blow her up in some spot so vital that she could not even send an SOS?

All these things were so improbable as to be ruled out, but nonetheless they were all investigated. There are no longer derelict ships drifting about in the North Atlantic, as there used to be. The vessel's trim was all right. She had a freeboard of 21 feet, and plenty of ballast neither too high nor too low in the hull. Her hull, boilers, engines and all her equipment were in thoroughly good order. It was inconceivable that the sea could overwhelm her. If she had collided with some other vessel, then either the other vessel would arrive somewhere to report the accident, or be lost also. No other vessel reported any collision in that area and no other vessel was lost there, or near there. As for submerged wreckage, sunken rocks and all that sort of thing, had she struck any of these she would not *suddenly* have been blotted out. She would have taken time to founder, and had some opportunity to get radio messages away and to launch her boats.

The loss of the *Anglo-Australian,* in its way, promised to become as great a mystery as the loss of the passenger steamer *Waratah,* or the inexplicable abandonment of the brigantine *Mary Celeste* in the same general area of the Azores, over sixty years earlier. The *Mary Celeste* matter had never been fully cleared up.

Incidentally, the *Mary Celeste* case has become the most misrepresented and loosely written-about sea 'mystery' of all time. The indisputable facts are startling enough and are worth recalling. The brigantine was found sailing without a crew on board, yet everything appeared to be in good seamanlike order except that one of the for'ard hatches had been removed, and there was a little damage to the running rigging. Her master had sailed with his wife and small child aboard. No trace was ever found of any of the persons who had been aboard, and their fate remains a mystery. There is almost equal mystery as to why the *Mary Celeste* should ever have been abandoned, but the consensus of informed opinion is that her cargo of industrial alcohol in drums had given trouble. Eight of the drums were found to be empty when the vessel reached Genoa, and

[267]

there must have been a lot of fumes in the unventilated hold while the little vessel was running before hard westerly weather out of New York towards the Azores. The *Mary Celeste* was found adrift at sea by the Nova Scotian brigantine *Dei Gratia*. There were neither people nor boats aboard. The wheel was not lashed, but the binnacle had been knocked over, probably by the sea, and the compass destroyed. She was under very short canvas—it had been blowing a bit—and her foresail and fore upper topsail were blown away. Most of her sails, however, were properly furled. The chronometer, sextant and ship's register were missing. The captain's bunk had been slept in, by a child, but not made. There were six months' provisions aboard but—contrary to many stories—there was not a meal on the cabin table and neither was there any cooked food in the galley. The ship's only boat was gone. The log was on a desk in the mate's cabin, but it threw no light on the mystery. It had not been kept for about a week. There was some water in the hold, but not enough to give any cause for alarm. It was soon pumped out and the mate of the *Dei Gratia,* with a few men, got the *Mary Celeste* under control again, heading away for Gibraltar. The *Mary Celeste*'s standing rigging, masts and spars were in good order and, indeed, the ship was described by one of the seamen who boarded her in the sea as "fit to go round the world."

Various theories were immediately put forward to account for the curious case of the *Mary Celeste*. It was suggested that there had been a mutiny, or that there had been no mutiny but a barefaced attempt to rob the insurers of ship and cargo through connivance with the *Dei Gratia,* which—according to this yarn—did not find the brigantine abandoned but hid her master, officers and crew, claimed the vessel as salvage and shared the criminal proceeds with the *Mary Celeste*'s ship's company at some never-discovered hideout afterwards. In that case, why was nothing ever found of the *Mary Celeste*'s crew? There were seven seamen aboard, good men all of them. Live men do not disappear into thin air, and crime will out—especially a 'crime' where the searchlight of the world was at once focussed, as it was in this case. No connivance was ever proven against the *Dei Gratia* nor was such ever suspected by seafaring men. The *Mary Celeste* was insured for $14,000 and appraised at $16,000. Her cargo was valued at $37,000, and the freight payable when it was safely delivered at Genoa was $3,400. These were not large sums, even if the *Dei Gratia's* people had secured the whole of them by murdering their alleged fellow-conspirators in the *Mary Celeste*. Even the seamen's pipes were found in the abandoned vessel. A seafarer conniving at anything would still take his pipe with him.

A thorough investigation of all the circumstances of the case was made at Gibraltar shortly after the *Dei Gratia* arrived there, but the mystery was never cleared up. Indeed, much of the matter was further obscured by various red herrings drawn across the trail by the investigators at Gibraltar. It was certain, however, that crime had nothing to do with the *Dei Gratia's* share in the mystery, either of piracy or fraud. Most likely, alcohol fumes when the fore hatch was lifted stampeded all hands into the abandonment of the *Mary Celeste,* and then they were lost in their boat. That could happen very easily. They would open the hatch only in good weather.*

Whether the *Anglo-Australian* had suddenly been confronted with the ghost of the *Mary Celeste* and taken refuge in the sea in her alarm will, perhaps, never be known, but such a 'theory' is as sound as many which were advanced to account for the strange abandonment of the little brigantine. The *Anglo-Australian,* in her turn, became a somewhat written-up 'mystery,' but with very much less cause. Indeed, the probable reason for her loss became apparent not long afterwards. About a month after she had gone missing, a Greek steamer, the *Mount Kyllene,* also in ballast, also west-bound

* The interested reader is referred to a book called MARY CELESTE, THE ODYSSEY OF AN ABANDONED SHIP, by Charles Edey Fay, published by The Peabody Museum of Salem, Massachusetts, in 1942. This is the best book on the subject.

in the North Atlantic and somewhere in the vicinity of the Azores, suddenly began to buckle and break in two. But she took her time about it, and the crew survived, even though the ship was in two pieces within fifteen minutes of the first sign of damage. The weather was not as bad then as it probably was at the time of the *Anglo-Australian*'s disappearance. Careful investigation showed that the *Mount Kyllene* broke in two because she had all her weight amidships—engines, water ballast and solid ballast—and she was suspended between the crests of two seas, with the heavily laden part of the hull temporarily unsupported by a sufficient volume of water. So she 'sagged.' Her middle—so to speak—fell out of her, and she disintegrated. A ship may be badly strained and, in exceptional cases, destroyed because of the bad distribution of heavy weight aboard, either at both ends of her or in the middle. If at both ends, she 'hogs'; in the middle, she 'sags.' The *Mount Kyllene* had sagged to death.

It was discovered that the *Anglo-Australian,* too, had her greatest concentration of weight amidships. With her bow and her stern suspended on the crests of a couple of big seas, this great weight amidships could have caused her to break her back. Contrary to the views expressed by the learned judge who heard the *Hopestar* civil case, this could happen quickly and perfectly well account for the complete disappearance of the vessel, without time or opportunity to get any message away. In the case of the *Mount Kyllene,* the concentration of weight amidships was greater than with the *Anglo-Australian,* but the weather was much worse at the time the British ship was lost. It is difficult to say what else could have caused her loss. With her back broken and her masts down, the battery-operated radio would not reach anyone. The nearest ship at the time was some 90 miles away. It would be unnecessary for both parts of the ship to sink at once for the whole to go missing, and it is not difficult to imagine circumstances—for example, with the deck officers in one section and the majority of the crew in the other, both sections rolling and lurching violently with their normal stability quite gone, until first one and then the other slipped down into the sea that was breaking right over them—when the men would have no chance at all to get a boat away, or to do anything else.

There is one awful feature of all these accidents ashore as well as at sea and that is, even as they happen, their complete incredibility to those who are caught in them. Accidents are events one reads about in newspapers or hears of on the radio. They happen to other ships, other aircraft, other trains, other automobiles— never to ours. And then one comes along which does happen to us and, before the first shocked astonishment has passed, the corpses are being counted, or the names of the lost written up on the long, long board which records those of the vast legion lost at sea. In a dreadful moment of rending steel, of smashing seas, of the alarming and utter disintegration of the ship one serves, trusts, lives in, and knows so well, it is all over. Who shall survive to tell of such things as these, when they happen in a gale of wind? Who shall put off in a boat?

And so the court found that the most probable cause of the loss of the *Anglo-Australian* was the buckling of the shelter-deck and consequent complete fracture from deck to keel. There was some evidence before the court indicating a lack of structural strength in the ship. Recurring cracks in the shelter-deck, it was said, were last repaired by welding not long before she sailed on her last voyage. Witnesses declared that this shelter-deck was known to show visible buckling amidships in heavy weather under ballast conditions. This, however, had always been regarded as minor damage—until the ship disappeared.

The public does not hear much about these missing vessels because they are tramps. It takes the sudden loss of a passenger ship to shock the great mass of landlubbers. They can see themselves in a passenger ship but they have little interest in tramps, even when the tramps belong to famous lines. The steamer *Vardulia,* for instance, was a unit in the well-known Donaldson Line which operates vessels on a Transatlantic service, including passenger vessels. The *Vardulia* was not one of the passenger carriers. She had been a cattle-carrier, bringing live steers across the North Atlantic to be slaughtered for English beef. Built as the *Verdun* by Russell and Company at Port Glasgow in 1917, she was a fine big steamer, 423 feet long and of nearly 6,000 tons. She had 6 watertight bulkheads, was 100A1 at Lloyd's, had always been well looked after in every way. She was bought by Donaldson's for £46,311 4s.4d. in 1929, and what the odd 4s.4d. was for is not recorded. Under the Donaldson flag she made many successful voyages. And yet she, too, disappeared, to be posted missing at Lloyd's and never afterwards traced.

The *Vardulia* sailed on her last voyage on the 12th of October, 1935. The port she then left was West Hartlepool, and she was properly loaded, adequately manned by a crew of thirty-seven (master, three mates, carpenter, six able seamen, one deckhand, two ordinary seamen and one apprentice on deck, with an adequate engine-room complement), and in thoroughly seaworthy condition. She had a cargo of general and coal. She had made sixteen previous Transatlantic voyages, with no record of any cargo having shifted. Radio messages received from her indicated that she was meeting bad weather, but that was the normal thing in the North Atlantic at that time of the year, and most other times, too. However, on Friday, the 18th, when she was less than a week at sea, she sent out a general urgent message—"Position 58 north 18.30 west: whole gale: ships in vicinity please indicate position"—which could only mean that she was in some kind of serious trouble. The wind in that position was north-west Force 9—a gale—with a high sea. The following morning, the *Vardulia* sent out an SOS, giving the same position and saying that she required immediate assistance as she had taken a dangerous list. This was followed by a further message "Now abandoning ship."

There was nothing more. There was no sign of the *Vardulia* either, though there were a good many ships in the vicinity and they raced to her aid—no sign of the *Vardulia,* no wreckage, and no boats. What had happened to cause her first to take the list, and then to disappear? She was a well-built ship and a well-found ship, with no history of any weakness. She was a well-run ship, with no history of adverse incidents of any kind. The coal was properly stowed, with shifting-boards.

The cause of the loss of the *Vardulia* must remain grounds for conjecture. The only certainty in her case was that she had taken a serious list and her people were given time to get an SOS away, which did not help them at all. There was an inquiry, but the only point the court uncovered was that the removal of the cattle decks above Nos. 1 and 2 hatches—which had been done in May of the year she was lost—had worried the master a little. Its finding, however, was that the cause of the loss "must remain a mystery of the sea."

Nor is the mysterious loss of the odd big tramp confined to vessels under the British flag, by any means. Since the end of the Second World War, Finnish, German, Norwegian, American, Turkish and Dutch tramps have gone missing. In the year 1953 alone, fifteen vessels of 12,506 tons, out of 223 vessels lost at sea from various causes, were posted missing, compared with 45 of some 50,000 tons, which foundered, and 32 of 48,000 tons, which went down in or after collisions. These figures are from Lloyd's Register of Shipping and they do not cover Russian shipping, or native vessels or small craft generally. They refer solely to seagoing registered ships, records of which are kept at or known to Lloyd's.

The American steamer *Pennsylvania* is one of the few big American vessels which have been posted missing in recent years, but in her case there is no mystery about what caused her fate. She split open when working, heavily laden, in a sea-way, and sank. The

Pennsylvania, built in 1944, was a cargo-carrier of 7,608 tons, owned by the States Steamship Company. With a crew of 46, she sailed from Vancouver on the 2nd day of January, 1952, and from Seattle three days later, bound for Yokohama. A week later she reported that she had developed serious cracks in the hull, and she then sent out an SOS. Her position was given as 51 north, 141 west —a lonely part of the North Pacific for a ship to be fighting for her life. On the 9th January, a message came from her that she was abandoning ship with four lifeboats. That was at half past four in the afternoon. Aircraft and surface vessels began at once to make a search, which was carried on exhaustively. Two of the boats were seen from the air, capsized and with no bodies near them or anywhere in the vicinity. The other boats and the ship herself were never seen, and there were no survivors.

Afterwards there was a most thorough inquiry conducted by the United States Coast Guard (which is charged with the supervision of the vessels of the American merchant marine), and this went on, at Seattle, for five days. Fifteen witnesses put 37 exhibits before the court, but pinned down nothing. There was no discoverable reason for the *Pennsylvania* to crack open.

The steamer *Edna,* of Mariehamn, was not big but she was also a tramp. Indeed she registered only 829 tons. She was built in 1905, so, when she went missing in the North Sea in the winter of 1952, she was 47 years old. But she was still 100A1 at Lloyd's. The Finns have a number of elderly vessels in their merchant service, but they chose them wisely and keep them up well. The *Edna* was carrying a full cargo of wood pulp from the Baltic for Preston, in Lancashire, when she sent out an SOS. She had a crew of seventeen men. Though a search was begun immediately the SOS was received and continued for a long time, nothing of the *Edna* or her crew was found.

The *Edna* was interesting because she belonged to the late Gustaf Erikson, the last owner of a big sailing-ship line. Captain Erikson ran anything between twelve and twenty square-rigged ships for years in the hardest of all trades, that around Cape Horn. They were old ships when he bought them and he ran them with youthful officers and boy crews. Yet none of these ships went missing. Now and again, one might be briefly overdue, but they always came in from their voyages, except for the loss at sea of the four-masted barque *Melbourne,* which was run down by an oil-tanker. It was odd, from all those voyages, that it should be the home-loving little steamer that disappeared on a humdrum run across the short North Sea.

On the other side of the North Atlantic, the 2,250-ton Canadian steamer *Novadoc,* of Fort William, Ontario, sailed from Digby, Nova Scotia, for New York on the 1st of March, 1947, reported herself as being 22 miles east of Portland, Maine, two days later, and then disappeared from the face of the earth with her crew of 24 men. There was no wreckage. Nothing was found. It is extraordinary how ships, big and small, can go out from port fit—apparently —for any conditions they might meet, move for a day or two or for weeks among other ships, and then disappear as utterly as if they had never been. The Belgian steamer *Tigris,* of Antwerp, 2,737 tons, which sailed from that port on the 18th of September, 1930, was seen off the Isle of Wight and then disappeared: the L.M.S. steamer *Calder,* 1,107 tons, which sailed from Hamburg on the 17th of April, 1931, passed Cuxhaven the following day and then disappeared: the *Broomfleet,* of Goole, on never-ending passage Goole for Ipswich: the *Paringa,* 1,360 tons, lost somehow in the sea between Melbourne and Sydney when on passage towards Japan to be broken up, in 1936: the *Dignitas,* of Genoa, 5,376 tons, which sailed from Bizerta in North Africa bound for Ymuiden on the 29th of October, 1931, passed Ushant on the 8th day of November and was never seen nor heard from again—where are all these? For they are all posted missing at Lloyd's. Big ships, small ships, old ships, new ships—all swallowed up somehow in the maw of the insatiable sea. . . . And yet surely a steamer of over 5,000 tons could hardly be lost without trace in waters so confined as those of the English Channel, as the *Dignitas* was lost?

The answer is that she *is* lost and—beyond a lifebuoy found on the beach at Rottingdean which may have been hers—nothing was ever found of her, or to throw any light on her probable fate. Nor are such mysteries things of the past, sea history, over and done with. They still happen—not often, of course, when seen against the great background of the safely completed voyages and the vast assemblage of ships of all kinds which never get into trouble at all. But, now and again, even very big ships still get on the 'overdue' list at Lloyd's, and the Lutine bell rings rarely for any of them.

Ships like the Argentine steamer *General San Martin,* for example, which—apart from the battleship *Sao Paulo*—is the largest vessel ever posted missing at Lloyd's (disregarding war losses). The *General San Martin,* a steamer of 9,589 tons built in 1918 as the French liner *Aurigny,* for Chargeurs Réunis, was a twin-screw 13-knot ship with accommodation for over a thousand passengers. She was 481 feet long, with a beam of 58 feet. She acquired Argentine nationality and her new name after a serious fire aboard in Buenos Aires, in 1941. She was rebuilt to some extent, after this, not as a passenger vessel, and she was carrying a crew of 54 but no passengers when she sailed from Buenos Aires for the last time on the 28th of August, 1954. She touched at Bahia Blanca to complete loading and left there on the 4th of September, bound via the Straits of Magellan for the port of San Antonio, in Chile—a coasting passage. Her cargo included some 10,000 tons of wheat in bulk and bags as well as general, in which were such things as casks of tallow, bales of wool, cans of lard, bags of yerba maté and so forth—none of it at all dangerous from the point of view of liability to shift, take fire or explode.

The *General San Martin* safely made the worst part of her passage, through the Straits of Magellan, and was last reported on the 12th of September as dropping her pilot after passing through channels in the Gulf of Peñas, on the coast of Southern Chile. The pilot reported that all was well aboard; yet the *General San Martin,* for all her strength and her bulk and her good engines and everything else, did not arrive at San Antonio. Nor did she send any SOS, or leave an identifiable trace of herself, anywhere. Intensive search by air and sea, begun as soon as she was overdue, yielded nothing beyond some oil patches on the sea and a bit of wreckage near Cape Raper. This was not identified as definitely belonging to the missing ship. No trace of her crew of fifty-four has been found. The *General San Martin* was posted at Lloyd's as a missing vessel on the 27th of October, 1954, and the precise reason for her fate remains a mystery.

Really insoluble mysteries of the sea are rare, though inexplicable occurrences are not. Sometimes odd stories drift about the seaports or in the daily press purporting to deal with this 'mystery' or that, but, on the whole, seamen have their own ideas as to the solution of most of these. A case in point was the 4,000-ton steamer *Haida,* built in 1909 as the *Burgeo Star,* which sailed from Seattle for Hong-Kong with a full cargo of sulphur, on the 24th of October, 1937, and never arrived. The *Haida* should have touched at Honolulu, but did not. She sent out no reports or messages of any kind, though she had full radio equipment. Hers was an unusual case in that she had sailed on a temporary certificate of British registry and she was not, at the time, classed at Lloyd's. Her complete silence was also unusual. There began to be stories about her, when she did not arrive, that she had been made away with by the Japanese Navy, or her crew had pirated her (as the *Dei Gratia's* crew were alleged to have stolen the *Mary Celeste*) and sold her and her sulphur cargo somewhere, probably in Japan. These stories, based on nothing, began to make the headlines. The Japanese were the bogeymen of the time, and one story about them was as good as another.

But then, one day weeks afterwards, the keeper of the Vancouver

Island Lighthouse was walking his beach when he picked up a life-buoy which had been some time in the sea. The name of the life-buoy could still be read. It was *Haida,* Shanghai. Of course possibly the 'pirates' had thrown the lifebuoy overboard, as a false clue. But the years passed and nothing was ever heard to throw any further light on the fate of the *Haida.* None of her crew was ever heard of. It appeared at last that the lifebuoy was genuine enough. The *Haida* had gone down in the sea.

If there is a genuine sea mystery, a really clueless case, it must be that of the London steamer *Asiatic Prince* which disappeared mys-teriously, also in the Pacific, early in 1928. Facts about the *Asiatic Prince* are few and hard to come by—hence the mystery, for where facts are fewest fancy always takes a hand. Such facts as are established include these: The *Asiatic Prince* was built in 1926 to Lloyd's highest class, for the cargo-carrying service of the Prince Line. She sailed from Los Angeles for Yokohama on the 16th of March, 1928, on a normal voyage in her company's service. Her crew of forty-eight under Captain Duncan included four youthful apprentices. Eight days after she sailed, a somewhat cryptic SOS signal was heard by the British steamer *City of Eastbourne* when somewhere off Honolulu, but the SOS was so peculiar that at first it was not known from which ship it came. For a while, it was thought to be from the British tanker *British Hussar.* The operators in the Transpacific passenger steamers *Niagara* and *Ventura* also picked up this message and, cryptic or not—the call-sign was not that of the *Asiatic Prince* but was very similar—search was set afoot. The message mentioned a "terrific storm." Three mine-sweepers of the United States Navy searched the area whence the message had come, and they searched thoroughly. They found nothing. In due course, the *Asiatic Prince* (from which nothing further had been heard) failed to arrive at her destination. She was posted overdue, and then advertised for. There was no news of her—no news any-where. In due course, she became yet another missing vessel.

1. The *Yewvalley* was a typical little North Sea coaster, like the *Yewarch*.

2. Plugging into a nasty head sea

3. At the pumps—backbreaking, heartbreaking work

4. The *Lalla Rookh* was fast, but she was once seriously overdue.

5. The *Red Rock*—only ship ever Posted Missing and later found again.

6. Sinking trawler off Greenland. The crew were saved from this one.

7. A typical distant-water trawlerman

8. A small Hollander, familiar in the North Sea trades

9. Little coaster: many such ships are Missing.

10. Hatches fill the main deck. They can be vulnerable.

11. The missing Brazilian battleship *Sao Paulo*

12. Group of Arctic trawlers in the fish dock at Hull

13. ABOVE RIGHT. A lot of room for ice—deck of a big trawler

14. RIGHT. Mizzen of a fisherman—small sail, but often a life-saver

15. Model of the Hull trawler *Roderigo*

16. Skipper George Coverdale

17. The *Lorella* was a beautiful, strong modern ship. But she went.

18. Norwegian sealer in Greenland packice

19. Elling Myklebust, lost with the sealers

20. Sealing captain from Brandal

21. The *Polarsel*—
typical modern sealer

22. Bottlenose whaler

23. The missing liner
Waratah

24. Four-mast barque *Ponape*

25. Missing school-ship— the magnificent *København*

26. The *Admiral Karpfanger*, missing near Cape Horn

27. Violent weather off Cape Horn. Square-riggers had to be able to take it.

28. Biscayan fisherman at Douarnenez

29. Concarneau tunnymen in the old days

30. At Concarneau today—modern fishermen. Six were lost.

31. The missing *General San Martin*

32. What happened to the *Hopestar?*

33. The *Samkey* must have rolled over.

34. The *Awahou*, missing in the Coral Sea

35. The new *Melanie Schulte* disappeared in the North Atlantic.

36. Dorymen of the *Joao Costa*, the day of their rescue

37. The *Joao Costa*

38. Dorymen are good small-boat sailors.

There were some odd points in the case of the *Asiatic Prince*. She was alleged to be carrying bullion, secret weapons and so forth, and it was even suggested by the wilder 'theorists' that a crew of pirates had managed to get aboard her in Los Angeles before she left (or in China: geography didn't bother these theorists much) and these had later seized the ship for her gold. This was a favourite story. Others suggested that possibly the ship was overwhelmed by a waterspout, struck by a meteorite, or swept under by some enormous tidal wave. Some pessimist, recalling that in 1908 a meteorite weighing several hundred tons had fallen on a lonely spot in Siberia and another had struck the earth somewhere in the United States, suggested that maybe a piece of a star from outer space had fallen on the lost ship, too. (This was in the days before alleged flying saucers were popular, or there would have been 'theories' that she was bombed from one of these.) The favourite story was the one about the pirates and, from time to time, that is still brought forward. The *Asiatic Prince,* according to the latest version of this yarn, was lost somewhere in the China Seas, not off the Hawaiian Islands, and the faint radio message received from her contained one decipherable word. The word was 'pirates.' No such message was received and the ship was not anywhere near the China Sea.

These rumour-mongers are perhaps encouraged by the really strange feature in this case, and that is the fact that no formal investigation was held. Many lives had been lost: the *Asiatic Prince* was a fine new motor-ship and—as in almost all other important cases of the kind—the nautical world was entitled to feel that a public inquiry was called for. There was, unfortunately, not the slightest doubt that the ship and all her people were missing. Why? Was this another *Waratah,* without the passengers?

The only official explanation which I have been able to obtain comes from the Public Relations Division of the Ministry of Transport, in London, under date 11th October, 1955.

After the *Asiatic Prince* was reported missing [it states], a Preliminary Inquiry was held under Section 465 of the Merchant Shipping Act, 1894, by the Board of Trade, which in 1928 was the Department responsible for the safety of navigation at sea. The main purpose of such Inquiries, which are confidential to the Department, is to enable the Minister to decide whether or not a Formal Investigation (i.e., Public Inquiry) should be held.

In deciding whether to hold a Formal Investigation, the Minister's main consideration is whether the circumstances of the casualty are such that a Court of Formal Investigation is likely to arrive at a conclusion as to its cause or whether it would be likely to arrive at findings which might lead to the prevention of similar occurrences in the future.

In the case of the *Asiatic Prince* there were no witnesses available who could establish any reliable facts. The case was, however, carefully reviewed but because of the lack of information it was decided that no useful purpose would be served by ordering a Formal Investigation.

And that is that, over a quarter of a century afterwards. But *no* witnesses? *No* reliable facts? After all, forty-eight men had died in a fine new ship, belonging to a well-known line. Was she carrying bullion? How stable was she? How was she laden? Could *no one* throw light on anything to do with this strangely lost 7,000-ton vessel? Apparently, no one could or, if they did, it was behind closed doors. Perhaps the shipping journalists are not to be blamed if they think there also may be a mystery here—or perhaps the Board of Trade accepted the theory that the *Asiatic Prince,* poor ship, had been 'bombed' by a meteorite. There would be little use in holding a formal investigation into an accident of that kind.

CHAPTER FIFTEEN

Must the Men Die Too?

THE West German tramp motor-ship *Melanie Schulte,* belonging to the firm of Schulte and Bruns, of Emden, was a remarkably fine vessel, a powerful big cargo-carrier fit to go anywhere and stand up to anything. She registered 6,357 tons gross and was 445 feet long. She was built in 1952 by the Nordseewerke G.m.b.H. and was classed 100 A 4E by Germanischer Lloyd's. She cost over eight million marks to build. Her equipment was the best that could be put into her. She had all the radio she could ever find use for, including a powerful main sending station and battery-run emergency sets for the boats. She had boats enough on both sides of the ship to get her whole crew—thirty-five men—away, and the davits and quick-release gear for the boats were of the latest pattern. She had ample life-jackets for everyone aboard, and to spare. She had four sister-ships—the *Henriette Schulte, Francisca Henrik Fisser, Carl Fisser,* and the *Herta Engeline Fritzen*—all of which did very well on all sorts of voyages at sea, and still do so.

The *Melanie Schulte* sailed on her maiden voyage from Emden to Quebec in the latter part of 1952. The weather was so bad when she left Borkum that she was unable to land the pilot, and he was carried on to Ymuiden in Holland. Here he went ashore with the remark that he should have known better than to pilot a vessel which had refused to leave the ways—a ship under an unlucky star. This was a jocular reference to the fact that, when she was being launched, the *Melanie Schulte* carried away part of the launching structure (simply because it had been insufficiently greased) and had to be forced into the water. The old salts looking on had regarded this as obvious reluctance on the ship's part to enter an element which was, they said, going to drown her. Nevertheless the *Melanie Schulte* made a successful maiden voyage, across the Atlantic westbound to Quebec and back to Germany with full cargo. She met plenty of bad weather and she behaved well, showing herself to be an excellent sea vessel. Westerly winds of Force 9 threw up a high and nasty sea in her face, off the Newfoundland Banks, and her people thought the new ship came through the hard test extremely well.

Yet the *Melanie Schulte* disappeared at sea on her very next passage, to become yet another of that all-too-familiar case of the fine big ship going down without sending out any indication that she was even in trouble, without leaving any survivors, without—apparently—the slightest clue as to what happened to her, or why it happened. It was the worst shock the German merchant service had had since the loss of the *Admiral Karpfanger,* fourteen years earlier. The *Melanie Schulte* loaded a full cargo, 9,307 metric tons, of iron ore at Narvik in the north of Norway and sailed with this on the 17th of December, 1952, bound towards Mobile in the Gulf of Mexico. The weather was bad, as was to be expected at that time of year, but she was well fitted to plug into it. She sent out her position on the 21st of December as 58.22 north, 9.33 west, adding that she was heading into deteriorating weather. She was then about 90 miles west of the Hebrides, off the west coast of Scotland—a bad place for wild weather. Captain Heinrich Rohde had no reason to be bothered over that.

But she sent no further messages at all. Nothing. Not an SOS—just complete silence. As she was required to report her position at frequent and regular intervals to her owners in Emden, there was soon some anxiety about her—incredible as it seemed to be, *something* might have happened to her. A search was immediately arranged by ships and by aircraft from the Royal Air Force. There was no sign of the *Melanie Schulte* anywhere. In too many cases such searches come late, but this search was made in good time and yet yielded nothing.

In due course, the ship was overdue at Mobile, and then the usual advertisements were inserted for news of her. For a while, she was officially rated as an overdue vessel at Lloyd's, and her name appeared on the casualty page of Lloyd's List and Shipping Gazette as follows:

OVERDUE VESSEL

MELANIE SCHULTE.—Hamburg, Jan. 7.—Motor vessel Melanie Schulte was due at Mobile on Tuesday (Jan. 6) from Narvik with a cargo of ore. British naval forces and aircraft which made a search for the vessel on Monday and Tuesday found no trace of her.—"Hamburger Anzeiger." (See under "Miscellaneous" in issue of Jan. 1, 3, 6 and 7.) _____ Emden, Jan. 7.—Motor vessel Melanie Schulte must be considered lost, West German shipping experts said here to-day. The Melanie Schulte carried the most modern equipment and was considered highly seaworthy.

Then, on the 25th of February, 1953, the *Melanie Schulte* was posted at Lloyd's as a missing vessel.

In the meantime, a lifebelt bearing her name was picked up on the beach on the western side of Benbecula Island, off the west coast of Scotland, on the 17th of February. The lifebelt was painted with the name *"Melanie Schulte,* Hamburg," and there could be little doubt as to its origin. It was identified in Emden as part of the original outfit of the vessel. But what story was it trying to tell? Why just a lifebelt? Where were Captain Rohde, and his thirty-four men, his three mates, his four highly competent engineers, his sixteen-year-old messboy, his radio officer, all the rest of them?

Later a broken hatch or two came ashore on the island of North Uist, in the Outer Hebrides, and the builders identified these as being probably from the missing vessel. Then on the 5th of February was found a small piece of wreckage from her radio-room. There were just these three clues, if they were clues—the lifebelt (which meant nothing, really, for lifebelts can be lost overboard without ships being in difficulties), the smashed hatch, the scrap from the radio-room. In due course an inquiry was held at Hamburg into the loss of the *Melanie Schulte,* and that was all there was to go on—these few things, a model of the ship, the builders', surveyors' and insurance bureau certificates and so forth. All these were in perfect order. No fault could be found with the ship, and the court inquired thoroughly. It was much the same sort of court as is held in Britain on such occasions, with a judge and four assessors, three of whom were experienced master mariners.

The court met in Hamburg on the 23rd of April, 1953 and—like so many other courts elsewhere—could in the end only leave the mystery unsolved. The *Melanie Schulte* had foundered for some reason. There could be no doubt as to that. But for what reason? Was there sabotage? Had she struck a mine? The court called expert evidence on both these points, especially the possibility of the vessel having been mined. This the experts regarded as remote in the extreme. Sabotage, then? But who would sabotage a tramp with a load of iron ore? Why? No, sabotage, like the mine, was too glib an 'explanation.' Dr. Rohewald, of the West German meteorological office, gave evidence that the weather west of Scotland on the night of the 21st of December was very bad, with westerly winds up to Force 10—a severe gale—and high seas.

There was one point of importance, and that was the manner in which the ship was loaded. Iron ore is an exceptionally heavy cargo. It does not take up much space in a ship, which means that, when the ship is fully loaded, there is still plenty of room in her holds for the ore to shift. If it does shift, it is heavy stuff. Being a new ship, there had been insufficient time to discover the best manner of loading the *Melanie Schulte.* Some ships are 'tender,' others 'stiff.' Some need more weight carried high in their holds, others less. The best and safest distribution of the extremely heavy weight of some 9,000 tons of metal ore, dumped into a steel hull which had cubic capacity for 20,000 tons of it, was a problem, made the more difficult because the steel hull carrying it was bound on a westwards crossing of the North Atlantic in the bad-weather month of December. It was certain that the hull would be thrown about to the greatest possible extent, and every conceivable degree of stress which a ramping, roaring sea could exert would be exerted. It was a hard way to find the best manner of loading. Masters and stevedores, too, may have their own ideas. Are they always right?

In fact, there was some question about the *Melanie Schulte's* loading. Maybe Captain Rohde had carried too much of his heavy cargo too high, as the *Samkey* had once taken in too much Thames ballast. Some experts seemed to think he had done this, others that he had not. He was a thoroughly experienced tramp master, and that was not his first cargo from Narvik. He had been in the Narvik-Emden trade for nearly two years, in a smaller vessel. But it was his new ship's first such cargo. She was a five-hold ship, like most fair-sized modern cargo-carriers. The ore was loaded only in four holds, the for'ard hold being left empty. There were—approximately—

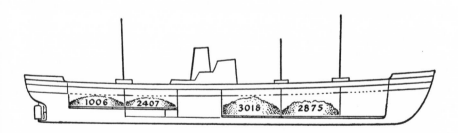

Fig. 7. Loading of the *Melanie Schulte*

2,875 tons in No. 2 hold; 3,018 tons in No. 3; 2,407 tons in No. 4; and 1,006 tons in the aftermost hold, No. 5. This gave a heavy concentration of weight round her heavy machinery amidships when the vessel was suspended (as the *Anglo-Australian* had once been, and the Greek *Mount Kyllene*) between the crests of two great seas. Did she somehow disintegrate? Or did some of her cargo fall down to leeward, with a violent lurch of the ship, and lead to the smashing-in of a hatch, perhaps of several hatches? Then the sea would pour in, and the ship—heavily laden as she was—would be very quickly gone.

Seamen will give their own answers to the questions. A court cannot deal with conjecture, but the broken hatch lying on the floor of the court, and the piece of smashed wood from the radio-room, were eloquent.

About the same time that the *Melanie Schulte* was being some-how overwhelmed in the savage sea, five thousand miles away, on the other side of the Atlantic, another iron-ore-laden steamer was also fighting a losing battle. This was the American Moore-McCormack steamer *Mormackite,* bringing 9,000 tons of iron ore from Vittoria to Baltimore. There were survivors from the *Mormackite,* not many but some—eleven from her crew of thirty-seven —and so it was known only too well what had happened to her. Her iron ore shifted and she capsized. The United States Coast Guard inquired fully into the accident and found that the dead master was at fault in (a) badly loading the ship, (b) making no preparations for abandoning the ship even when her position was precarious and (c) failing to order the radio officer to send out an SOS. But for that handful of survivors, the *Mormackite* would have been a missing vessel, too—as another bulk-carrier, the *Southern Districts,* was later to become, somewhere off the coast of South Carolina.

The *Southern Districts* was a former United States Navy LST— Landing Ship, Tanks—converted for bulk-cargo carrying after the end of the Second World War. LST's were intended as purely war-winning vessels and it was never contemplated that they might afterwards be used for purposes other than those for which they were designed, especially not for ordinary cargo-carrying. As vehicular ferries—yes, they might be very suitable for that, because they had large bow-doors which swung open to allow tanks and other vehicles to be loaded from beaches or to be driven out onto other beaches. LST's were built in great numbers in the United States, and there is no doubt that they played a considerable part in making the winning of the war possible. They were able to move armour without harbours. They could also move considerable bodies of troops with reasonable comfort on short distances. As tank carriers, large-scale removers of transport of all kinds and as troop-carriers, they served both the United States and the British navies (under Lend-Lease) very well. At the end of the war, they were surplus. The British Lend-Lease ships were returned to America. Many LST's were sold to operate not only under their own American flag but others, including the Liberian and the Panamanian.

Before very long, one or two were in serious trouble. The converted LST *Southern Isles,* for example, foundered in a heavy October gale while carrying a cargo of iron ore from Puerto Rico to Chester, in Pennsylvania, despite the fact that she had been strengthened as a cargo-carrier. After that, LST's under the Amer-

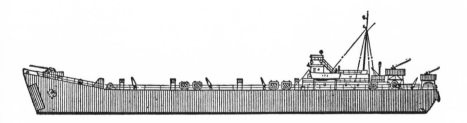

FIG. 8. American LST

ican flag were required to be further strengthened, and their owners were forbidden to load them with cargoes with a greater density than 26 cubic feet to the ton. This put LST's out of the heavy ore trade. As war-built and expendable vessels, LST's had not the scantlings to continue handling such heavy stuff.

The *Southern Districts* was built as an all-welded, steel-hull, diesel-driven LST of standard type at Leavenworth, in Kansas, during 1944. She was 328 feet long by 50 feet beam and 24.1 feet in depth. Her gross register tonnage was 3,338 tons, and her power-plant was that ordinarily found in American LST's (there also were a few British-built LST's of different design, with steam turbines), a pair of General Motors diesels each of which could develop 900 h.p. She was purchased from the U.S. Maritime Administration at the end of 1948, by the Philadelphia and Norfolk Steamship Company, and converted by them to be a cargo-carrier. Although in their design and specifications it had never been intended that LST's should be used for such a purpose, when the end of the war was near it was obvious that many former combatant vessels would be surplus, and they would be sold. The U.S. Coast Guard, being the responsible authority, therefore drew up plans and specifications for such conversions, to the best of its ability in what, after all, was a new—and problematic—field. The *Southern Districts'* conversion was in accordance with Coast-Guard-approved plans, and she duly went off to sea. Her license was to trade as a cargo vessel in coastwise service only, which included the coasts of both North and South America, and the West Indies. The bow-door, which (with her ability to beach) had been her principal asset in time of war, was welded up, and she was given various sloping bulkheads designed to make her, as far as possible, a self-trimming bulk-carrier. Eight hatches were cut into the main-deck, a new collision bulk-head and a transverse bulk-head between her two new cargo holds were installed and she was fitted with four sets of king posts which carried gear, not to work the cargo, but to raise and lower the steel 'lids' of her hatches. She was given steel hatch-covers made in one piece, not the older type of steel beams and wooden covers to fit into them. When all this had been done, the *Southern Districts* was to all intents and purposes an excellent bulk-cargo carrier and, as such, she was duly certified, after inspection at Norfolk, Virginia, in July, 1949.

Then the *Southern Isles*—a similarly converted vessel—went down, and the Coast Guard, always energetic to act and forceful where safety at sea is concerned, notified her owners that the *Southern Districts* must be further radically strengthened or she could not continue in trade. The additional strengthening was done and, in February, 1952, the ship went back into service again after once again being certified. This time she was not allowed to handle any cargoes which would put a weight exceeding 1,900 pounds per square foot on her tank tops. There were plenty of bulk cargoes to carry which complied with this requirement—commodities such as sulphur, phosphate rock, commercial fertilisers of one sort and another—and the *Southern Districts* carried such things for the best part of the following two years. She was inspected, and passed, on the 24th of February, 1953, and again on the 9th of January, 1954. She was four times in dry-dock during those two years.

The last annual inspection took ten days and was very thorough, for the Coast Guard (which not only had the responsibility for seeing that ships did not get into trouble but also had to rescue them and their people if they did get into difficulties) liked to be sure that these converted LST's were all right. It did not want any more cases like the loss of the *Southern Isles*. During this last inspection a good deal of work was done. Life-saving equipment, navigation gear, including the steering system, fire-fighting gear, were all seen to be properly efficient, and the hull, both internally and externally, was in order. The vessel had two 22-foot lifeboats, each capable of carrying thirty-one people, which was eight more than her total crew. These boats had been lowered, loaded and put into the water

[289]

during the survey, and everything was found in perfect order, including the portable radio.

After this inspection the vessel went back into the bulk-cargo trade on the Atlantic coast, West Indies and Gulf of Mexico. She continued in this without incident, except for touching the ground once when carrying a full cargo of sulphur in bulk from Port Sulphur, Louisiana, to Tampa, Florida. A couple of tugs and her own power got her off the ground again, and she appeared to have suffered no damage. This was by no means taken for granted and, when the vessel arrived at Tampa, she was surveyed independently by surveyors from the American Bureau of Shipping and the Coast Guard, as well as by a U.S. Salvage representative. The vessel was making no water and, apart from a minor defect in the starboard main engine, which was put right, everything seemed in order. The vessel then loaded phosphate rock at Tampa for New Orleans but, when this was being discharged, it was found that over 400 tons of it were damp and there were four feet of water in the No. 1 hold. When the cargo was out, a survey showed that the water had come in through holed bottom plating and had made its way through a worn place in a tank top. The *Southern Districts* was then dry-docked at the Todd Shipyard in New Orleans. This was towards the end of November, 1954.

Again a surveyor from the American Bureau of Shipping went over her, together with a Coast Guard inspector, paying particular attention to the condition of the under-water body. Sundry repairs were ordered to be done, for some of the bottom plates were holed (despite the fact that the ship had passed strict survey about nine months earlier). These small holes were attributed to grounding damage. One of the double-bottom tank tops was found holed and wasted in several places, and this was not grounding damage. All these things were put right and, indeed, a good deal of expensive work was done on the vessel, including the renewal of several plates

[290]

in her bottom. By December 2, all the work had been done to the surveyors' satisfaction, and the vessel was ready to sail.

It is a curious feature that, though the surveyors—who are notoriously hard men to please—were satisfied with the state of the vessel as repaired, and they certified her as seaworthy, three members of the deck crew did not share their view. They walked off the ship, refusing to sail with her, and as things turned out it was a good thing for them that they did so. They declared that the bottom damage made good was not all the injury the *Southern Districts* had sustained. She had, they said, frequent steering trouble at sea, and main-engine breakdowns also occurred. There had been cracks in the main-deck at sea, and these had been repaired by welding. They also declared that a fish bolt had been inserted in a hole in wasted bottom shell plating while the vessel was afloat at Corpus Christi, and they did not consider this a proper way to repair a vessel which was required to make long hauls in the Atlantic at all seasons of the year, even coastwise hauls. So the three crewmen walked away and the *Southern Districts,* patched up once more, went off to Port Sulphur to load a full cargo for discharge in Bucksport, Maine.

She duly loaded this cargo and no more members of her crew walked ashore—as far as is known, for the master did not leave a crew list when he sailed, as he should have done—the inference being that the others were satisfied with the ship in all respects. These included all the more experienced men. The sulphur was loaded properly and the vessel was not overloaded. She was in good trim (apart from a slight list, easily corrected) when she sailed on the 2nd of December, 1954, and the river and bar pilots afterwards reported that everything was normal aboard her. Neither the master nor any member of the crew indicated in any way to either pilot that there was anything wrong with the vessel.

But that was the last time the *Southern Districts* ever sailed from anywhere. She, too, disappeared—completely, with all her crew, her boats and everything else. She, too, sent no SOS, no signals, no indication that anything was wrong. She was sighted by several vessels as she proceeded on her coasting passage, which should have taken about a week to complete. An oil-tanker overhauled her, and reported that she was in no observable difficulty of any kind. Not long after noon on the 5th of December, when she was well in the Gulf Stream going northwards off the coast of South Carolina, the *Southern Districts* sent a routine radio message which indicated no difficulty. Yet the very next day she was not to be found. She would not have been missed so soon, since the master's instructions were to communicate with his owners only forty-eight hours before his expected time of arrival at the discharging port, but a radiogram was filed ashore for dispatch to a member of the crew. It was to deliver this that the *Southern Districts* was called and called again. She did not answer, which was thought strange, but no official notice was taken at the time. She just might not be listening, though she should have been keeping radio watch. However, the *Southern Districts* failed to arrive at Bucksport, or to put in anywhere else. As the weather had been bad, her owners were not immediately concerned about her failure to communicate with them or to arrive, but they, too, tried vainly to raise their ship by W/T. They did not succeed. No one succeeded. The *Southern Districts* was then already gone.

It was not until the 11th of December that the Coast Guard was informed of any real fears for the vessel's safety. The Coast Guard immediately organized its usual thorough search by sea and air. This search was continued almost until Christmas. Aircraft covered an area of 262,000 square miles of sea, and surface craft covered 9,000 square miles over the whole of the route the vessel would have taken from the point where she was last reported to Bucksport. Nothing was found. Later, the SS *Tullahoma*, while on passage from Paulsboro, New Jersey, to Beaumont, Texas, sighted a discarded lifebelt in the Florida Straits. This lifebelt was not picked up but it was passed less than thirty feet off the *Tullahoma*'s starboard bow, in good weather. The name on it was *Southern Districts*. The cover of this lifebelt was torn on one side.

How came a lifebelt from the lost ship to be there, in the Straits of Florida? The vessel was further north than that when she sent her last message, in a north-going stream—the great Gulf Stream which, like a mighty river in the sea, sweeps its warm water at the rate of knots to the nor'ard there and off the whole Atlantic seaboard of the United States, until it swings out wide towards Europe from a little north of Cape Hatteras. How could a lifebelt drift *south* in a north-going stream?

The answer was—very obviously—that it had not. That lifebelt had been thrown over, for some unknown reason, from the lost ship *before* she was lost. Perhaps, because it was torn a little in one part of the coverings, it was regarded as being worn out. The ideas of some crew members on what constitutes fair wear and tear are curious in these days, not only in American ships. At any rate, it was certain that the lifebelt seen there adrift in the blue Gulf Stream was not a relic of whatever tragedy had befallen the *Southern Districts*. She had passed that place before she could have been lost.

What sort of tragedy could this have been? The Coast Guard convened a comprehensive inquiry, which was held at New Orleans. This found that violent winds had blown in the area where the *Southern Districts* must have been on the day she was last heard from. Other ships—there were plenty of other ships there—reported that fresh south-easterlies (which would help north-bound ships) had suddenly chopped round to north-north-east, bringing up so broken and thoroughly nasty a sea that even large ships had done their best to get out of the main strength of the Stream as quickly as they could. In such conditions the Gulf Stream is notorious, for the wind, blowing against the relentless mass of the water as it pushes northwards, causes the sea to break and jump and leap in an angry torment. This was made much worse by the fresh south-easterlies which had previously been blowing, for these would have set up their own sea, their own wave-pattern, which the north-north-easterly would do its best to knock down. The wind was reported to have blown at fresh gale strength that night.

It would appear, on the face of it, that this was too much for the patched-up, much-surveyed and much-certified old LST, and she was overwhelmed. Though she was then only eight years old, that is old for a 3,000-tonner built to be flung upon an enemy beach and, surviving such shot and shell and mines and bombs as may be thrown at her, disgorge a swarm of tanks to support a landing. To have done that once could be life enough.

Immediately they realized that the ship was lost, Coast Guard reaction was swift and thorough. The certificates of seaworthiness granted to all such ships under the American flag were immediately cancelled, even before there had been time for the Committee of Lloyd's, far away in London, to post the *Southern Districts* as a missing vessel. This was done on the 5th of January, 1955, after the usual procedure. The Coast Guard's Board of Investigation, re-marking that the owners should have given more timely notice that their ship had not arrived, recommended that all vessels on coast-wise or foreign passages should be required to report their positions at least once each forty-eight hours. And, because there never could be hundred percent certainty that the twenty-three seafarers thought to be aboard the ship when she sailed (though they left, between them, twelve widows, including one an oiler had married in Yugoslavia only the previous May and had not since seen) were in fact aboard, and lost, *all* ships must furnish the Coast Guard with crew lists showing all persons actually on board and sailing whenever they left port to make a passage. The Board criticized the inspectors who, being aware that there were numerous small holes in the bottom plating and that at least one tank top was holed from deterioration, failed to go further to make a more thorough investigation of the entire bottom shell plating, as well as the tank tops.

These recommendations, which according to Coast Guard custom were listed as 'opinions,' were passed on to the Coast Guard
Commandant, who did not uphold the censure. The precise cause
of the disappearance of the *Southern Districts,* said the Commandant, would never be known, but it was probable that the structural
conditions of the vessel "contributed thereto," and it would appear
that "to some extent an incorrect assessment had been made of the
structural qualities of the ship for the practical operation of such
vessel in the bulk carrier trade."

The great fleet of the LST had played their part in winning
the war. Built at all kinds of yards, many of which had built nothing
bigger than a river barge before and some nothing at all, far up
rivers and on lakes, manned by three-month mariners who gained
their first real experience with the ships, sent into action after action, briefed always to do the job allotted them first and worry
about getting off the beach afterwards, designed—unlike all other
ocean-going vessels—to be run up bows first with a stern anchor
out which might pull them off, and might not, ships of this type had
done splendidly in almost every landing of importance throughout
the war, in all its theatres. Much had been asked of them, and much
given. But perhaps to make them into bulk-cargo-carrying merchantmen afterwards and expect them to run for years was another
thing. The dry-dock and repairs record of the *Southern Districts,*
looked at impartially, is hardly the story of a fully seaworthy vessel
only a few years old. Perhaps she resented the bulk loads of sulphur
and fertilisers and concentrates that were so frequently being poured
into her, and took herself and her crew down to the depths of the
sea the first real chance she had.

In the aggregate, a good many seafarers and others have lost
their lives in ships big and small which have gone missing since the
end of the Second World War, that is, in the past ten years. Over
a thousand have died in registered ships whose cases are mentioned

[295]

in this book, which is not meant to be exhaustive—43 in the *Samkey,* 40 in the *Hopestar,* 46 in the *Pennsylvania,* 35 in the *Melanie Schulte,* 54 in the *General San Martin,* 23 in the *Southern Districts,* 40 in the trawlers *Lorella* and *Roderigo,* 275 in the *Sir Harvey Adamson* (including the passengers), 101 in the *Monique,* of Noumea, (again including the passengers) and so on. Did all these people have to die? The ships must go, or some of them: but why always all the men? The sea may always claim its victims in ships and in men, but it would seem that the serious loss of life reflected here ought at least in some part to be avoidable.

All these ships had conventional life-saving gear, in abundance. The question inevitably arises as to just how useful this may be when it comes to survival in the sea. The lifeboats themselves should be all right, *if* they get away and are properly handled. But it looks as if the chances of the conventional ship's lifeboat making a useful getaway from a sudden serious casualty are somewhat slim. The boats are not designed to be self-launching, which would solve some of the difficulties. Getting them into the sea is a labour of skilled seamanship. They are usually carried high up in the ship, secured in chocks and held by gripes—they have to be, or they would do themselves damage with the motion of the safest of ships—and this problem of getting them safely away, from a heaving, lurching vessel that is being violently assailed in some raging sea, is sometimes insoluble. Lifeboats become heavier and heavier, and the gear to handle them is mechanised in various ways, to simplify their handling. But the very mechanisation is in itself a possible danger, for its source of power may break down. How is a heavy boat to be put into the sea safely then? As far as is known, not a single boat got away from any of those missing vessels, except from the *Pennsylvania,* despite properly conducted boat drills, inspections, regulations *ad infinitum,* the best of equipment and all the rest of it. Is there no answer, then?

What, for instance, about some kind of raft? Not just a box to

cling to, but a raft offering shelter as well as buoyancy. A man begins to die the moment he is thrown into the sea, especially in the
Arctic or under winter North Atlantic conditions. He must be
sheltered as well as just kept out of the water.

There is another disability which weighs against the chances of
the modern seafarer when his ship sinks under him, and that is—
too often—his plain unhandiness in a boat, if ever he does get in
one. The older seaman was not like this. He was usually a man used
to boats from boyhood, and his ship was small enough to give him a
real feeling of being at sea. But many of today's seafarers have
never been in a boat until they get—very briefly—to some pre-sea
training-school and, in many big ships, modern seafaring becomes
increasingly an indoors profession, except for a few men on deck.
One is reminded, as an example of the worth of retaining something
at least of the older outlook, of the experience of the Portuguese
dory fishermen on the Grand Banks and off Greenland.

The Portuguese operate a fleet of between forty-five and fifty
hand-lining fishing vessels on these banks every year, most of the
ships being auxiliary schooners—not broken-down old schooners
but modern vessels. They do not trawl but catch their fish by means
of one-man dories, and the larger of them carry anything from fifty
to eighty men who go out each day, for a period of six months, and
fish from these dories on the open sea. Naturally such men are
superb boatmen. Theirs is a hazardous calling. They risk being lost
in fog, overwhelmed by sudden squalls, being run down by large
vessels. They have to load their dories heavily if they are ever to
fill their ship. Yet the loss of life from drowning among these dorymen is infinitesimal. Each year at least one schooner is lost, either
to ice or fire or some other hazard of the sea. Yet since the end of
the First World War not a single one of these Portuguese ships is
missing—that is, over a period of more than thirty-five years, in a
branch of seafaring recognised as unusually hazardous, for the ships
have no shelter and they fish through the West Indies hurricane

season, too—and, in the past seven years, *not a single man has been lost* from any one of the eleven Portuguese dory-fishing schooners and small motor-ships which have foundered, been crushed by ice or burned out in that time. And this despite the fact that eight of those eleven ships foundered in the North Atlantic, usually in October, when caught in very bad weather while homeward-bound deeply laden with a full cargo of fish, and *none of them had any lifeboats* —as such—at all. The men got away in the dories. The dories floated off. They didn't have to be launched. The dories, which are flat-bottomed open boats about 14 feet long, were as buoyant as rafts and the dorymen were so accustomed to them that they required no other boats or shelter. Moreover, they were able to get away in the dories without being first immersed in the sea. Another feature—and an important one—is that these men were so accustomed to the motion of the dories that they were not seasick in them, and so wasted no vital body fluids by throwing up. (A great many seafarers are accustomed only to the motion of large ships: small boats make them seasick.)

Consider for example the case of the little dory-fishing motor-ship *Joao Costa,* a wooden vessel of 774 gross register tons, built at Murraceira in Portugal in 1945 and sailing out of the fishing port of Figueira da Foz. If ever there should have been a missing ship, it was this one. The *Joao Costa* was not an auxiliary schooner but a full-powered motor-ship, carrying a little steadying sail. Like the other dory-fishermen, her business was to sail over from her home port in the early spring of the year, anchor on some convenient point on the Grand Banks (preferably on foul ground, in order to avoid the too-numerous big trawlers which also work there) and, sending out her fifty-five dorymen in their fifty-five little boats each day for the following six or seven months, fill herself with fine fat cod which were salted down aboard. Then she brought this cargo home, where it was treated, and marketed. For six years the *Joao Costa* did this, very well. She was commanded by a young master with the same name of the ship, though he did not own her. She was named for his father, not him. Like most of the modern masters he had not himself been a doryman, but he was a fine seaman and an able fisherman.

On the seventh voyage, the *Joao Costa* foundered. She was coming back alone from the banks off the west coast of Greenland when she was caught in a very bad blow, near the Azores—in that same area where the *Anglo-Australian* and the *Samkey* had disappeared, and the *Sao Paulo* had also gone missing. She opened up, took in more water than the pumps could cope with (she was deeply laden) and, within a few hours of the leak first becoming serious, she went down. At the time her radio was temporarily out of order and, before it could be repaired, she had gone. So no message was sent away. As she was not due at Lisbon for four more days, she was not missed. She had been gone a week before a search was begun for her, for it was known that she must have passed through much bad weather and, at first, her failure to arrive was put down to delay caused by this.

A week after the *Joao Costa* had gone down, the American Liberty ship *Compass,* eastbound from the Atlantic seaboard of the United States toward the Mediterranean, chanced to steam into the area. The sea was still lumpy, after running high the whole week. Suddenly those in the *Compass* sighted a small boat adrift on the sea—three small boats, six small boats, dozens of them! They were strange little boats, painted yellow, each with a large number on its side, painted in white. In the boats were men, waving. The little boats were jumping and leaping in the sea so much that the *Compass* had difficulty getting the men out of them, and the men had to jump for the bottom of a rope ladder dangling in the sea. Thirty, forty, forty-five men were picked up. They were the dorymen of the *Joao Costa,* and they had been a week in those dories—a week without food and only such moisture as they could squeeze from the rain which soaked their stocking caps.

In the meantime, not far away, the German motor-ship *Henriette Schulte*—a sister to the ill-fated *Melanie*—was also finding herself suddenly among more of the dorymen adrift in the North Atlantic and she and the steamer *Steel Executive*—summoned by radio to assist—picked up the balance of the *Joao Costa*'s crew. Not just the survivors, *all* of them! The youthful master, a slim young man with a face like a priest, the deckboys, the handful of engineers, the cook and his mate, every single doryman, every single soul who had been aboard. The master had kept the majority of the men together, and the mate had led the rest, when they were split up by the continuous bad weather.

Those men were not all skilled dorymen. The officers, the deckboys and the engineers rarely went in a dory on the banks because that was not their work. But they were all used to dories, all skillful small-boat sailors and superb seamen, used to hardship, and the dorymen were also used to accepting the risk of being adrift in a dory at sea. There was one other quality which kept these men together and helped them to survive. This was that they prayed and they believed in the praying.

It is a curious feature of this case that the master of the *Henriette Schulte* who helped to pick those dorymen out of the sea, was to become the master of the *Melanie Schulte* the very next voyage and be missing in the sea himself, before the end of the year. Perhaps if he had had enough dories instead of lifeboats, he might have lived, and all his crew would not have been lost.

Every seaman is not a doryman, by any means, nor could he become one overnight. Nor would a dory save a man for long under conditions of extreme cold or extreme heat. It would seem, however, that there is a case for alteration in at least some life-saving equipment now traditionally taken to sea in ships. The standard, ministry-backed lifeboat has let too many men die. It has its uses, and a ship should carry at least one or two such boats. But the modern inflatable rubber raft, developed from the air-borne dinghies used in the Second World War, would appear to have a value, too. An inflatable raft could be launched as easily as a dory is and it would float off a doomed ship, right side up, as a stack of dories does. There are excellent such rafts on the market now which can be thrown in the sea by two men, and inflate themselves by the tripping of a line. They automatically right themselves no matter how they fall in the water. They offer shelter and safety to more than twenty men. Such a raft, in the stowed position, takes up no more room than a large cork fender. It is stowed aboard in a cylindrical valise, and it will inflate itself out of this if it is simply thrown overboard. It can neither capsize nor become waterlogged. It has a double-walled canopy, carried on two inflating arches, and this canopy serves to keep out both the heat and the cold.

Experiments under Arctic conditions (made by the British Admiralty and not by the manufacturers) showed that men would quickly warm up inside this canopy, even after being immersed in the sea. A group of volunteers swam to an inflatable raft in waters off Tromsø, well within the Arctic Circle. They clambered into the raft shivering but, with the raft's ventilation sleeves closed to give the minimum ventilation (which most sailors rather like anyway), the air inside rapidly became saturated and then warmed up from the body heat given off by the men. They warmed up, too, even though they were still wet, and the conditions outside were extremely cold.

Such a raft has its own disadvantages, but these do not include flimsiness. It is much less likely to damage than the ordinary rigid lifeboat because it is yielding, and the fabric from which it is made has stood exhaustive tests. It cannot be propelled very well; it makes men seasick; it cannot carry vast quantities of water and food. But seasickness can largely be overcome by the use of various preparations, particularly the drug Hyoscine, which is very effective. As for its powers of propulsion, it is often the best course, when a ship goes down, for the rafts or boats to stay in the vicinity, and the closer they do so remain the better are their chances of being seen and the people rescued, particularly in these days of air search. A group of bright yellow rafts, bunched together near the last reported position of whatever casualty they came from, should not have to wait long for rescue in these days, almost anywhere. The rescue facilities exist in abundance. It is the problem of getting away from the ship which so often causes loss of life.

As for the other disadvantage, that they cannot carry much in the way of fresh water or food, a big life-raft can carry emergency packs enough to support its contingent of men for as long as they are likely to survive. Experiments official and personal, Dr. Bombard's and the British Admiralty's Personnel Research Committee's among others, have shown that fit men can survive for long periods on very little, without emulating the famous Chinese who lived as a castaway on a raft with nothing for upwards of a hundred days, during the Second World War. (There was an idea afterwards that he had perhaps eaten his fellow survivors.) British experiments, for example, have shown that a daily intake of 500 cubic centimeters of water, a mouthful of sweetened condensed milk and a few boiled sweets will keep a man going in full vigour for at least five days. Fresh water is heavy stuff, but rations for twenty at this rate could be carried in a standard inflatable raft, to last for ten or twenty days.

Each autumn and winter bring their quota of seafarers lost at sea because the boats failed them in some way or other. Of the crew of forty men in the Hain Line motor-ship *Tresillian,* which foundered not forty miles from the coast of Ireland in a gale during November, 1954, only sixteen survived. The *Tresillian* was a motor-ship of considerably over 7,000 tons, built in 1944, and she was eastbound on a normal North Atlantic voyage, with all the life-saving equipment the Shipping Act requires. She had two lifeboats on each side, carried amidships. They were the best possible type of standard lifeboats, and the crew had been properly exercised in their use. But, before she foundered, the *Tresillian* had taken a heavy list to port and the sea then washed the two lifeboats on that side away. When they were needed, the other boats were on the ship's high side and could not be properly launched. And so many of the crew died, though help was near at hand. The *Tresillian* foundered in a busy part of a busy steamer lane, and the Shell tanker *Liparis* was standing by to pick up survivors. All the men had life-jackets. It is a reasonable supposition that, had the *Tresillian* carried one or two inflatable rafts, the loss of life may not have been so heavy, for such rafts can be launched at the last moment.

The British Royal yacht *Britannia* is among vessels already fitted with inflatable life-rafts, in addition to her quota of traditional boats. At present, British Ministry regulations insist upon rigid boats being carried in all seagoing vessels. Before there is any radical change in this policy it is obvious that there will have to be further investigation and research into the whole problem of survival at sea, and it is good to know that this is being carried forward steadily by the Ministry of Transport as well as the Admiralty.*

Nine ships gone missing in a day, with everyone aboard—two poor trawlers iced up and rolled over, going about their daily work in the bitter waters north of Iceland, and everybody drowned—a thousand persons lost from missing ships only since the end of the war! Though safety at sea has improved out of all recognition over the past fifty years, one may be pardoned for suggesting that there seems room for improvement still—a good deal of improvement.

* In May, 1956, the British Ministry of Transport and Civil Aviation made new regulations which will compel U.K. registered fishing vessels over 50 feet in length to carry inflatable liferafts. Such rafts may also be carried in coastwise passenger ships, and in yachts. This is a beginning. The thirteen crewmen of the Grimsby trawler *Osako,* which foundered in bad weather off the Faeroes on the night of April 21, 1956, were all rescued by means of inflatable liferafts floated to them by another Grimsby trawler, the *Thessalonian.*

[303]

The Lutine bell at Lloyd's rings too seldom to announce good tidings from ships overdue and thought to be lost. When they are overdue they are also lost, far too often, and their people have gone with them.

Index

NOTE: Page numbers in parentheses refer to maps.

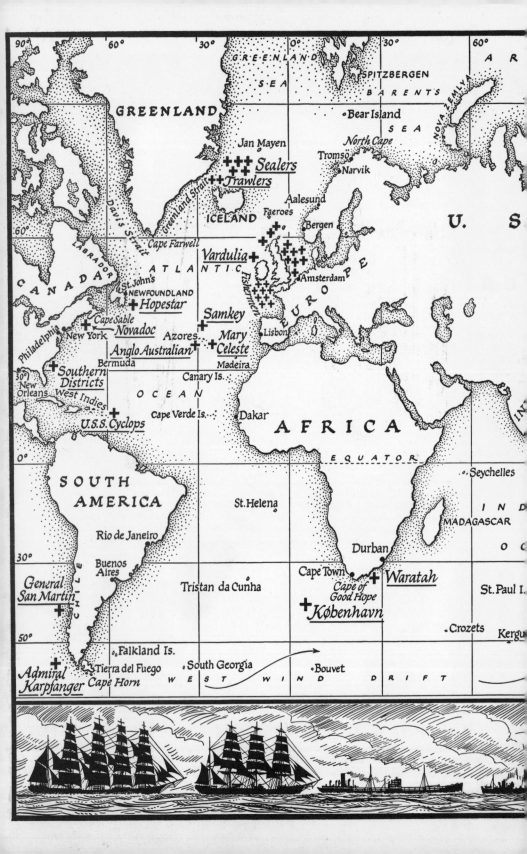